Capital Punishment and the Judicial Process

Third Edition

2008 Supplement

Randall Coyne

University of Oklahoma College of Law

Lyn Entzeroth

University of Tulsa College of Law

Carolina Academic Press

Durham, North Carolina

ISBN 978-1-59460-626-7

Carolina Academic Press
700 Kent Street
Durham, NC 27701
Phone 919-489-7486
Fax 919-493-5668
www.cap-press.com

TABLE OF CONTENTS

CHAPTER 1   THE GREAT DEBATE OVER CAPITAL PUNISHMENT

F.   Other Issues in the Death Penalty Debate

1.   Risk of Executing the Innocent

Page 35. Insert before Note and Questions on Procedural Bar and Claims of Innocence:

Note on Kansas v. Marsh, 548 U.S. 163 (2006)

In *Kansas v. Marsh*, 548 U.S. 163 (2006), Justice Scalia, in a concurring opinion, and Justice Souter, in a dissenting opinion, discussed the degree of risk that each justice perceived existed with respect to wrongful executions of actually innocent persons, and the role the Court and the law should play in preventing or minimizing that risk. Excerpts of the justices' discussion on this issue follow.

Kansas v. Marsh
548 U.S. 163 (2006)

Justice SCALIA, concurring.

I join the opinion of the Court. I write separately to clarify briefly the import of my joinder, and to respond at somewhat greater length . . . to Justice Souter's claims about risks inherent in capital punishment. . . .

III

. . . The dissent's suggestion that capital defendants are *especially* liable to suffer from the lack of 100% perfection in our criminal justice system is implausible. Capital cases are given especially close scrutiny at every level, which is why in most cases many years elapse before the sentence is executed. And of course capital cases receive special attention in the application of executive clemency. Indeed, one of the arguments made by abolitionists is that the process of finally completing all the appeals and reexaminations of capital sentences is so lengthy, and thus so expensive for the State, that the game is not worth the candle. The proof of the pudding, of course, is that as far as anyone can determine (and many are looking), *none* of cases included in the .027% error rate for American verdicts involved a capital defendant erroneously executed.

Since 1976 there have been approximately a half million murders in the United States. In that time, 7,000 murderers have been sentenced to death; about 950 of them have been executed; and about 3,700 inmates are currently on death row. See Marquis, The Myth of Innocence, 95 J.Crim. L. & C. 501, 518 (2006). As a consequence of the sensitivity of the criminal justice system to the due-process rights of defendants sentenced to death, almost two-thirds of all death sentences are overturned. "Virtually none" of these reversals, however, are attributable to a defendant's "actual innocence." Most are based on legal errors that have little or nothing to do with guilt. The studies cited by the dissent demonstrate nothing more.

Like other human institutions, courts and juries are not perfect. One cannot have a system of criminal punishment without accepting the possibility that someone will be punished mistakenly. That is a truism, not a revelation. But with regard to the punishment of death in the current American system, that possibility has been reduced to an insignificant minimum. This explains why those ideologically driven to ferret out and proclaim a mistaken modern execution have not a single verifiable case to point to, whereas it is easy as pie to identify plainly guilty murderers who have been set free. The American people have determined that the good to be derived from capital punishment – in deterrence, and perhaps most of all in the meting out of condign justice for horrible crimes – outweighs the risk of error. It is no proper part of the business of this Court, or of its Justices, to second-guess that judgment, much less to impugn it before the world, and less still to frustrate it by imposing judicially invented obstacles to its execution.

Justice SOUTER, with whom Justice Stevens, Justice Ginsburg, and Justice Breyer join, dissenting.

III

. . . Today, a new body of fact must be accounted for in deciding what, in practical terms, the Eighth Amendment guarantees should tolerate, for the period starting in 1989 has seen repeated exonerations of convicts under death sentences, in numbers never imagined before the development of DNA tests. We cannot face up to these facts and still hold that the guarantee of morally justifiable sentencing is hollow enough to allow maximizing death sentences, by requiring them when juries fail to find the worst degree of culpability: when, by a State's own standards and a State's own characterization, the case for death is "doubtful."

A few numbers from a growing literature will give a sense of the reality that must be addressed. When the Governor of Illinois imposed a moratorium on executions in 2000, 13 prisoners under death sentences had been released since 1977 after a number of them were shown to be innocent, as described in a report which used their examples to illustrate a theme common to all 13, of "relatively little solid evidence connecting the charged defendants to the crimes." During the same period, 12 condemned convicts had been executed. Subsequently the Governor determined that 4 more death row inmates were innocent.[2] Illinois had thus wrongly

---

[2]The Illinois Report emphasizes the difference between exoneration of a convict because of actual innocence, and reversal of a judgment because of legal error affecting conviction or sentence but not inconsistent with guilt in fact. See Report 9 (noting that, apart from the 13 released men, a "broader review" discloses that more than half of the State's death penalty cases "were reversed at some point in the process"). More importantly, it takes only a cursory reading of the Report to recognize that it describes men released who were demonstrably innocent or convicted on grossly unreliable evidence. Of one, the Report notes "two other persons were subsequently convicted in Wisconsin of" the murders. Of two others, the Report states that they were released after "DNA tests

convicted and condemned even more capital defendants than it had executed, but it may well not have been otherwise unique; one recent study reports that between 1989 and 2003, 74 American prisoners condemned to death were exonerated, Gross, Jacoby, Matheson, Montgomery, & Patil, Exonerations in the United States 1989 Through 2003, 95 J.Crim. L. & C. 523, 531 (2006) (hereinafter Gross), many of them cleared by DNA evidence. Another report states that "more than 110" death row prisoners have been released since 1973 upon findings that they were innocent of the crimes charged, and "[h]undreds of additional wrongful convictions in potentially capital cases have been documented over the past century." Lanier & Acker, Capital Punishment, the Moratorium Movement, and Empirical Questions, 10 Psychology, Public Policy & Law 577, 593 (2004). Most of these wrongful convictions and sentences resulted from eyewitness misidentification, false confession, and (most frequently) perjury, and the total shows that among all prosecutions homicide cases suffer an unusually high incidence of false conviction, probably owing to the combined difficulty of investigating without help from the victim, intense pressure to get convictions in homicide cases, and the corresponding incentive for the guilty to frame the innocent.

We are thus in a period of new empirical argument about how "death is different,": not only would these false verdicts defy correction after the fatal moment, the Illinois experience shows them to be remarkable in number, and they are probably disproportionately high in capital cases. . . .

---

revealed that none of them were the source of the semen found in the victim. That same year, two other men confessed to the crime, pleaded guilty and were sentenced to life in prison, and a third was tried and convicted for the crime." Of yet another, the Report says that "another man subsequently confessed to the crime for which [the released man] was convicted. He entered a plea of guilty and is currently serving a prison term for that crime."

A number were subject to judgments as close to innocence as any judgments courts normally render. In the case of one of the released men, the Supreme Court of Illinois found the evidence insufficient to support his conviction. See *People v. Smith,* 185 Ill.2d 532, 236 Ill.Dec. 779, 708 N.E.2d 365 (1999). Several others obtained acquittals, and still more simply had the charges against them dropped, after receiving orders for new trials.

At least 2 of the 13 were released at the initiative of the executive. We can reasonably assume that a State under no obligation to do so would not release into the public a person against whom it had a valid conviction and sentence unless it were certain beyond all doubt that the person in custody was not the perpetrator of the crime. The reason that the State would forgo even a judicial forum in which defendants would demonstrate grounds for vacating their convictions is a matter of common sense: evidence going to innocence was conclusive.

Page 36. Insert at the end of Note and Questions on Procedural Bar and Claims of Innocence:

Note on House v. Bell, 547 U.S. 518 (2006)

The United States Supreme Court in *House v. Bell*, 547 U.S. 518 (2006), found that Paul Gregory House, who had been convicted and sentenced to death for the murder of Carolyn Muncey, had presented sufficient evidence to demonstrate actual innocence so as to allow a federal court to hear a claim that otherwise had been procedurally defaulted in state court. In reaching this determination, the Court focused on the evidence presented at trial and the evidence subsequently developed.

House v. Bell
547 U.S. 518 (2006)

IV
DNA Evidence

First, in direct contradiction of evidence presented at trial, DNA testing has established that the semen on Mrs. Muncey's nightgown and panties came from her husband, Mr. Muncey, not from House. The State, though conceding this point, insists this new evidence is immaterial. At the guilt phase at least, neither sexual contact nor motive were elements of the offense, so in the State's view the evidence, or lack of evidence, of sexual assault or sexual advance is of no consequence. We disagree. In fact we consider the new disclosure of central importance.

From beginning to end the case is about who committed the crime. When identity is in question, motive is key. The point, indeed, was not lost on the prosecution, for it introduced the evidence and relied on it in the final guilt-phase closing argument. Referring to "evidence at the scene," the prosecutor suggested that House committed, or attempted to commit, some "indignity" on Mrs. Muncey that neither she "nor any mother on that road would want to do with Mr. House." Particularly in a case like this where the proof was, as the State Supreme Court observed, circumstantial, we think a jury would have given this evidence great weight. Quite apart from providing proof of motive, it was the only forensic evidence at the scene that would link House to the murder.

Law and society, as they ought to do, demand accountability when a sexual offense has been committed, so not only did this evidence link House to the crime; it likely was a factor in persuading the jury not to let him go free. At sentencing, moreover, the jury came to the unanimous conclusion, beyond a reasonable doubt, that the murder was committed in the course of a rape or kidnaping. The alleged sexual motivation relates to both those determinations. This is particularly so given that, at the sentencing phase, the jury was advised that House had a previous conviction for sexual assault.

A jury informed that fluids on Mrs. Muncey's garments could have come from House might have found that House trekked the nearly two miles to the victim's home and lured her away in order to commit a sexual offense. By contrast a jury acting without the assumption that the semen could have come from House would have found it necessary to establish some different motive, or, if the same motive, an intent far more speculative. When the only direct evidence of sexual assault drops out of the case, so, too, does a central theme in the State's narrative linking House to the crime. In that light, furthermore, House's odd evening walk and his false statements to authorities, while still potentially incriminating, might appear less suspicious.

Bloodstains

The other relevant forensic evidence is the blood on House's pants, which appears in small, even minute, stains in scattered places. As the prosecutor told the jury, they were stains that, due to their small size, "you or I might not detect[,] [m]ight not see, but which the FBI lab was able to find on [House's] jeans." The stains appear inside the right pocket, outside that pocket, near the inside button, on the left thigh and outside leg, on the seat of the pants, and on the right bottom cuff, including inside the pants. Due to testing by the FBI, cuttings now appear on the pants in several places where stains evidently were found. (The cuttings were destroyed in the testing process, and defense experts were unable to replicate the tests.) At trial, the government argued "nothing that the defense has introduced in this case explains what blood is doing on his jeans, all over [House's] jeans, that is scientifically, completely different from his blood." House, though not disputing at this point that the blood is Mrs. Muncey's, now presents an alternative explanation that, if credited, would undermine the probative value of the blood evidence.

During House's habeas proceedings, Dr. Cleland Blake, an Assistant Chief Medical Examiner for the State of Tennessee and a consultant in forensic pathology to the TBI for 22 years, testified that the blood on House's pants was chemically too degraded, and too similar to blood collected during the autopsy, to have come from Mrs. Muncey's body on the night of the crime. The blood samples collected during the autopsy were placed in test tubes without preservative. Under such conditions, according to Dr. Blake, "you will have enzyme degradation. You will have different blood group degradation, blood marker degradation." The problem of decay, moreover, would have been compounded by the body's long exposure to the elements, sitting outside for the better part of a summer day. In contrast, if blood is preserved on cloth, "it will stay there for years,"; indeed, Dr. Blake said he deliberately places blood drops on gauze during autopsies to preserve it for later testing. The blood on House's pants, judging by Agent Bigbee's tests, showed "similar deterioration, breakdown of certain of the named numbered enzymes" as in the autopsy samples. "[I]f the victim's blood had spilled on the jeans while the victim was alive and this blood had dried," Dr. Blake stated, "the deterioration would not have occurred," and "you would expect [the blood on the jeans] to be different than what was in the tube." Dr. Blake thus concluded the blood on the jeans came from the autopsy samples, not from Mrs. Muncey's live (or recently killed) body.

5

Other evidence confirms that blood did in fact spill from the vials. It appears the vials passed from Dr. Carabia, who performed the autopsy, into the hands of two local law enforcement officers, who transported it to the FBI, where Agent Bigbee performed the enzyme tests. The blood was contained in four vials, evidently with neither preservative nor a proper seal. The vials, in turn, were stored in a styrofoam box, but nothing indicates the box was kept cool. Rather, in what an evidence protocol expert at the habeas hearing described as a violation of proper procedure, the styrofoam box was packed in the same cardboard box as other evidence including House's pants (apparently in a paper bag) and other clothing (in separate bags). The cardboard box was then carried in the officers' car while they made the 10-hour journey from Tennessee to the FBI lab. Dr. Blake stated that blood vials in hot conditions (such as a car trunk in the summer) could blow open; and in fact, by the time the blood reached the FBI it had hemolyzed, or spoiled, due to heat exposure. By the time the blood passed from the FBI to a defense expert, roughly a vial and a half were empty, though Agent Bigbee testified he used at most a quarter of one vial. Blood, moreover, had seeped onto one corner of the styrofoam box and onto packing gauze inside the box below the vials.

In addition, although the pants apparently were packaged initially in a paper bag and FBI records suggest they arrived at the FBI in one, the record does not contain the paper bag but does contain a plastic bag with a label listing the pants and Agent Scott's name – and the plastic bag has blood on it. The blood appears in a forked streak roughly five inches long and two inches wide running down the bag's outside front. Though testing by House's expert confirmed the stain was blood, the expert could not determine the blood's source. Speculations about when and how the blood got there add to the confusion regarding the origins of the stains on House's pants.

Faced with these indications of, at best, poor evidence control, the State attempted to establish at the habeas hearing that all blood spillage occurred after Agent Bigbee examined the pants. Were that the case, of course, then blood would have been detected on the pants before any spill – which would tend to undermine Dr. Blake's analysis and support using the bloodstains to infer House's guilt. In support of this theory the State put on testimony by a blood spatter expert who believed the "majority" of the stains were "transfer stains," that is, stains resulting from "wip[ing] across the surface of the pants" rather than seeping or spillage. Regarding the spillage in the styrofoam box, the expert noted that yellow "Tennessee Crime Laboratory" tape running around the box and down all four sides did not line up when the bloodstains on the box's corner were aligned. The inference was that the FBI received the box from Tennessee authorities, opened it, and resealed it before the spillage occurred. Reinforcing this theory, Agent Bigbee testified that he observed no blood spillage in the styrofoam box and that had he detected such signs of evidence contamination, FBI policy would have required immediate return of the evidence.

In response House argued that even assuming the tape alignment showed spillage occurring after FBI testing, spillage on one or more earlier occasions was likely. In fact even the State's spatter expert declined to suggest the blood in the box and on the packing gauze accounted for the full vial and a quarter missing. And when the defense expert opened the box and discovered the spills, the bulk of the blood-caked gauze was located around and underneath the half-full vial, which was also located near the stained corner. No gauze immediately surrounding the completely empty vial was stained. The tape, moreover, circled the box in two layers, one underneath the other, and in one spot the underlying layer stops cleanly at the lid's edge, as if cut with a razor, and does not continue onto the body of the box below. In House's view this clean cut suggests the double layers could not have resulted simply from wrapping the tape around twice, as the spatter expert claimed; rather, someone possessing Tennessee Crime Lab tape – perhaps the officers transporting the blood and pants – must have cut the box open and resealed it, possibly creating an opportunity for spillage. Supporting the same inference, a label on the box's lid lists both blood and vaginal secretions as the box's contents, though Agent Bigbee's records show the vaginal fluids arrived at the FBI in a separate envelope. Finally, cross-examination revealed that Agent Bigbee's practice did not always match the letter of FBI policy. Although Mrs. Muncey's bra and housecoat were packed together in a single bag, creating, according to Agent Bigbee, a risk of "cross contamination," he did not return them; nor did he note the discrepancy between the "[b]lood and [v]aginal secretions" label and the styrofoam box's actual contents, though he insisted his customary practice was to match labels with contents immediately upon opening an evidence box.

The State challenged Dr. Blake's scientific conclusions, and to do so it called Agent Bigbee as a witness. Agent Bigbee defended the testimony he had given at the trial. To begin with, he suggested Dr. Blake had misconstrued the term "inc" in Agent Bigbee's trial report, interpreting it to mean "incomplete" when it in fact meant "inconclusive." Dr. Blake, however, replied "[s]ame difference" when asked whether his opinion would change if "inc" meant "inconclusive." Agent Bigbee further asserted that, whereas Dr. Blake (in Bigbee's view) construed the results to mean the enzyme was not present at all, in fact the results indicated only that Bigbee could not identify the marker type on whatever enzymes were present. Yet the State did not cross-examine Dr. Blake on this point, nor did the District Court resolve the dispute one way or the other, so on this record it seems possible that Dr. Blake meant only to suggest the blood was too degraded to permit conclusive typing. The State, moreover, does not ask us to question Dr. Blake's basic premise about the durability of blood chemicals deposited on cotton – a premise Agent Bigbee appeared to accept as a general matter. Given the record as it stands, then, we cannot say Dr. Blake's conclusions have been discredited; if other objections might be adduced, they must await further proceedings. At the least, the record before us contains credible testimony suggesting that the missing enzyme markers are generally better preserved on cloth than in poorly kept test tubes, and that principle could support House's spillage theory for the blood's origin.

In this Court, as a further attack on House's showing, the State suggests that, given the spatter expert's testimony, House's theory would require a jury to surmise that Tennessee officials donned the pants and deliberately spread blood over them. We disagree. This should be a matter for the trier of fact to consider in the first instance, but we can note a line of argument that could refute the State's position. It is correct that the State's spatter expert opined that the stains resulted from wiping or smearing rather than direct spillage; and she further stated that the distribution of stains in some spots suggests the pants were "folded in some manner or creased in some manner" when the transfers occurred. While the expert described this pattern, at least with respect to stains on the lap of the pants, as "consistent" with the pants being worn at the time of the staining, her testimony, as we understand it, does not refute the hypothesis that the packaging of the pants for transport was what caused them to be folded or creased. It seems permissible, moreover, to conclude that the small size and wide distribution of stains – inside the right pocket, outside that pocket, near the inside button, on the left thigh and outside leg, on the seat of the pants, and on the right bottom cuff, including inside the pants – fits as well with spillage in transport as with wiping and smearing from bloody objects at the crime scene, as the State proposes. (As has been noted, no blood was found on House's shoes.)

The District Court discounted Dr. Blake's opinion, not on account of Blake's substantive approach, but based on testimony from Agent Scott indicating he saw, as the District Court put it, "what appeared to be bloodstains on Mr. House's blue jeans when the jeans were removed from the laundry hamper at Ms. Turner's trailer." This inference seems at least open to question, however. Agent Scott stated only that he "saw reddish brownish stains [he] suspected to be blood"; he admitted that he "didn't thoroughly examine the blue jeans at that time." The pants were in fact extensively soiled with mud and reddish stains, only small portions of which are blood.

In sum, considering "all the evidence," on this issue, we think the evidentiary disarray surrounding the blood, taken together with Dr. Blake's testimony and the limited rebuttal of it in the present record, would prevent reasonable jurors from placing significant reliance on the blood evidence. We now know, though the trial jury did not, that an Assistant Chief Medical Examiner believes the blood on House's jeans must have come from autopsy samples; that a vial and a quarter of autopsy blood is unaccounted for; that the blood was transported to the FBI together with the pants in conditions that could have caused vials to spill; that the blood did indeed spill at least once during its journey from Tennessee authorities through FBI hands to a defense expert; that the pants were stored in a plastic bag bearing both a large blood stain and a label with TBI Agent Scott's name; and that the styrofoam box containing the blood samples may well have been opened before it arrived at the FBI lab. Thus, whereas the bloodstains, emphasized by the prosecution, seemed strong evidence of House's guilt at trial, the record now raises substantial questions about the blood's origin.

A Different Suspect

Were House's challenge to the State's case limited to the questions he has raised about the blood and semen, the other evidence favoring the prosecution might well suffice to bar relief. There is, however, more; for in the post-trial proceedings House presented troubling evidence that Mr. Muncey, the victim's husband, himself could have been the murderer.

At trial, as has been noted, the jury heard that roughly two weeks before the murder Mrs. Muncey's brother received a frightened phone call from his sister indicating that she and Mr. Muncey had been fighting, that she was scared, and that she wanted to leave him. The jury also learned that the brother once saw Mr. Muncey "smac[k]" the victim. House now has produced evidence from multiple sources suggesting that Mr. Muncey regularly abused his wife. For example, one witness – Kathy Parker, a lifelong area resident who denied any animosity towards Mr. Muncey – recalled that Mrs. Muncey "was constantly with black eyes and busted mouth." In addition Hazel Miller, who is Kathy Parker's mother and a lifelong acquaintance of Mr. Muncey, testified at the habeas hearing that two or three months before the victim's death Mr. Muncey came to Miller's home and "tried to get my daughter [Parker] to go out with him.". (Parker had dated Mr. Muncey at age 14.) According to Miller, Muncey said "[h]e was upset with his wife, that they had had an argument and he said he was going to get rid of that woman one way or the other."

Another witness – Mary Atkins, also an area native who "grew up" with Mr. Muncey and professed no hard feelings – claims she saw Mr. Muncey "backhan[d]" Mrs. Muncey on the very night of the murder. Atkins recalled that during a break in the recreation center dance, she saw Mr. Muncey and his wife arguing in the parking lot. Mr. Muncey "grabbed her and he just backhanded her." After that, Mrs. Muncey "left walking." There was also testimony from Atkins' mother, named Artie Lawson. A self-described "good friend" of Mr. Muncey, Lawson said Mr. Muncey visited her the morning after the murder, before the body was found. According to Lawson, Mr. Muncey asked her to tell anyone who inquired not only that she had been at the dance the evening before and had seen him, but also that he had breakfasted at her home at 6 o'clock that morning. Lawson had not in fact been at the dance, nor had Mr. Muncey been with her so early.

Of most importance is the testimony of Kathy Parker and her sister Penny Letner. They testified at the habeas hearing that, around the time of House's trial, Mr. Muncey had confessed to the crime. Parker recalled that she and "some family members and some friends [were] sitting around drinking" at Parker's trailer when Mr. Muncey "just walked in and sit down." Muncey, who had evidently been drinking heavily, began "rambling off . . . [t]alking about what happened to his wife and how it happened and he didn't mean to do it." According to Parker, Mr. Muncey "said they had been into [an] argument and he slapped her and she fell and hit her head and it killed her and he didn't mean for it to happen." Parker said she "freaked out and run him off."

Letner similarly recalled that at some point either "during [House's] trial or just before," Mr. Muncey intruded on a gathering at Parker's home. Appearing "pretty well blistered," Muncey "went to crying and was talking about his wife and her death and he was saying that he didn't mean to do it." "[D]idn't mean to do what[?]," Letner asked, at which point Mr. Muncey explained:

"[S]he was 'bitching him out' because he didn't take her fishing that night, that he went to the dance instead. He said when he come home that she was still on him pretty heavily 'bitching him out' again and that he smacked her and that she fell and hit her head. He said I didn't mean to do it, but I had to get rid of her, because I didn't want to be charged with murder."

Letner, who was then 19 years old with a small child, said Mr. Muncey's statement "scared [her] quite badly," so she "got out of there immediately." Asked whether she reported the incident to the authorities, Letner stated, "I was frightened, you know. . . . I figured me being 19 year old they wouldn't listen to anything I had to say." Parker, on the other hand, claimed she (Parker) in fact went to the Sherriff's Department, but no one would listen:

"I tried to speak to the Sheriff but he was real busy. He sent me to a deputy. The deputy told me to go upstairs to the courtroom and talk to this guy, I can't remember his name. I never did really get to talk to anybody."

Parker said she did not discuss the matter further because "[t]hey had it all signed, sealed and delivered. We didn't know anything to do until we heard that they reopened [House's] trial." Parker's mother, Hazel Miller, confirmed she had driven Parker to the courthouse, where Parker "went to talk to some of the people about this case."

Other testimony suggests Mr. Muncey had the opportunity to commit the crime. According to Dennis Wallace, a local law enforcement official who provided security at the dance on the night of the murder, Mr. Muncey left the dance "around 10:00, 10:30, 9:30 to 10:30." Although Mr. Muncey told law enforcement officials just after the murder that he left the dance only briefly and returned, Wallace could not recall seeing him back there again. Later that evening, Wallace responded to Mr. Muncey's report that his wife was missing. Muncey denied he and his wife had been "a fussing or a fighting"; he claimed his wife had been "kidnapped." Wallace did not recall seeing any blood, disarray, or knocked-over furniture, although he admitted he "didn't pay too much attention" to whether the floor appeared especially clean. According to Wallace, Mr. Muncey said "let's search for her" and then led Wallace out to search "in the weeds" around the home and the driveway (not out on the road where the body was found).

In the habeas proceedings, then, two different witnesses (Parker and Letner) described a confession by Mr. Muncey; two more (Atkins and Lawson) described suspicious behavior (a fight and an attempt to construct a false alibi) around the time of the crime; and still other witnesses described a history of abuse.

As to Parker and Letner, the District Court noted that it was "not impressed with the allegations of individuals who wait over ten years to come forward with their evidence," especially considering that "there was no physical evidence in the Munceys' kitchen to corroborate [Mr. Muncey's] alleged confession that he killed [his wife] there." Parker and Letner, however, did attempt to explain their delay coming forward, and the record indicates no reason why these two women, both lifelong acquaintances of Mr. Muncey, would have wanted either to frame him or to help House. Furthermore, the record includes at least some independent support for the statements Parker and Letner attributed to Mr. Muncey. The supposed explanation for the fatal fight – that his wife was complaining about going fishing – fits with Mrs. Muncey's statement to Luttrell earlier that evening that her husband's absence was "all right, because she was going to make him take her fishing the next day." And Dr. Blake testified, in only partial contradiction of Dr. Carabia, that Mrs. Muncey's head injury resulted from "a surface with an edge" or "a hard surface with a corner," not from a fist. (Dr. Carabia had said either a fist or some other object could have been the cause.)

Mr. Muncey testified at the habeas hearing, and the District Court did not question his credibility. Though Mr. Muncey said he seemed to remember visiting Lawson the day after the murder, he denied either killing his wife or confessing to doing so. Yet Mr. Muncey also claimed, contrary to Constable Wallace's testimony and to his own prior statement, that he left the dance on the night of the crime only when it ended at midnight. Mr. Muncey, moreover, denied ever hitting Mrs. Muncey; the State itself had to impeach him with a prior statement on this point.

It bears emphasis, finally, that Parker's and Letner's testimony is not comparable to the sort of eleventh-hour affidavit vouching for a defendant and incriminating a conveniently absent suspect that Justice O'Connor described in her concurring opinion in *Herrera* as "unfortunate" and "not uncommon" in capital cases; nor was the confession Parker and Letner described induced under pressure of interrogation. The confession evidence here involves an alleged spontaneous statement recounted by two eyewitnesses with no evident motive to lie. For this reason it has more probative value than, for example, incriminating testimony from inmates, suspects, or friends or relations of the accused.

The evidence pointing to Mr. Muncey is by no means conclusive. If considered in isolation, a reasonable jury might well disregard it. In combination, however, with the challenges to the blood evidence and the lack of motive with respect to House, the evidence pointing to Mr. Muncey likely would reinforce other doubts as to House's guilt.

Other Evidence

Certain other details were presented at the habeas hearing. First, Dr. Blake, in addition to testifying about the blood evidence and the victim's head injury, examined photographs of House's bruises and scratches and concluded, based on 35 years' experience monitoring the development and healing of bruises, that they were too old to have resulted from the crime. In addition Dr. Blake claimed that the injury on House's right knuckle was indicative of "[g]etting mashed"; it was not consistent with striking someone. (That of course would also eliminate the explanation that the injury came from the blow House supposedly told Turner he gave to his unidentified assailant.)

The victim's daughter, Lora Muncey (now Lora Tharp), also testified at the habeas hearing. She repeated her recollection of hearing a man with a deep voice like her grandfather's and a statement that her father had had a wreck down by the creek. She also denied seeing any signs of struggle or hearing a fight between her parents, though she also said she could not recall her parents ever fighting physically. The District Court found her credible, and this testimony certainly cuts in favor of the State.

Finally, House himself testified at the habeas proceedings. He essentially repeated the story he allegedly told Turner about getting attacked on the road. The District Court found, however, based on House's demeanor, that he "was not a credible witness."

Conclusion

This is not a case of conclusive exoneration. Some aspects of the State's evidence – Lora Muncey's memory of a deep voice, House's bizarre evening walk, his lie to law enforcement, his appearance near the body, and the blood on his pants – still support an inference of guilt. Yet the central forensic proof connecting House to the crime – the blood and the semen – has been called into question, and House has put forward substantial evidence pointing to a different suspect. Accordingly, and although the issue is close, we conclude that this is the rare case where – had the jury heard all the conflicting testimony – it is more likely than not that no reasonable juror viewing the record as a whole would lack reasonable doubt.

Note

1. Eventually, the federal district court ordered Tennessee to retry Mr. House or release him from custody. On July 3, 2008, Mr. House, who suffers from multiple sclerosis, was released to the custody of his mother after bail was posted on his behalf pending retrial. Tennessee has indicated that it will not seek death in the retrial. *See* http://blogs.amnestyusa.org/death-penalty.

2. Two recent books detail the exoneration of two men convicted of murder in Oklahoma: Ron Williamson, who was convicted of murder and sentenced to death, and his co-defendant Dennis Fritz, who was convicted of murder and sentenced to life imprisonment. The books are: John Grisham, THE INNOCENT MAN: MURDER AND INJUSTICE IN A SMALL TOWN (Doubleday) (2006) and Dennis Fritz, JOURNEY TOWARDS JUSTICE (Seven Locks Press) (2006).

CHAPTER 2 PROHIBITION AGAINST CRUEL AND UNUSUAL PUNISHMENT

B. Proportionality as a Limitation on Punishment

Note on Punishing Child Rape and Other Sex Crimes by Death

Page 72. Substitute for Louisiana v. Wilson:

Kennedy v. Louisiana
2008 WL 2511282

KENNEDY, J., delivered the opinion of the Court, in which Stevens, Souter, Ginsburg, and Breyer, JJ., joined.

I

Petitioner's crime was one that cannot be recounted in these pages in a way sufficient to capture in full the hurt and horror inflicted on his victim or to convey the revulsion society, and the jury that represents it, sought to express by sentencing petitioner to death. At 9:18 a.m. on March 2, 1998, petitioner called 911 to report that his [8-year-old] stepdaughter, referred to here as L. H., had been raped. He told the 911 operator that L.H. had been in the garage while he readied his son for school. Upon hearing loud screaming, petitioner said, he ran outside and found L.H. in the side yard. Two neighborhood boys, petitioner told the operator, had dragged L.H. from the garage to the yard, pushed her down, and raped her. Petitioner claimed he saw one of the boys riding away on a blue 10-speed bicycle.

When police arrived at petitioner's home between 9:20 and 9:30 a.m., they found L.H. on her bed, wearing a T-shirt and wrapped in a bloody blanket. She was bleeding profusely from the vaginal area. Petitioner told police he had carried her from the yard to the bathtub and then to the bed. Consistent with this explanation, police found a thin line of blood drops in the garage on the way to the house and then up the stairs. Once in the bedroom, petitioner had used a basin of water and a cloth to wipe blood from the victim. This later prevented medical personnel from collecting a reliable DNA sample.

L.H. was transported to the Children's Hospital. An expert in pediatric forensic medicine testified that L. H.'s injuries were the most severe he had seen from a sexual assault in his four years of practice. A laceration to the left wall of the vagina had separated her cervix from the back of her vagina, causing her rectum to protrude into the vaginal structure. Her entire perineum was torn from the posterior fourchette to the anus. The injuries required emergency surgery.

At the scene of the crime, at the hospital, and in the first weeks that followed, both L.H. and petitioner maintained in their accounts to investigators that L.H. had been raped by two neighborhood boys. One of L. H.'s doctors testified at trial that L.H. told all hospital personnel

13

the same version of the rape, although she reportedly told one family member that petitioner raped her. L.H. was interviewed several days after the rape by a psychologist. The interview was videotaped, lasted three hours over two days, and was introduced into evidence at trial. On the tape one can see that L.H. had difficulty discussing the subject of the rape. She spoke haltingly and with long pauses and frequent movement. Early in the interview, L.H. expressed reservations about the questions being asked:

> "I'm going to tell the same story. They just want me to change it .... They want me to say my Dad did it . . . . I don't want to say it . . . . I tell them the same, same story."

She told the psychologist that she had been playing in the garage when a boy came over and asked her about Girl Scout cookies she was selling; and that the boy "pulled [her by the legs to] the backyard," where he placed his hand over her mouth, "pulled down [her] shorts," and raped her.

Eight days after the crime, and despite L. H.'s insistence that petitioner was not the offender, petitioner was arrested for the rape. The State's investigation had drawn the accuracy of petitioner and L. H.'s story into question. Though the defense at trial proffered alternative explanations, the case for the prosecution, credited by the jury, was based upon the following evidence: An inspection of the side yard immediately after the assault was inconsistent with a rape having occurred there, the grass having been found mostly undisturbed but for a small patch of coagulated blood. Petitioner said that one of the perpetrators fled the crime scene on a blue 10-speed bicycle but gave inconsistent descriptions of the bicycle's features, such as its handlebars. Investigators found a bicycle matching petitioner and L. H.'s description in tall grass behind a nearby apartment, and petitioner identified it as the bicycle one of the perpetrators was riding. Yet its tires were flat, it did not have gears, and it was covered in spider webs. In addition police found blood on the underside of L. H.'s mattress. This convinced them the rape took place in her bedroom, not outside the house.

Police also found that petitioner made two telephone calls on the morning of the rape. Sometime before 6:15 a.m., petitioner called his employer and left a message that he was unavailable to work that day. Petitioner called back between 6:30 and 7:30 a.m. to ask a colleague how to get blood out of a white carpet because his daughter had "just become a young lady." At 7:37 a.m., petitioner called B & B Carpet Cleaning and requested urgent assistance in removing bloodstains from a carpet. Petitioner did not call 911 until about an hour and a half later.

About a month after petitioner's arrest L.H. was removed from the custody of her mother, who had maintained until that point that petitioner was not involved in the rape. On June 22, 1998, L.H. was returned home and told her mother for the first time that petitioner had raped her. And on December 16, 1999, about 21 months after the rape, L.H. recorded her accusation in a videotaped interview with the Child Advocacy Center.

The State charged petitioner with aggravated rape of a child under La. Stat. Ann. § 14:42 (West 1997 and Supp. 1998) and sought the death penalty. At all times relevant to petitioner's case, the statute provided:

"A. Aggravated rape is a rape committed ... where the anal or vaginal sexual intercourse is deemed to be without lawful consent of the victim because it is committed under any one or more of the following circumstances:
. . . . .
"(4) When the victim is under the age of twelve years. Lack of knowledge of the victim's age shall not be a defense.
. . . . .
"D. Whoever commits the crime of aggravated rape shall be punished by life imprisonment at hard labor without benefit of parole, probation, or suspension of sentence.

"(1) However, if the victim was under the age of twelve years, as provided by Paragraph A(4) of this Section:

"(a) And if the district attorney seeks a capital verdict, the offender shall be punished by death or life imprisonment at hard labor without benefit of parole, probation, or suspension of sentence, in accordance with the determination of the jury."

(Since petitioner was convicted and sentenced, the statute has been amended to include oral intercourse within the definition of aggravated rape and to increase the age of the victim from 12 to 13. See La. Stat. Ann. § 14:42 (West Supp. 2007).)

Aggravating circumstances are set forth in La.Code Crim. Proc. Ann., Art. 905.4 (West 1997 Supp.). In pertinent part and at all times relevant to petitioner's case, the provision stated:

"A. The following shall be considered aggravating circumstances:

"(1) The offender was engaged in the perpetration or attempted perpetration of aggravated rape, forcible rape, aggravated kidnapping, second degree kidnapping, aggravated burglary, aggravated arson, aggravated escape, assault by drive-by shooting, armed robbery, first degree robbery, or simple robbery.
. . . . .

"(10) The victim was under the age of twelve years or sixty-five years of age or older."

The trial began in August 2003. L.H. was then 13 years old. She testified that she "woke up one morning and Patrick was on top of [her]." She remembered petitioner bringing her "[a] cup of orange juice and pills chopped up in it" after the rape and overhearing him on the telephone saying she had become a "young lady." L.H. acknowledged that she had accused two neighborhood boys but testified petitioner told her to say this and that it was untrue.

The jury having found petitioner guilty of aggravated rape, the penalty phase ensued. The State presented the testimony of S.L., who is the cousin and goddaughter of petitioner's ex-wife. S.L. testified that petitioner sexually abused her three times when she was eight years old and that the last time involved sexual intercourse. She did not tell anyone until two years later and did not pursue legal action.

The jury unanimously determined that petitioner should be sentenced to death. The Supreme Court of Louisiana affirmed. The court rejected petitioner's reliance on *Coker v. Georgia,* 433 U.S. 584 (1977), noting that, while *Coker* bars the use of the death penalty as punishment for the rape of an adult woman, it left open the question which, if any, other nonhomicide crimes can be punished by death consistent with the Eighth Amendment. Because "children are a class that need special protection," the state court reasoned, the rape of a child is unique in terms of the harm it inflicts upon the victim and our society.

The court acknowledged that petitioner would be the first person executed for committing child rape since La. Stat. Ann. § 14:42 was amended in 1995 and that Louisiana is in the minority of jurisdictions that authorize the death penalty for the crime of child rape. But following the approach of *Roper v. Simmons,* 543 U.S. 551 (2005), and *Atkins v. Virginia,* 536 U.S. 304 (2002), it found significant not the "numerical counting of which [S]tates . . . stand for or against a particular capital prosecution," but "the direction of change." Since 1993, the court explained, four more States – Oklahoma, South Carolina, Montana, and Georgia – had capitalized the crime of child rape and at least eight States had authorized capital punishment for other nonhomicide crimes. By its count, 14 of the then-38 States permitting capital punishment, plus the Federal Government, allowed the death penalty for nonhomicide crimes and 5 allowed the death penalty for the crime of child rape.

The state court next asked whether "child rapists rank among the worst offenders." It noted the severity of the crime; that the execution of child rapists would serve the goals of deterrence and retribution; and that, unlike in *Atkins* and *Roper,* there were no characteristics of petitioner that tended to mitigate his moral culpability. It concluded: "[S]hort of first-degree murder, we can think of no other non-homicide crime more deserving [of capital punishment]."

On this reasoning the Supreme Court of Louisiana rejected petitioner's argument that the death penalty for the rape of a child under 12 years is disproportionate and upheld the constitutionality of the statute. Chief Justice Calogero dissented. *Coker, supra,* and *Eberheart v. Georgia,* 433 U.S. 917 (1977), in his view, "set out a bright-line and easily administered rule" that the Eighth Amendment precludes capital punishment for any offense that does not involve the death of the victim. . . .

II

The Eighth Amendment, applicable to the States through the Fourteenth Amendment, provides that "[e]xcessive bail shall not be required, nor excessive fines imposed, nor cruel and unusual punishments inflicted." The Amendment proscribes "all excessive punishments, as well as cruel and unusual punishments that may or may not be excessive." *Atkins,* 536 U.S., at 311, n. 7. The Court explained in *Atkins* and *Roper* that the Eighth Amendment's protection against excessive or cruel and unusual punishments flows from the basic "precept of justice that punishment for [a] crime should be graduated and proportioned to [the] offense." *Weems v. United States,* 217 U.S. 349, 367 (1910). Whether this requirement has been fulfilled is determined not by the standards that prevailed when the Eighth Amendment was adopted in 1791 but by the norms that "currently prevail." *Atkins, supra,* at 311. The Amendment "draw[s] its meaning from the evolving standards of decency that mark the progress of a maturing society." *Trop v. Dulles,* 356 U.S. 86, 101 (1958) (plurality opinion). This is because "[t]he standard of extreme cruelty is not merely descriptive, but necessarily embodies a moral judgment. The standard itself remains the same, but its applicability must change as the basic mores of society change." *Furman v. Georgia,* 408 U.S. 238, 382 (1972) (Burger, C. J., dissenting).

Evolving standards of decency must embrace and express respect for the dignity of the person, and the punishment of criminals must conform to that rule. As we shall discuss, punishment is justified under one or more of three principal rationales: rehabilitation, deterrence, and retribution. It is the last of these, retribution, that most often can contradict the law's own ends. This is of particular concern when the Court interprets the meaning of the Eighth Amendment in capital cases. When the law punishes by death, it risks its own sudden descent into brutality, transgressing the constitutional commitment to decency and restraint.

For these reasons we have explained that capital punishment must "be limited to those offenders who commit 'a narrow category of the most serious crimes' and whose extreme culpability makes them 'the most deserving of execution.'" *Roper, supra,* at 568 (quoting *Atkins, supra,* at 319). Though the death penalty is not invariably unconstitutional, the Court insists upon confining the instances in which the punishment can be imposed.

Applying this principle, we held in *Roper* and *Atkins* that the execution of juveniles and mentally retarded persons are punishments violative of the Eighth Amendment because the offender had a diminished personal responsibility for the crime. The Court further has held that the death penalty can be disproportionate to the crime itself where the crime did not result, or was not intended to result, in death of the victim. In *Coker,* for instance, the Court held it would be unconstitutional to execute an offender who had raped an adult woman. See also *Eberheart, supra* (holding unconstitutional in light of *Coker* a sentence of death for the kidnaping and rape

17

of an adult woman). And in *Enmund v. Florida,* 458 U.S. 782 (1982), the Court overturned the capital sentence of a defendant who aided and abetted a robbery during which a murder was committed but did not himself kill, attempt to kill, or intend that a killing would take place. On the other hand, in *Tison v. Arizona,* 481 U.S. 137 (1987), the Court allowed the defendants' death sentences to stand where they did not themselves kill the victims but their involvement in the events leading up to the murders was active, recklessly indifferent, and substantial.

In these cases the Court has been guided by "objective indicia of society's standards, as expressed in legislative enactments and state practice with respect to executions."*Roper,* 543 U.S., at 563; see also *Coker, supra,* at 593-597 (plurality opinion) (finding that both legislatures and juries had firmly rejected the penalty of death for the rape of an adult woman); *Enmund, supra,* at 788 (looking to "historical development of the punishment at issue, legislative judgments, international opinion, and the sentencing decisions juries have made"). The inquiry does not end there, however. Consensus is not dispositive. Whether the death penalty is disproportionate to the crime committed depends as well upon the standards elaborated by controlling precedents and by the Court's own understanding and interpretation of the Eighth Amendment's text, history, meaning, and purpose.

Based both on consensus and our own independent judgment, our holding is that a death sentence for one who raped but did not kill a child, and who did not intend to assist another in killing the child, is unconstitutional under the Eighth and Fourteenth Amendments.

III
A

The existence of objective indicia of consensus against making a crime punishable by death was a relevant concern in *Roper, Atkins, Coker,* and *Enmund,* and we follow the approach of those cases here.

. . . Definitive resolution of state-law issues is for the States' own courts, and there may be disagreement over the statistics. It is further true that some States, including States that have addressed the issue in just the last few years, have made child rape a capital offense. The summary recited here, however, does allow us to make certain comparisons with the data cited in the *Atkins, Roper,* and *Enmund* cases.

When *Atkins* was decided in 2002, 30 States, including 12 noncapital jurisdictions, prohibited the death penalty for mentally retarded offenders; 20 permitted it. When *Roper* was decided in 2005, the numbers disclosed a similar division among the States: 30 States prohibited the death penalty for juveniles, 18 of which permitted the death penalty for other offenders; and 20 States authorized it. Both in *Atkins* and in *Roper,* we noted that the practice of executing mentally retarded and juvenile offenders was infrequent. Only five States had executed an offender known to have an IQ below 70 between 1989 and 2002, and only three States had executed a juvenile offender between 1995 and 2005.

The statistics in *Enmund* bear an even greater similarity to the instant case. There eight jurisdictions had authorized imposition of the death penalty solely for participation in a robbery during which an accomplice committed murder, and six defendants between 1954 and 1982 had been sentenced to death for felony murder where the defendant did not personally commit the homicidal assault. These facts, the Court concluded, "weigh[ed] on the side of rejecting capital punishment for the crime."

The evidence of a national consensus with respect to the death penalty for child rapists, as with respect to juveniles, mentally retarded offenders, and vicarious felony murderers, shows divided opinion but, on balance, an opinion against it. Thirty-seven jurisdictions – 36 States plus the Federal Government – have the death penalty. As mentioned above, only six of those jurisdictions authorize the death penalty for rape of a child. Though our review of national consensus is not confined to tallying the number of States with applicable death penalty legislation, it is of significance that, in 45 jurisdictions, petitioner could not be executed for child rape of any kind. That number surpasses the 30 States in *Atkins* and *Roper* and the 42 States in *Enmund* that prohibited the death penalty under the circumstances those cases considered.

B

At least one difference between this case and our Eighth Amendment proportionality precedents must be addressed. Respondent and its *amici* suggest that some States have an "erroneous understanding of this Court's Eighth Amendment jurisprudence. They submit that the general propositions set out in *Coker,* contrasting murder and rape, have been interpreted in too expansive a way, leading some state legislatures to conclude that *Coker* applies to child rape when in fact its reasoning does not, or ought not, apply to that specific crime.

This argument seems logical at first, but in the end it is unsound. In *Coker,* a four-Member plurality of the Court, plus Justice Brennan and Justice Marshall in concurrence, held that a sentence of death for the rape of a 16-year-old woman, who was a minor under Georgia law, see Ga.Code Ann. § 74-104 (1973), yet was characterized by the Court as an adult, was disproportionate and excessive under the Eighth Amendment. (The Court did not explain why the 16-year-old victim qualified as an adult, but it may be of some significance that she was married, had a home of her own, and had given birth to a son three weeks prior to the rape.)

. . . *Coker's* analysis of the Eighth Amendment is susceptible of a reading that would prohibit making child rape a capital offense. In context, however, *Coker's* holding was narrower than some of its language read in isolation. The *Coker* plurality framed the question as whether, "with respect to rape of an adult woman," the death penalty is disproportionate punishment. And it repeated the phrase "an adult woman" or "an adult female" in discussing the act of rape or the victim of rape eight times in its opinion. The distinction between adult and child rape was not merely rhetorical; it was central to the Court's reasoning. The opinion does not speak to the constitutionality of the death penalty for child rape, an issue not then before the Court. . . .

We conclude . . . that there is no clear indication that state legislatures have misinterpreted *Coker* to hold that the death penalty for child rape is unconstitutional. The small number of States that have enacted this penalty, then, is relevant to determining whether there is a consensus against capital punishment for this crime.

C

Respondent insists that the six States where child rape is a capital offense, along with the States that have proposed but not yet enacted applicable death penalty legislation, reflect a consistent direction of change in support of the death penalty for child rape. Consistent change might counterbalance an otherwise weak demonstration of consensus. See *Atkins,* 536 U.S., at 315 ("It is not so much the number of these States that is significant, but the consistency of the direction of change"); *Roper,* 543 U.S., at 565 ("Impressive in *Atkins* was the rate of abolition of the death penalty for the mentally retarded"). But whatever the significance of consistent change where it is cited to show emerging support for expanding the scope of the death penalty, no showing of consistent change has been made in this case.

Respondent and its *amici* identify five States where, in their view, legislation authorizing capital punishment for child rape is pending. It is not our practice, nor is it sound, to find contemporary norms based upon state legislation that has been proposed but not yet enacted. There are compelling reasons not to do so here. Since the briefs were submitted by the parties, legislation in two of the five States has failed. In Tennessee, the house bills were rejected almost a year ago, and the senate bills appear to have died in committee. And in Missouri, the 2008 legislative session has ended, tabling the pending legislation.

Aside from pending legislation, it is true that in the last 13 years there has been change towards making child rape a capital offense. This is evidenced by six new death penalty statutes, three enacted in the last two years. But this showing is not as significant as the data in *Atkins,* where 18 States between 1986 and 2001 had enacted legislation prohibiting the execution of mentally retarded persons. Respondent argues the instant case is like *Roper* because, there, only five States had shifted their positions between 1989 and 2005, one less State than here. But in *Roper,* we emphasized that, though the pace of abolition was not as great as in *Atkins,* it was counterbalanced by the total number of States that had recognized the impropriety of executing juvenile offenders. When we decided *Stanford v. Kentucky,* 492 U.S. 361 (1989), 12 death penalty States already prohibited the execution of any juvenile under 18, and 15 prohibited the execution of any juvenile under 17. Here, the total number of States to have made child rape a capital offense after *Furman* is six. This is not an indication of a trend or change in direction comparable to the one supported by data in *Roper.* The evidence here bears a closer resemblance to the evidence of state activity in *Enmund,* where we found a national consensus against the death penalty for vicarious felony murder despite eight jurisdictions having authorized the practice.

D

There are measures of consensus other than legislation. Statistics about the number of executions may inform the consideration whether capital punishment for the crime of child rape is regarded as unacceptable in our society. These statistics confirm our determination from our review of state statutes that there is a social consensus against the death penalty for the crime of child rape.

Nine States – Florida, Georgia, Louisiana, Mississippi, Montana, Oklahoma, South Carolina, Tennessee, and Texas – have permitted capital punishment for adult or child rape for some length of time between the Court's 1972 decision in *Furman* and today. Yet no individual has been executed for the rape of an adult or child since 1964, and no execution for any other nonhomicide offense has been conducted since 1963. See Historical Statistics of the United States, at 5-262 to 5-263 (Table Ec343-357). Cf. *Thompson v. Oklahoma,* 487 U.S. 815, 852-853 (1988) (O'Connor, J., concurring in judgment) (that "four decades have gone by since the last execution of a defendant who was younger than 16 at the time of the offense . . . support[s] the inference of a national consensus opposing the death penalty for 15-year-olds").

Louisiana is the only State since 1964 that has sentenced an individual to death for the crime of child rape; and petitioner and Richard Davis, who was convicted and sentenced to death for the aggravated rape of a 5-year-old child by a Louisiana jury in December 2007, are the only two individuals now on death row in the United States for a nonhomicide offense.

After reviewing the authorities informed by contemporary norms, including the history of the death penalty for this and other nonhomicide crimes, current state statutes and new enactments, and the number of executions since 1964, we conclude there is a national consensus against capital punishment for the crime of child rape.

IV

A

As we have said in other Eighth Amendment cases, objective evidence of contemporary values as it relates to punishment for child rape is entitled to great weight, but it does not end our inquiry. "[T]he Constitution contemplates that in the end our own judgment will be brought to bear on the question of the acceptability of the death penalty under the Eighth Amendment." *Coker, supra,* at 597 (plurality opinion); see also *Roper, supra,* at 563; *Enmund, supra,* at 797 ("[I]t is for us ultimately to judge whether the Eighth Amendment permits imposition of the death penalty"). We turn, then, to the resolution of the question before us, which is informed by our precedents and our own understanding of the Constitution and the rights it secures.

It must be acknowledged that there are moral grounds to question a rule barring capital punishment for a crime against an individual that did not result in death. These facts illustrate the point. Here the victim's fright, the sense of betrayal, and the nature of her injuries caused more prolonged physical and mental suffering than, say, a sudden killing by an unseen assassin. The attack was not just on her but on her childhood. For this reason, we should be most reluctant to rely upon the language of the plurality in *Coker,* which posited that, for the victim of rape, "life may not be nearly so happy as it was" but it is not beyond repair. Rape has a permanent psychological, emotional, and sometimes physical impact on the child. We cannot dismiss the years of long anguish that must be endured by the victim of child rape.

It does not follow, though, that capital punishment is a proportionate penalty for the crime. The constitutional prohibition against excessive or cruel and unusual punishments mandates that the State's power to punish "be exercised within the limits of civilized standards." Evolving standards of decency that mark the progress of a maturing society counsel us to be most hesitant before interpreting the Eighth Amendment to allow the extension of the death penalty, a hesitation that has special force where no life was taken in the commission of the crime. It is an established principle that decency, in its essence, presumes respect for the individual and thus moderation or restraint in the application of capital punishment.

. . . Our concern here is limited to crimes against individual persons. We do not address, for example, crimes defining and punishing treason, espionage, terrorism, and drug kingpin activity, which are offenses against the State. As it relates to crimes against individuals, though, the death penalty should not be expanded to instances where the victim's life was not taken. We said in *Coker* of adult rape:

> "We do not discount the seriousness of rape as a crime. It is highly reprehensible, both in a moral sense and in its almost total contempt for the personal integrity and autonomy of the female victim .... Short of homicide, it is the 'ultimate violation of self.' . . .[But] [t]he murderer kills; the rapist, if no more than that, does not. . . . We have the abiding conviction that the death penalty, which 'is unique in its severity and irrevocability,' is an excessive penalty for the rapist who, as such, does not take human life." 433 U.S., at 597-598 (plurality opinion) (citation omitted).

The same distinction between homicide and other serious violent offenses against the individual informed the Court's analysis in *Enmund,* 458 U.S. 782, where the Court held that the death penalty for the crime of vicarious felony murder is disproportionate to the offense. The Court repeated there the fundamental, moral distinction between a "murderer" and a "robber," noting that while "robbery is a serious crime deserving serious punishment," it is not like death in its "severity and irrevocability."

Consistent with evolving standards of decency and the teachings of our precedents we conclude that, in determining whether the death penalty is excessive, there is a distinction between intentional first-degree murder on the one hand and nonhomicide crimes against individual persons, even including child rape, on the other. The latter crimes may be devastating in their harm, as here, but "in terms of moral depravity and of the injury to the person and to the public" they cannot be compared to murder in their "severity and irrevocability."

In reaching our conclusion we find significant the number of executions that would be allowed under respondent's approach. The crime of child rape, considering its reported incidents, occurs more often than first-degree murder. Approximately 5,702 incidents of vaginal, anal, or oral rape of a child under the age of 12 were reported nationwide in 2005; this is almost twice the total incidents of intentional murder for victims of all ages (3,405) reported during the same period. Although we have no reliable statistics on convictions for child rape, we can surmise that, each year, there are hundreds, or more, of these convictions just in jurisdictions that permit capital punishment. As a result of existing rules, see generally *Godfrey,* 446 U.S., at 428-433 (plurality opinion), only 2.2% of convicted first-degree murderers are sentenced to death. But under respondent's approach, the 36 States that permit the death penalty could sentence to death all persons convicted of raping a child less than 12 years of age. This could not be reconciled with our evolving standards of decency and the necessity to constrain the use of the death penalty.

It might be said that narrowing aggravators could be used in this context, as with murder offenses, to ensure the death penalty's restrained application. We find it difficult to identify standards that would guide the decisionmaker so the penalty is reserved for the most severe cases of child rape and yet not imposed in an arbitrary way. Even were we to forbid, say, the execution of first-time child rapists, or require as an aggravating factor a finding that the perpetrator's instant rape offense involved multiple victims, the jury still must balance, in its discretion, those aggravating factors against mitigating circumstances. In this context, which involves a crime that in many cases will overwhelm a decent person's judgment, we have no confidence that the imposition of the death penalty would not be so arbitrary as to be "freakis[h]," *Furman,* 408 U.S., at 310 (Stewart, J., concurring). We cannot sanction this result when the harm to the victim, though grave, cannot be quantified in the same way as death of the victim.

. . . [T]he resulting imprecision and the tension between evaluating the individual circumstances and consistency of treatment have been tolerated where the victim dies. It should not be introduced into our justice system, though, where death has not occurred.

Our concerns are all the more pronounced where, as here, the death penalty for this crime has been most infrequent. We have developed a foundational jurisprudence in the case of capital murder to guide the States and juries in imposing the death penalty. Starting with *Gregg,* 428 U.S. 153, we have spent more than 32 years articulating limiting factors that channel the jury's discretion to avoid the death penalty's arbitrary imposition in the case of capital murder. Though that practice remains sound, beginning the same process for crimes for which no one has been executed in more than 40 years would require experimentation in an area where a failed experiment would result in the execution of individuals undeserving of the death penalty. Evolving standards of decency are difficult to reconcile with a regime that seeks to expand the death penalty to an area where standards to confine its use are indefinite and obscure.

B

Our decision is consistent with the justifications offered for the death penalty. *Gregg* instructs that capital punishment is excessive when it is grossly out of proportion to the crime or it does not fulfill the two distinct social purposes served by the death penalty: retribution and deterrence of capital crimes.

As in *Coker,* here it cannot be said with any certainty that the death penalty for child rape serves no deterrent or retributive function. See *id.,* at 593, n. 4 (concluding that the death penalty for rape might serve "legitimate ends of punishment" but nevertheless is disproportionate to the crime). Cf. *Gregg, supra,* at 185-186 (joint opinion of Stewart, Powell, and Stevens, JJ.) ("[T]here is no convincing empirical evidence either supporting or refuting th[e] view [that the death penalty serves as a significantly greater deterrent than lesser penalties]. We may nevertheless assume safely that there are murderers . . . for whom . . . the death penalty undoubtedly is a significant deterrent"); *id.,* at 186 (the value of capital punishment, and its contribution to acceptable penological goals, typically is a "complex factual issue the resolution of which properly rests with the legislatures"). This argument does not overcome other objections, however. The incongruity between the crime of child rape and the harshness of the death penalty poses risks of overpunishment and counsels against a constitutional ruling that the death penalty can be expanded to include this offense.

The goal of retribution, which reflects society's and the victim's interests in seeing that the offender is repaid for the hurt he caused, does not justify the harshness of the death penalty here. In measuring retribution, as well as other objectives of criminal law, it is appropriate to distinguish between a particularly depraved murder that merits death as a form of retribution and the crime of child rape.

There is an additional reason for our conclusion that imposing the death penalty for child rape would not further retributive purposes. In considering whether retribution is served, among other factors we have looked to whether capital punishment "has the potential . . . to allow the community as a whole, including the surviving family and friends of the victim, to affirm its own judgment that the culpability of the prisoner is so serious that the ultimate penalty must be sought and imposed." *Panetti v. Quarterman,* 127 S.Ct. 2842, ____ (2007). In considering the death penalty for nonhomicide offenses this inquiry necessarily also must include the question whether the death penalty balances the wrong to the victim.

It is not at all evident that the child rape victim's hurt is lessened when the law permits the death of the perpetrator. Capital cases require a long-term commitment by those who testify for the prosecution, especially when guilt and sentencing determinations are in multiple proceedings. In cases like this the key testimony is not just from the family but from the victim herself. During formative years of her adolescence, made all the more daunting for having to come to terms with the brutality of her experience, L.H. was required to discuss the case at length with law enforcement personnel. In a public trial she was required to recount once more all the details of the crime to a jury as the State pursued the death of her stepfather. And in the end the State made L.H. a central figure in its decision to seek the death penalty, telling the jury in closing statements: "[L. H.] is asking you, asking you to set up a time and place when he dies."

Society's desire to inflict the death penalty for child rape by enlisting the child victim to assist it over the course of years in asking for capital punishment forces a moral choice on the child, who is not of mature age to make that choice. The way the death penalty here involves the child victim in its enforcement can compromise a decent legal system; and this is but a subset of fundamental difficulties capital punishment can cause in the administration and enforcement of laws proscribing child rape.

There are, moreover, serious systemic concerns in prosecuting the crime of child rape that are relevant to the constitutionality of making it a capital offense. The problem of unreliable, induced, and even imagined child testimony means there is a "special risk of wrongful execution" in some child rape cases. This undermines, at least to some degree, the meaningful contribution of the death penalty to legitimate goals of punishment. Studies conclude that children are highly susceptible to suggestive questioning techniques like repetition, guided imagery, and selective reinforcement. See Ceci & Friedman, The Suggestibility of Children: Scientific Research and Legal Implications, 86 Cornell L.Rev. 33, 47 (2000) (there is "strong evidence that children, especially young children, are suggestible to a significant degree-even on abuse-related questions"); Gross, Jacoby, Matheson, Montgomery, & Patil, Exonerations in the United States 1989 Through 2003, 95 J.Crim. L. & C. 523, 539 (2005) (discussing allegations of abuse at the Little Rascals Day Care Center); see also Quas, Davis, Goodman, & Myers, Repeated Questions, Deception, and Children's True and False Reports of Body Touch, 12 Child Maltreatment 60, 61-66 (2007) (finding that 4- to 7-year-olds "were able to maintain [a] lie about body touch fairly effectively when asked repeated, direct questions during a mock forensic interview").

Similar criticisms pertain to other cases involving child witnesses; but child rape cases present heightened concerns because the central narrative and account of the crime often comes from the child herself. She and the accused are, in most instances, the only ones present when the crime was committed. And the question in a capital case is not just the fact of the crime, including, say, proof of rape as distinct from abuse short of rape, but details bearing upon brutality in its commission. These matters are subject to fabrication or exaggeration, or both. Although capital punishment does bring retribution, and the legislature here has chosen to use it for this end, its judgment must be weighed, in deciding the constitutional question, against the special risks of unreliable testimony with respect to this crime.

With respect to deterrence, if the death penalty adds to the risk of non-reporting, that, too, diminishes the penalty's objectives. Underreporting is a common problem with respect to child sexual abuse. See Hanson, Resnick, Saunders, Kilpatrick, & Best, Factors Related to the Reporting of Childhood Rape, 23 Child Abuse & Neglect 559, 564 (1999) (finding that about 88% of female rape victims under the age of 18 did not disclose their abuse to authorities); Smith et al., Delay in Disclosure of Childhood Rape: Results From A National Survey, 24 Child Abuse & Neglect 273, 278-279 (2000) (finding that 72% of women raped as children disclosed their abuse to someone, but that only 12% of the victims reported the rape to authorities). Although we know little about what differentiates those who report from those who do not report, one of the most commonly cited reasons for nondisclosure is fear of negative consequences for the perpetrator, a concern that has special force where the abuser is a family member, see Goodman-Brown, Edelstein, Goodman, Jones, & Gordon, Why Children Tell: A Model of Children's Disclosure of Sexual Abuse, 27 Child Abuse & Neglect 525, 527-528 (2003); *Smith, supra,* at 283-284 (finding that, where there was a relationship between perpetrator and victim, the victim was likely to keep the abuse a secret for a longer period of time, perhaps because of a "greater sense of loyalty or emotional bond"). The experience of the *amici* who work with child victims indicates that, when the punishment is death, both the victim and the victim's family members may be more likely to shield the perpetrator from discovery, thus increasing underreporting. As a result, punishment by death may not result in more deterrence or more effective enforcement.

In addition, by in effect making the punishment for child rape and murder equivalent, a State that punishes child rape by death may remove a strong incentive for the rapist not to kill the victim. Assuming the offender behaves in a rational way, as one must to justify the penalty on grounds of deterrence, the penalty in some respects gives less protection, not more, to the victim, who is often the sole witness to the crime. It might be argued that, even if the death penalty results in a marginal increase in the incentive to kill, this is counterbalanced by a marginally increased deterrent to commit the crime at all. Whatever balance the legislature strikes, however, uncertainty on the point makes the argument for the penalty less compelling than for homicide crimes.

Each of these propositions, standing alone, might not establish the unconstitutionality of the death penalty for the crime of child rape. Taken in sum, however, they demonstrate the serious negative consequences of making child rape a capital offense. These considerations lead us to conclude, in our independent judgment, that the death penalty is not a proportional punishment for the rape of a child.

V

Our determination that there is a consensus against the death penalty for child rape raises the question whether the Court's own institutional position and its holding will have the effect of blocking further or later consensus in favor of the penalty from developing. The Court, it will be argued, by the act of addressing the constitutionality of the death penalty, intrudes upon the consensus-making process. By imposing a negative restraint, the argument runs, the Court makes it more difficult for consensus to change or emerge. The Court, according to the criticism, itself becomes enmeshed in the process, part judge and part the maker of that which it judges.

These concerns overlook the meaning and full substance of the established proposition that the Eighth Amendment is defined by "the evolving standards of decency that mark the progress of a maturing society." Confirmed by repeated, consistent rulings of this Court, this principle requires that use of the death penalty be restrained. The rule of evolving standards of decency with specific marks on the way to full progress and mature judgment means that resort to the penalty must be reserved for the worst of crimes and limited in its instances of application. In most cases justice is not better served by terminating the life of the perpetrator rather than confining him and preserving the possibility that he and the system will find ways to allow him to understand the enormity of his offense. Difficulties in administering the penalty to ensure against its arbitrary and capricious application require adherence to a rule reserving its use, at this stage of evolving standards and in cases of crimes against individuals, for crimes that take the life of the victim.

The judgment of the Supreme Court of Louisiana upholding the capital sentence is reversed. This case is remanded for further proceedings not inconsistent with this opinion.

E.   Modern Methods of Execution

6.   Lethal Injection

Page 129. Insert before Note on Eighth Amendment Challenge to the Use of Pavulon in Lethal Injections:

Hill v. McDonough
547 U.S. 573 (2006)

Justice KENNEDY delivered the opinion of the Court.

Petitioner Clarence E. Hill challenges the constitutionality of a three-drug sequence the State of Florida likely would use to execute him by lethal injection. Seeking to enjoin the procedure, he filed this action in the United States District Court for the Northern District of Florida, pursuant to the Civil Rights Act of 1871, as amended, 42 U.S.C. § 1983. The District Court and the Court of Appeals for the Eleventh Circuit construed the action as a petition for a writ of habeas corpus and ordered it dismissed for noncompliance with the requirements for a second and successive petition. The question before us is whether Hill's claim must be brought by an action for a writ of habeas corpus under the statute authorizing that writ, 28 U.S.C. § 2254, or whether it may proceed as an action for relief under 42 U.S.C. § 1983.

This is not the first time we have found it necessary to discuss which of the two statutes governs an action brought by a prisoner alleging a constitutional violation. See, *e.g., Nelson v. Campbell,* 541 U.S. 637 (2004); *Heck v. Humphrey,* 512 U.S. 477 (1994); *Preiser v. Rodriguez,* 411 U.S. 475 (1973). Hill's suit, we now determine, is comparable in its essentials to the action the Court allowed to proceed under § 1983 in *Nelson.* In accord with that precedent we now reverse.

I

In the year 1983, Hill was convicted of first-degree murder and sentenced to death. When his conviction and sentence became final some five years later, the method of execution then prescribed by Florida law was electrocution. On January 14, 2000 – four days after the conclusion of Hill's first, unsuccessful round of federal habeas corpus litigation – Florida amended the controlling statute to provide: "A death sentence shall be executed by lethal injection, unless the person sentenced to death affirmatively elects to be executed by electrocution." § 922.105(1) (2003). The now-controlling statute, which has not been changed in any relevant respect, does not specify a particular lethal-injection procedure. Implementation is the responsibility of the Florida Department of Corrections. The department has not issued rules establishing a specific lethal-injection protocol, and its implementing policies and procedures appear exempt from Florida's Administrative Procedure Act.

After the statute was amended to provide for lethal injection, the Florida Supreme Court heard a death row inmate's claim that the execution procedure violated the Eighth Amendment's prohibition of cruel and unusual punishments. In *Sims* [*v. State,* 754 So.2d 657 (Fla. 2000) (per curiam)], the complainant, who had acquired detailed information about the procedure from the State, contended the planned three-drug sequence of injections would cause great pain if the drugs were not administered properly. The Florida Supreme Court rejected this argument as too speculative.

On November 29, 2005, the Governor of Florida signed Hill's death warrant, which ordered him to be executed on January 24, 2006. Hill requested information about the lethal injection protocol, but the department provided none. Hill then challenged, for the first time, the State's lethal injection procedure. On December 15, 2005, he filed a successive postconviction petition in state court, relying upon the Eighth Amendment. The trial court denied Hill's request for an evidentiary hearing and dismissed his claim as procedurally barred. The Florida Supreme Court affirmed on January 17, 2006.

Three days later – and four days before his scheduled execution – Hill brought this action in District Court pursuant to 42 U.S.C. § 1983. Assuming the State would use the procedure discussed at length in the *Sims* decision, Hill alleged that the first drug injected, sodium pentothal, would not be a sufficient anesthetic to render painless the administration of the second and third drugs, pancuronium bromide and potassium chloride. There was an ensuing risk, Hill alleged, that he could remain conscious and suffer severe pain as the pancuronium paralyzed his lungs and body and the potassium chloride caused muscle cramping and a fatal heart attack. The complaint sought an injunction "barring defendants from executing Plaintiff in the manner they currently intend."

The District Court found that under controlling Eleventh Circuit precedent the § 1983 claim was the functional equivalent of a petition for writ of habeas corpus. Because Hill had sought federal habeas corpus relief in an earlier action, the District Court deemed his petition successive and thus barred for failure to obtain leave to file from the Court of Appeals as required by 28 U.S.C. § 2244(b). On the day of the scheduled execution the Court of Appeals affirmed. It held that Hill's action was a successive petition and that it would deny any application for leave to file a successive petition because § 2244(b)(2) would not allow his claim to proceed. After issuing a temporary stay of execution, this Court granted Hill's petition for certiorari and continued the stay pending our resolution of the case.

II

"Federal law opens two main avenues to relief on complaints related to imprisonment: a petition for habeas corpus, 28 U.S.C. § 2254, and a complaint under the Civil Rights Act of 1871, as amended, 42 U.S.C. § 1983. Challenges to the lawfulness of confinement or to particulars affecting its duration are the province of habeas corpus." An inmate's challenge to the circumstances of his confinement, however, may be brought under § 1983.

In *Nelson v. Campbell,* we addressed whether a challenge to a lethal injection procedure must proceed as a habeas corpus action. The complainant had severely compromised peripheral veins, and Alabama planned to apply an invasive procedure on his arm or leg to enable the injection. He sought to enjoin the procedure, alleging it would violate the Eighth Amendment. The Court observed that the question whether a general challenge to a method of execution must proceed under habeas was a difficult one. The claim was not easily described as a challenge to the fact or duration of a sentence; yet in a State where the legislature has established lethal injection as the method of execution, "a constitutional challenge seeking to permanently enjoin the use of lethal injection may amount to a challenge to the fact of the sentence itself."

Nelson did not decide this question. The lawsuit at issue, as the Court understood the case, did not require an injunction that would challenge the sentence itself. The invasive procedure in *Nelson* was not mandated by law, and the inmate appeared willing to concede the existence of an acceptable alternative procedure. Absent a finding that the challenged procedure was necessary to the lethal injection, the Court concluded, injunctive relief would not prevent the State from implementing the sentence. Consequently, the suit as presented would not be deemed a challenge to the fact of the sentence itself.

The decision in *Nelson* also observed that its holding was congruent with the Court's precedents addressing civil rights suits for damages that implicate habeas relief. Those cases provide that prisoners' suits for damages can be barred from proceeding under § 1983 when a judgment in the prisoner's favor necessarily implies the invalidity of the prisoner's sentence. The action in *Nelson,* however, was not analogous to a damages suit filed to circumvent the limits imposed by the habeas statute. The suit did not challenge an execution procedure required by law, so granting relief would not imply the unlawfulness of the lethal injection sentence.

In the case before us we conclude that Hill's § 1983 action is controlled by the holding in *Nelson.* Here, as in *Nelson,* Hill's action if successful would not necessarily prevent the State from executing him by lethal injection. The complaint does not challenge the lethal injection sentence as a general matter but seeks instead only to enjoin the respondents "from executing [Hill] in the manner they currently intend." The specific objection is that the anticipated protocol allegedly causes "a foreseeable risk of . . . gratuitous and unnecessary" pain. Hill concedes that "other methods of lethal injection the Department could choose to use would be constitutional," and respondents do not contend, at least to this point in the litigation, that granting Hill's injunction would leave the State without any other practicable, legal method of executing Hill by lethal injection. Florida law, moreover, does not require the Department of Corrections to use the challenged procedure. Hill's challenge appears to leave the State free to use an alternative lethal injection procedure. Under these circumstances a grant of injunctive relief could not be seen as barring the execution of Hill's sentence.

One difference between the present case and *Nelson,* of course, is that Hill challenges the chemical injection sequence rather than a surgical procedure preliminary to the lethal injection. In *Nelson,* however, the State argued that the invasive procedure was not a medical operation separable from the lethal injection but rather a "necessary prerequisite to, and thus an indispensable part of, any lethal injection procedure." The Court reasoned that although venous access was necessary for lethal injection, it did not follow that the State's chosen means of access were necessary; "the gravamen of petitioner's entire claim" was that the procedure was "gratuitous." The same is true here. Although the injection of lethal chemicals is an obvious necessity for the execution, Hill alleges that the challenged procedure presents a risk of pain the State can avoid while still being able to enforce the sentence ordering a lethal injection.

One concern is that the foregoing analysis may be more theoretical than real based on the practicalities of the case. A procedure that avoids the harms Hill alleges, for instance, may be susceptible to attack for other purported risks of its own. Respondents and their supporting *amici* thus contend that the legal distinction between habeas corpus and § 1983 actions must account for the practical reality of capital litigation tactics: Inmates file these actions intending to forestall execution, and *Nelson*'s emphasis on whether a suit challenges something "necessary" to the execution provides no endpoint to piecemeal litigation aimed at delaying the execution. Viewed in isolation, no single component of a given execution procedure may be strictly necessary, the argument goes, and a capital litigant may put off execution by challenging one aspect of a procedure after another. The *amici* States point to *Nelson*'s aftermath as a cautionary example, contending that on remand the District Court allowed Nelson to amend his complaint and that litigation over the constitutionality of Alabama's adopted alternative – one that Nelson had previously proposed – continues to this day.

Respondents and their supporting *amici* conclude that two different rules should follow from these practical considerations. The United States as *amicus curiae* contends that a capital litigant's § 1983 action can proceed if, as in *Nelson*, the prisoner identifies an alternative, authorized method of execution. A suit like Hill's that fails to do so, the United States maintains, is more like a claim challenging the imposition of any method of execution – which is to say, the execution itself – because it shows the complainant is unable or unwilling to concede acceptable alternatives "[e]xcept in the abstract."

Although we agree courts should not tolerate abusive litigation tactics, even if the United States' proposed limitation were likely to be effective we could not accept it. It is true that the *Nelson* plaintiff's affirmative identification of an acceptable alternative supported our conclusion that the suit need not proceed as a habeas action. That fact, however, was not decisive. *Nelson* did not change the traditional pleading requirements for § 1983 actions. If the relief sought would foreclose execution, recharacterizing a complaint as an action for habeas corpus might be proper. Imposition of heightened pleading requirements, however, is quite a different matter. Specific pleading requirements are mandated by the Federal Rules of Civil Procedure, and not, as a general rule, through case-by-case determinations of the federal courts.

Respondents and the States as *amici* frame their argument differently. While not asking the Court in explicit terms to overrule *Nelson,* they contend a challenge to a procedure implicating the direct administration of an execution must proceed as a habeas action. They rely on cases barring § 1983 damages actions that, if successful, would imply the invalidation of an existing sentence or confinement. Those cases, they contend, demonstrate that the test of whether an action would undermine a sentence must "be applied functionally." By the same logic, it is said, a suit should be brought in habeas if it would frustrate the execution as a practical matter.

This argument cannot be squared with *Nelson*'s observation that its criterion – whether a grant of relief to the inmate would necessarily bar the execution – is consistent with *Heck*'s and *Balisok*'s approach to damages actions that implicate habeas relief. In those cases the question is whether "the nature of the challenge to the procedures could be such as necessarily to imply the invalidity" of the confinement or sentence. As discussed above, and at this stage of the litigation, the injunction Hill seeks would not necessarily foreclose the State from implementing the lethal injection sentence under present law, and thus it could not be said that the suit seeks to establish "unlawfulness [that] would render a conviction or sentence invalid." Any incidental delay caused by allowing Hill to file suit does not cast on his sentence the kind of negative legal implication that would require him to proceed in a habeas action.

III

Filing an action that can proceed under § 1983 does not entitle the complainant to an order staying an execution as a matter of course. Both the State and the victims of crime have an important interest in the timely enforcement of a sentence. Our conclusions today do not diminish that interest, nor do they deprive federal courts of the means to protect it.

We state again, as we did in *Nelson,* that a stay of execution is an equitable remedy. It is not available as a matter of right, and equity must be sensitive to the State's strong interest in enforcing its criminal judgments without undue interference from the federal courts. Thus, like other stay applicants, inmates seeking time to challenge the manner in which the State plans to execute them must satisfy all of the requirements for a stay, including a showing of a significant possibility of success on the merits.

A court considering a stay must also apply "a strong equitable presumption against the grant of a stay where a claim could have been brought at such a time as to allow consideration of the merits without requiring entry of a stay."

After *Nelson* a number of federal courts have invoked their equitable powers to dismiss suits they saw as speculative or filed too late in the day. Although the particular determinations made in those cases are not before us, we recognize that the problem they address is significant. Repetitive or piecemeal litigation presumably would raise similar concerns. The federal courts can and should protect States from dilatory or speculative suits, but it is not necessary to reject *Nelson* to do so.

The equities and the merits of Hill's underlying action are also not before us. We reverse the judgment of the Court of Appeals and remand the case for further proceedings consistent with this opinion.

Baze v. Rees
128 S.Ct. 1520 (2008)

ROBERTS, Chief Justice, announced the judgment of the Court, and issued an opinion, in which Kennedy, J., and Alito, J., joined.

I
C

. . . Petitioners Ralph Baze and Thomas C. Bowling were each convicted of two counts of capital murder and sentenced to death. The Kentucky Supreme Court upheld their convictions and sentences on direct appeal.

After exhausting their state and federal collateral remedies, Baze and Bowling sued three state officials in the Franklin Circuit Court for the Commonwealth of Kentucky, seeking to have Kentucky's lethal injection protocol declared unconstitutional. After a 7-day bench trial during which the trial court received the testimony of approximately 20 witnesses, including numerous experts, the court upheld the protocol, finding there to be minimal risk of various claims of improper administration of the protocol. On appeal, the Kentucky Supreme Court stated that a method of execution violates the Eighth Amendment when it "creates a substantial risk of wanton and unnecessary infliction of pain, torture or lingering death." Applying that standard, the court affirmed.

We granted certiorari to determine whether Kentucky's lethal injection protocol satisfies the Eighth Amendment. We hold that it does.

II

The Eighth Amendment to the Constitution, applicable to the States through the Due Process Clause of the Fourteenth Amendment, *see Robinson v. California,* 370 U.S. 660, 666 (1962), provides that "[e]xcessive bail shall not be required, nor excessive fines imposed, nor cruel and unusual punishments inflicted." We begin with the principle, settled by *Gregg,* that capital punishment is constitutional. *See* 428 U.S., at 177 (joint opinion of Stewart, Powell, and Stevens, JJ.). It necessarily follows that there must be a means of carrying it out. Some risk of pain is inherent in any method of execution – no matter how humane – if only from the prospect of error in following the required procedure. It is clear, then, that the Constitution does not demand the avoidance of all risk of pain in carrying out executions.

Petitioners do not claim that it does. Rather, they contend that the Eighth Amendment prohibits procedures that create an "unnecessary risk" of pain. Specifically, they argue that courts must evaluate "(a) the severity of pain risked, (b) the likelihood of that pain occurring, and (c) the extent to which alternative means are feasible, either by modifying existing execution procedures or adopting alternative procedures." Petitioners envision that the quantum of risk necessary to make out an Eighth Amendment claim will vary according to the severity of the pain and the availability of alternatives, but that the risk must be "significant" to trigger Eighth Amendment scrutiny.

Kentucky responds that this "unnecessary risk" standard is tantamount to a requirement that States adopt the "least risk" alternative in carrying out an execution, a standard the Commonwealth contends will cast recurring constitutional doubt on any procedure adopted by the States. Instead, Kentucky urges the Court to approve the "substantial risk" test used by the courts below.

A

This Court has never invalidated a State's chosen procedure for carrying out a sentence of death as the infliction of cruel and unusual punishment. In *Wilkerson v. Utah,* 99 U.S. 130

33

(1879), we upheld a sentence to death by firing squad imposed by a territorial court, rejecting the argument that such a sentence constituted cruel and unusual punishment. We noted there the difficulty of "defin[ing] with exactness the extent of the constitutional provision which provides that cruel and unusual punishments shall not be inflicted." Rather than undertake such an effort, the *Wilkerson* Court simply noted that "it is safe to affirm that punishments of torture, . . . and all others in the same line of unnecessary cruelty, are forbidden" by the Eighth Amendment. By way of example, the Court cited cases from England in which "terror, pain, or disgrace were sometimes superadded" to the sentence, such as where the condemned was "embowelled alive, beheaded, and quartered," or instances of "public dissection in murder, and burning alive." In contrast, we observed that the firing squad was routinely used as a method of execution for military officers. What each of the forbidden punishments had in common was the deliberate infliction of pain for the sake of pain-"superadd [ing]" pain to the death sentence through torture and the like.

We carried these principles further in *In re Kemmler,* 136 U.S. 436 (1890). There we rejected an opportunity to incorporate the Eighth Amendment against the States in a challenge to the first execution by electrocution, to be carried out by the State of New York. In passing over that question, however, we observed that "[p]unishments are cruel when they involve torture or a lingering death; but the punishment of death is not cruel within the meaning of that word as used in the Constitution. It implies there something inhuman and barbarous, something more than the mere extinguishment of life." We noted that the New York statute adopting electrocution as a method of execution "was passed in the effort to devise a more humane method of reaching the result."

B

Petitioners do not claim that lethal injection or the proper administration of the particular protocol adopted by Kentucky by themselves constitute the cruel or wanton infliction of pain. Quite the contrary, they concede that "if performed properly," an execution carried out under Kentucky's procedures would be "humane and constitutional." That is because, as counsel for petitioners admitted at oral argument, proper administration of the first drug, sodium thiopental, eliminates any meaningful risk that a prisoner would experience pain from the subsequent injections of pancuronium and potassium chloride.

Instead, petitioners claim that there is a significant risk that the procedures will *not* be properly followed-in particular, that the sodium thiopental will not be properly administered to achieve its intended effect-resulting in severe pain when the other chemicals are administered. Our cases recognize that subjecting individuals to a risk of future harm-not simply actually inflicting pain-can qualify as cruel and unusual punishment. To establish that such exposure violates the Eighth Amendment, however, the conditions presenting the risk must be "*sure or very likely* to cause serious illness and needless suffering," and give rise to "sufficiently *imminent* dangers." *Helling v. McKinney,* 509 U.S. 25, 33, 34-35 (1993) (emphasis added). We have explained that to prevail on such a claim there must be a "substantial risk of serious harm," an "objectively intolerable risk of harm" that prevents prison officials from pleading that they were "subjectively blameless for purposes of the Eighth Amendment." *Farmer v. Brennan,* 511 U.S. 825, 842, 846, and n. 9 (1994).

Simply because an execution method may result in pain, either by accident or as an inescapable consequence of death, does not establish the sort of "objectively intolerable risk of harm" that qualifies as cruel and unusual. In *Louisiana ex rel. Francis v. Resweber,* 329 U.S. 459 (1947), a plurality of the Court upheld a second attempt at executing a prisoner by electrocution after a mechanical malfunction had interfered with the first attempt. The principal opinion noted that "[a]ccidents happen for which no man is to blame," *id.,* at 462, and concluded that such "an accident, with no suggestion of malevolence," did not give rise to an Eighth Amendment violation.

C

Much of petitioners' case rests on the contention that they have identified a significant risk of harm that can be eliminated by adopting alternative procedures, such as a one-drug protocol that dispenses with the use of pancuronium and potassium chloride, and additional monitoring by trained personnel to ensure that the first dose of sodium thiopental has been adequately delivered. Given what our cases have said about the nature of the risk of harm that is actionable under the Eighth Amendment, a condemned prisoner cannot successfully challenge a State's method of execution merely by showing a slightly or marginally safer alternative.

Permitting an Eighth Amendment violation to be established on such a showing would threaten to transform courts into boards of inquiry charged with determining "best practices" for executions, with each ruling supplanted by another round of litigation touting a new and improved methodology. Such an approach finds no support in our cases, would embroil the courts in ongoing scientific controversies beyond their expertise, and would substantially intrude on the role of state legislatures in implementing their execution procedures-a role that by all accounts the States have fulfilled with an earnest desire to provide for a progressively more humane manner of death. Accordingly, we reject petitioners' proposed "unnecessary risk" standard, as well as the dissent's "untoward" risk variation.

Instead, the proffered alternatives must effectively address a "substantial risk of serious harm." *Farmer, supra,* at 842. To qualify, the alternative procedure must be feasible, readily implemented, and in fact significantly reduce a substantial risk of severe pain. If a State refuses to adopt such an alternative in the face of these documented advantages, without a legitimate penological justification for adhering to its current method of execution, then a State's refusal to change its method can be viewed as "cruel and unusual" under the Eighth Amendment.

III

In applying these standards to the facts of this case, we note at the outset that it is difficult to regard a practice as "objectively intolerable" when it is in fact widely tolerated. Thirty-six States that sanction capital punishment have adopted lethal injection as the preferred method of execution. The Federal Government uses lethal injection as well. This broad consensus goes not just to the method of execution, but also to the specific three-drug combination used by Kentucky. Thirty States, as well as the Federal Government, use a series of sodium thiopental, pancuronium bromide, and potassium chloride, in varying amounts. No State uses or has ever used the alternative one-drug protocol belatedly urged by petitioners. This consensus is probative but not conclusive with respect to that aspect of the alternatives proposed by petitioners.

In order to meet their "heavy burden" of showing that Kentucky's procedure is "cruelly inhumane," *Gregg,* 428 U.S., at 175 (joint opinion of Stewart, Powell, and Stevens, JJ.), petitioners point to numerous aspects of the protocol that they contend create opportunities for error. Their claim hinges on the improper administration of the first drug, sodium thiopental. It is uncontested that, failing a proper dose of sodium thiopental that would render the prisoner unconscious, there is a substantial, constitutionally unacceptable risk of suffocation from the administration of pancuronium bromide and pain from the injection of potassium chloride. We agree with the state trial court and State Supreme Court, however, that petitioners have not shown that the risk of an inadequate dose of the first drug is substantial. And we reject the argument that the Eighth Amendment requires Kentucky to adopt the untested alternative procedures petitioners have identified.

A

Petitioners contend that there is a risk of improper administration of thiopental because the doses are difficult to mix into solution form and load into syringes; because the protocol fails to establish a rate of injection, which could lead to a failure of the IV; because it is possible that the IV catheters will infiltrate into surrounding tissue, causing an inadequate dose to be delivered to the vein; because of inadequate facilities and training; and because Kentucky has no reliable means of monitoring the anesthetic depth of the prisoner after the sodium thiopental has been administered.

As for the risk that the sodium thiopental would be improperly prepared, petitioners contend that Kentucky employs untrained personnel who are unqualified to calculate and mix an adequate dose, especially in light of the omission of volume and concentration amounts from the written protocol. The state trial court, however, specifically found that "[i]f the manufacturers' instructions for reconstitution of Sodium Thiopental are followed, . . . there would be minimal risk of improper mixing, despite converse testimony that a layperson would have difficulty performing this task." We cannot say that this finding is clearly erroneous, particularly when that finding is substantiated by expert testimony describing the task of reconstituting powder sodium thiopental into solution form as "[n]ot difficult at all. . . . You take a liquid, you inject it into a vial with the powder, then you shake it up until the powder dissolves and, you're done. The instructions are on the package insert."

Likewise, the asserted problems related to the IV lines do not establish a sufficiently substantial risk of harm to meet the requirements of the Eighth Amendment. Kentucky has put in place several important safeguards to ensure that an adequate dose of sodium thiopental is delivered to the condemned prisoner. The most significant of these is the written protocol's requirement that members of the IV team must have at least one year of professional experience as a certified medical assistant, phlebotomist, EMT, paramedic, or military corpsman. Kentucky currently uses a phlebotomist and an EMT, personnel who have daily experience establishing IV catheters for inmates in Kentucky's prison population. Moreover, these IV team members, along with the rest of the execution team, participate in at least 10 practice sessions per year. These sessions, required by the written protocol, encompass a complete walk-through of the execution procedures, including the siting of IV catheters into volunteers. In addition, the protocol calls for the IV team to establish both primary and backup lines and to prepare two sets of the lethal injection drugs before the execution commences. These redundant measures ensure that if an insufficient dose of sodium thiopental is initially administered through the primary line, an additional dose can be given through the backup line before the last two drugs are injected.

The IV team has one hour to establish both the primary and backup IVs, a length of time the trial court found to be "not excessive but rather necessary," contrary to petitioners' claim that using an IV inserted after any "more than ten or fifteen minutes of unsuccessful attempts is dangerous because the IV is almost certain to be unreliable." And, in any event, merely because the protocol gives the IV team one hour to establish intravenous access does not mean that team members are required to spend the entire hour in a futile attempt to do so. The qualifications of the IV team also substantially reduce the risk of IV infiltration.

In addition, the presence of the warden and deputy warden in the execution chamber with the prisoner allows them to watch for signs of IV problems, including infiltration. Three of the Commonwealth's medical experts testified that identifying signs of infiltration would be "very obvious," even to the average person, because of the swelling that would result. Kentucky's protocol specifically requires the warden to redirect the flow of chemicals to the backup IV site if the prisoner does not lose consciousness within 60 seconds. In light of these safeguards, we cannot say that the risks identified by petitioners are so substantial or imminent as to amount to an Eighth Amendment violation.

B

Nor does Kentucky's failure to adopt petitioners' proposed alternatives demonstrate that the Commonwealth's execution procedure is cruel and unusual.

First, petitioners contend that Kentucky could switch from a three-drug protocol to a one-drug protocol by using a single dose of sodium thiopental or other barbiturate. That alternative was not proposed to the state courts below. As a result, we are left without any findings on the effectiveness of petitioners' barbiturate-only protocol, despite scattered references in the trial testimony to the sole use of sodium thiopental or pentobarbital as a preferred method of execution.

In any event, the Commonwealth's continued use of the three-drug protocol cannot be viewed as posing an "objectively intolerable risk" when no other State has adopted the one-drug method and petitioners proffered no study showing that it is an equally effective manner of imposing a death sentence. Indeed, the State of Tennessee, after reviewing its execution procedures, rejected a proposal to adopt a one-drug protocol using sodium thiopental. The State concluded that the one-drug alternative would take longer than the three-drug method and that the "required dosage of sodium thiopental would be less predictable and more variable when it is used as the sole mechanism for producing death. . . ." *Workman v. Bredesen,* 486 F.3d 896, 919 (6th Cir. 2007). We need not endorse the accuracy of those conclusions to note simply that the comparative efficacy of a one-drug method of execution is not so well established that Kentucky's failure to adopt it constitutes a violation of the Eighth Amendment.

Petitioners also contend that Kentucky should omit the second drug, pancuronium bromide, because it serves no therapeutic purpose while suppressing muscle movements that could reveal an inadequate administration of the first drug. The state trial court, however, specifically found that pancuronium serves two purposes. First, it prevents involuntary physical movements during unconsciousness that may accompany the injection of potassium chloride. The Commonwealth has an interest in preserving the dignity of the procedure, especially where convulsions or seizures could be misperceived as signs of consciousness or distress. Second, pancuronium stops respiration, hastening death. Kentucky's decision to include the drug does not offend the Eighth Amendment.

Petitioners' barbiturate-only protocol, they contend, is not untested; it is used routinely by veterinarians in putting animals to sleep. Moreover, 23 States, including Kentucky, bar veterinarians from using a neuromuscular paralytic agent like pancuronium bromide, either expressly or, like Kentucky, by specifically directing the use of a drug like sodium pentobarbital. If pancuronium is too cruel for animals, the argument goes, then it must be too cruel for the condemned inmate. Whatever rhetorical force the argument carries, it overlooks the States' legitimate interest in providing for a quick, certain death. In the Netherlands, for example, where physician-assisted euthanasia is permitted, the Royal Dutch Society for the Advancement of Pharmacy recommends the use of a muscle relaxant (such as pancuronium dibromide) in addition to thiopental in order to prevent a prolonged, undignified death. That concern may be less compelling in the veterinary context, and in any event other methods approved by veterinarians – such as stunning the animal or severing its spinal cord, make clear that veterinary practice for animals is not an appropriate guide to humane practices for humans.

Petitioners also fault the Kentucky protocol for lacking a systematic mechanism for monitoring the "anesthetic depth" of the prisoner. Under petitioners' scheme, qualified personnel would employ monitoring equipment, such as a Bispectral Index (BIS) monitor, blood pressure cuff, or EKG to verify that a prisoner has achieved sufficient unconsciousness before injecting the final two drugs. The visual inspection performed by the warden and deputy warden, they maintain, is an inadequate substitute for the more sophisticated procedures they envision.

At the outset, it is important to reemphasize that a proper dose of thiopental obviates the concern that a prisoner will not be sufficiently sedated. All the experts who testified at trial agreed on this point. The risks of failing to adopt additional monitoring procedures are thus even more "remote" and attenuated than the risks posed by the alleged inadequacies of Kentucky's procedures designed to ensure the delivery of thiopental.

But more than this, Kentucky's expert testified that a blood pressure cuff would have no utility in assessing the level of the prisoner's unconsciousness following the introduction of sodium thiopental, which depresses circulation. Furthermore, the medical community has yet to endorse the use of a BIS monitor, which measures brain function, as an indication of anesthetic awareness. The asserted need for a professional anesthesiologist to interpret the BIS monitor readings is nothing more than an argument against the entire procedure, given that both Kentucky law, and the American Society of Anesthesiologists' own ethical guidelines, prohibit anesthesiologists from participating in capital punishment. Nor is it pertinent that the use of a blood pressure cuff and EKG is "the standard of care in surgery requiring anesthesia," as the dissent points out. Petitioners have not shown that these supplementary procedures, drawn from a different context, are necessary to avoid a substantial risk of suffering.

The dissent believes that rough-and-ready tests for checking consciousness – calling the inmate's name, brushing his eyelashes, or presenting him with strong, noxious odors – could materially decrease the risk of administering the second and third drugs before the sodium thiopental has taken effect. Again, the risk at issue is already attenuated, given the steps Kentucky has taken to ensure the proper administration of the first drug. Moreover, the scenario the dissent posits involves a level of unconsciousness allegedly sufficient to avoid detection of improper administration of the anesthesia under Kentucky's procedure, but not sufficient to prevent pain. There is no indication that the basic tests the dissent advocates can make such fine distinctions. If these tests are effective only in determining whether the sodium thiopental has entered the inmate's bloodstream, the record confirms that the visual inspection of the IV site under Kentucky's procedure achieves that objective.

The dissent would continue the stay of these executions (and presumably the many others held in abeyance pending decision in this case) and send the case back to the lower courts to determine whether such added measures redress an "untoward" risk of pain. But an inmate cannot succeed on an Eighth Amendment claim simply by showing one more step the State could take as a failsafe for other, independently adequate measures. This approach would serve no meaningful purpose and would frustrate the State's legitimate interest in carrying out a sentence of death in a timely manner.

Justice Stevens suggests that our opinion leaves the disposition of other cases uncertain, but the standard we set forth here resolves more challenges than he acknowledges. A stay of execution may not be granted on grounds such as those asserted here unless the condemned prisoner establishes that the State's lethal injection protocol creates a demonstrated risk of severe pain. He must show that the risk is substantial when compared to the known and available alternatives. A State with a lethal injection protocol substantially similar to the protocol we uphold today would not create a risk that meets this standard.

. . . Reasonable people of good faith disagree on the morality and efficacy of capital punishment, and for many who oppose it, no method of execution would ever be acceptable. But as Justice Frankfurter stressed in *Resweber,* "[o]ne must be on guard against finding in personal disapproval a reflection of more or less prevailing condemnation." 329 U.S., at 471 (concurring opinion). This Court has ruled that capital punishment is not prohibited under our Constitution, and that the States may enact laws specifying that sanction. "[T]he power of a State to pass laws means little if the State cannot enforce them." *McCleskey v. Zant,* 499 U.S. 467, 491 (1991). State efforts to implement capital punishment must certainly comply with the Eighth Amendment, but what that Amendment prohibits is wanton exposure to "objectively intolerable risk," *Farmer,* 511 U.S., at 846, not simply the possibility of pain.

Kentucky has adopted a method of execution believed to be the most humane available, one it shares with 35 other States. Petitioners agree that, if administered as intended, that procedure will result in a painless death. The risks of maladministration they have suggested-such as improper mixing of chemicals and improper setting of IVs by trained and experienced personnel-cannot remotely be characterized as "objectively intolerable." Kentucky's decision to adhere to its protocol despite these asserted risks, while adopting safeguards to protect against them, cannot be viewed as probative of the wanton infliction of pain under the Eighth Amendment. Finally, the alternative that petitioners belatedly propose has problems of its own, and has never been tried by a single State.

Throughout our history, whenever a method of execution has been challenged in this Court as cruel and unusual, the Court has rejected the challenge. Our society has nonetheless steadily moved to more humane methods of carrying out capital punishment. The firing squad, hanging, the electric chair, and the gas chamber have each in turn given way to more humane methods, culminating in today's consensus on lethal injection. The broad framework of the Eighth Amendment has accommodated this progress toward more humane methods of execution, and our approval of a particular method in the past has not precluded legislatures from taking the steps they deem appropriate, in light of new developments, to ensure humane capital punishment. There is no reason to suppose that today's decision will be any different.

The judgment below concluding that Kentucky's procedure is consistent with the Eighth Amendment is, accordingly, affirmed.

Justice ALITO, concurring.

II

In order to show that a modification of a lethal injection protocol is required by the Eighth Amendment, a prisoner must demonstrate that the modification would "*significantly* reduce a *substantial* risk of *severe* pain." (Emphasis added). Showing merely that a modification would result in some reduction in risk is insufficient. Moreover, an inmate should be required to do more than simply offer the testimony of a few experts or a few studies. Instead, an inmate challenging a method of execution should point to a well-established scientific consensus. Only if a State refused to change its method in the face of such evidence would the State's conduct be comparable to circumstances that the Court has previously held to be in violation of the Eighth Amendment. *See Farmer v. Brennan,* 511 U.S. 825, 836 (1994).

Justice STEVENS, concurring in the judgment.

When we granted certiorari in this case, I assumed that our decision would bring the debate about lethal injection as a method of execution to a close. It now seems clear that it will not. The question whether a similar three-drug protocol may be used in other States remains open, and may well be answered differently in a future case on the basis of a more complete record. Instead of ending the controversy, I am now convinced that this case will generate debate not only about the constitutionality of the three-drug protocol, and specifically about the justification for the use of the paralytic agent, pancuronium bromide, but also about the justification for the death penalty itself.

I

Because it masks any outward sign of distress, pancuronium bromide creates a risk that the inmate will suffer excruciating pain before death occurs. There is a general understanding among veterinarians that the risk of pain is sufficiently serious that the use of the drug should be proscribed when an animal's life is being terminated. As a result of this understanding among knowledgeable professionals, several States – including Kentucky – have enacted legislation prohibiting use of the drug in animal euthanasia. *See* 2 Ky. Admin. Regs., tit. 201, ch. 16:090, § 5(1) (2004). It is unseemly – to say the least – that Kentucky may well kill petitioners using a drug that it would not permit to be used on their pets.

Use of pancuronium bromide is particularly disturbing because-as the trial court specifically found in this case-it serves "no therapeutic purpose." The drug's primary use is to prevent involuntary muscle movements, and its secondary use is to stop respiration. In my view, neither of these purposes is sufficient to justify the risk inherent in the use of the drug.

The plurality believes that preventing involuntary movement is a legitimate justification for using pancuronium bromide because "[t]he Commonwealth has an interest in preserving the dignity of the procedure, especially where convulsions or seizures could be misperceived as signs of consciousness or distress." This is a woefully inadequate justification. Whatever minimal interest there may be in ensuring that a condemned inmate dies a dignified death, and that witnesses to the execution are not made uncomfortable by an incorrect belief (which could easily be corrected) that the inmate is in pain, is vastly outweighed by the risk that the inmate is actually experiencing excruciating pain that no one can detect. Nor is there any necessity for pancuronium bromide to be included in the cocktail to inhibit respiration when it is immediately followed by potassium chloride, which causes death quickly by stopping the inmate's heart.

Moreover, there is no nationwide endorsement of the use of pancuronium bromide that merits any special presumption of respect. While state legislatures have approved lethal injection as a humane method of execution, the majority have not enacted legislation specifically approving the use of pancuronium bromide, or any given combination of drugs. And when the Colorado Legislature focused on the issue, it specified a one-drug protocol consisting solely of sodium thiopental. *See* Colo.Rev.Stat. Ann. § 18-1.3-1202 (2007). In the majority of States that use the three-drug protocol, the drugs were selected by unelected Department of Correction officials with no specialized medical knowledge and without the benefit of expert assistance or guidance. As such, their drug selections are not entitled to the kind of deference afforded legislative decisions.

Nor should the failure of other state legislatures, or of Congress, to outlaw the use of the drug on condemned prisoners be viewed as a nationwide endorsement of an unnecessarily dangerous practice. Even in those States where the legislature specifically approved the use of a paralytic agent, review of the decisions that led to the adoption of the three-drug protocol has persuaded me that they are the product of "administrative convenience" and a "stereotyped reaction" to an issue, rather than a careful analysis of relevant considerations favoring or disfavoring a conclusion. Indeed, the trial court found that "the various States simply fell in line" behind Oklahoma, adopting the protocol without any critical analysis of whether it was the best available alternative.

It is striking that when this state agency-with some specialized medical knowledge and with the benefit of some expert assistance and guidance-focused on the issue, it disagreed with the legislature's "stereotyped reaction," *Mathews,* 427 U.S., at 520, 521 (Stevens, J., dissenting), and specified a two-drug protocol that omitted pancuronium bromide.[8]

In my view, therefore, States wishing to decrease the risk that future litigation will delay

---

[8] Further, concerns about this issue may have played a role in New Jersey's subsequent decisions to create a New Jersey Death Penalty Study Commission in 2006, and ultimately to abolish the death penalty in 2007.

executions or invalidate their protocols would do well to reconsider their continued use of pancuronium bromide.

Justice THOMAS, with whom Justice Scalia joins, concurring in the judgment.

Although I agree that petitioners have failed to establish that Kentucky's lethal injection protocol violates the Eighth Amendment, I write separately because I cannot subscribe to the plurality opinion's formulation of the governing standard. As I understand it, that opinion would hold that a method of execution violates the Eighth Amendment if it poses a substantial risk of severe pain that could be significantly reduced by adopting readily available alternative procedures. This standard-along with petitioners' proposed "unnecessary risk" standard and the dissent's "untoward risk" standard, finds no support in the original understanding of the Cruel and Unusual Punishments Clause or in our previous method-of-execution cases; casts constitutional doubt on long-accepted methods of execution; and injects the Court into matters it has no institutional capacity to resolve. Because, in my view, a method of execution violates the Eighth Amendment only if it is deliberately designed to inflict pain, I concur only in the judgment.

I

The Eighth Amendment's prohibition on the "inflict[ion]" of "cruel and unusual punishments" must be understood in light of the historical practices that led the Framers to include it in the Bill of Rights. Justice Stevens' ruminations notwithstanding, it is clear that the Eighth Amendment does not prohibit the death penalty. That is evident both from the ubiquity of the death penalty in the founding era, *see* S. Banner, The Death Penalty: An American History 23 (2002) (hereinafter Banner) (noting that, in the late 18th century, the death penalty was "the standard penalty for all serious crimes"), and from the Constitution's express provision for capital punishment, (requiring an indictment or presentment of a grand jury to hold a person for "a capital, or otherwise infamous crime," and prohibiting deprivation of "life" without due process of law).

That the Constitution permits capital punishment in principle does not, of course, mean that all methods of execution are constitutional. In English and early colonial practice, the death penalty was not a uniform punishment, but rather a range of punishments, some of which the Framers likely regarded as cruel and unusual. Death by hanging was the most common mode of execution both before and after 1791, and there is no doubt that it remained a permissible punishment after enactment of the Eighth Amendment. "An ordinary death by hanging was not, however, the harshest penalty at the disposal of the seventeenth- and eighteenth-century state." In addition to hanging, which was intended to, and often did, result in a quick and painless death, "[o]fficials also wielded a set of tools capable of *intensifying* a death sentence," that is, "ways of producing a punishment worse than death."

One such "tool" was burning at the stake. Because burning, unlike hanging, was always painful and destroyed the body, it was considered "a form of super-capital punishment, worse than death itself." Reserved for offenders whose crimes were thought to pose an especially grave threat to the social order – such as slaves who killed their masters and women who killed their husbands – burning a person alive was so dreadful a punishment that sheriffs sometimes hanged the offender first "as an act of charity."

Other methods of intensifying a death sentence included "gibbeting," or hanging the condemned in an iron cage so that his body would decompose in public view, and "public dissection," a punishment Blackstone associated with murder, 4 W. Blackstone, Commentaries 376 (1769) (hereinafter Blackstone). But none of these was the worst fate a criminal could meet. That was reserved for the most dangerous and reprobate offenders-traitors. "The punishment of high treason," Blackstone wrote, was "very solemn and terrible," and involved "embowelling alive, beheading, and quartering," Thus, the following death sentence could be pronounced on seven men convicted of high treason in England:

> "That you and each of you, be taken to the place from whence you came, and from thence be drawn on a hurdle to the place of execution, where you shall be hanged by the necks, not till you are dead; that you be severally taken down, while yet alive, and your bowels be taken out and burnt before your faces-that your heads be then cut off, and your bodies cut in four quarters, to be at the King's disposal. And God Almighty have mercy on your souls." G. Scott, History of Capital Punishment 179 (1950).[*]

The principal object of these aggravated forms of capital punishment was to terrorize the criminal, and thereby more effectively deter the crime. Their defining characteristic was that they were purposely designed to inflict pain and suffering beyond that necessary to cause death. As Blackstone put it, "in very atrocious crimes, other circumstances of terror, pain, or disgrace [were] superadded." These "superadded" circumstances "were carefully handed out to apply terror where it was thought to be most needed," and were designed "to ensure that death would be slow and painful, and thus all the more frightening to contemplate."

Although the Eighth Amendment was not the subject of extensive discussion during the

---

[*] As gruesome as these methods of execution were, they were not the worst punishments the Framers would have been acquainted with. After surveying the various "superadd[itions]" to the death penalty in English law, as well as lesser punishments such as "mutilation or dismembering, by cutting off the hand or ears" and stigmatizing the offender "by slitting the nostrils, or branding in the hand or cheek," Blackstone was able to congratulate his countrymen on their refinement, in contrast to the barbarism on the Continent: "Disgusting as this catalogue may seem, it will afford pleasure to an English reader, and do honor to the English law, to compare it with that shocking apparatus of death and torment to be met with in the criminal codes of almost every other nation in Europe." 4 Blackstone 377.

44

debates on the Bill of Rights, there is good reason to believe that the Framers viewed such enhancements to the death penalty as falling within the prohibition of the Cruel and Unusual Punishments Clause. By the late 18th century, the more violent modes of execution had "dwindled away," and would for that reason have been "unusual" in the sense that they were no longer "regularly or customarily employed," *Harmelin v. Michigan,* 501 U.S. 957, 976 (1991) (opinion of Scalia, J.). Embellishments upon the death penalty designed to inflict pain for pain's sake also would have fallen comfortably within the ordinary meaning of the word "cruel." *See* 1 S. Johnson, A Dictionary of the English Language 459 (1773) (defining "cruel" to mean "[p]leased with hurting others; inhuman; hard-hearted; void of pity; wanting compassion; savage; barbarous; unrelenting"); 1 N. Webster, An American Dictionary of the English Language 52 (1828) (defining "cruel" as "[d]isposed to give pain to others, in body or mind; willing or pleased to torment, vex or afflict; inhuman; destitute of pity, compassion or kindness").

Moreover, the evidence we do have from the debates on the Constitution confirms that the Eighth Amendment was intended to disable Congress from imposing torturous punishments. It was the absence of such a restriction on Congress' power in the Constitution as drafted in Philadelphia in 1787 that led one delegate at the Massachusetts ratifying convention to complain that Congress was "nowhere restrained from inventing the most cruel and unheard-of punishments, and annexing them to crimes; and there is no constitutional check on them, but that *racks* and *gibbets* may be amongst the most mild instruments of their discipline." 2 J. Elliot, The Debates in the Several State Conventions on the Adoption of the Federal Constitution 111 (2d ed. 1891). Similarly, during the ratification debate in Virginia, Patrick Henry objected to the lack of a Bill of Rights, in part because there was nothing to prevent Congress from inflicting "tortures, or cruel and barbarous punishment[s]."

Early commentators on the Constitution likewise interpreted the Cruel and Unusual Punishments Clause as referring to torturous punishments. One commentator viewed the Eighth Amendment as prohibiting "horrid modes of torture":

> "The prohibition of cruel and unusual punishments, marks the improved spirit of the age, which would not tolerate the use of the rack or the stake, or any of those horrid modes of torture, devised by human ingenuity for the gratification of fiendish passion." J. Bayard, A Brief Exposition of the Constitution of the United States 154 (2d ed. 1840).

Similarly, another commentator found "sufficient reasons" for the Eighth Amendment in the "barbarous and cruel punishments" inflicted in less enlightened countries:

> "Under the [Eighth] amendment the infliction of cruel and unusual punishments, is also prohibited. The various barbarous and cruel punishments inflicted under the laws of some other countries, and which profess not to be behind the most enlightened nations on earth in

civilization and refinement, furnish sufficient reasons for this express prohibition. Breaking on the wheel, flaying alive, rending asunder with horses, various species of horrible tortures inflicted in the inquisition, maiming, mutilating and scourging to death, are wholly alien to the spirit of our humane general constitution."

So barbaric were the punishments prohibited by the Eighth Amendment that Joseph Story thought the provision "wholly unnecessary in a free government, since it is scarcely possible, that any department of such a government should authorize, or justify such atrocious conduct." 3 J. Story, Commentaries on the Constitution of the United States 750 (1833).

II

Consistent with the original understanding of the Cruel and Unusual Punishments Clause, this Court's cases have repeatedly taken the view that the Framers intended to prohibit torturous modes of punishment akin to those that formed the historical backdrop of the Eighth Amendment. *See, e.g., Estelle v. Gamble,* 429 U.S. 97, 102 (1976) ("[T]he primary concern of the drafters was to proscribe 'torture[s]' and other 'barbar [ous]' methods of punishment"); *Weems,* 217 U.S., at 390 (White, J., dissenting) ("[I]t may not be doubted, and indeed is not questioned by any one, that the cruel punishments against which the bill of rights provided were the atrocious, sanguinary and inhuman punishments which had been inflicted in the past upon the persons of criminals"). That view has permeated our method-of-execution cases. Thrice the Court has considered a challenge to a modern method of execution, and thrice it has rejected the challenge, each time emphasizing that the Eighth Amendment is aimed at methods of execution purposely designed to inflict pain.

In the first case, *Wilkerson v. Utah,* 99 U.S. 130 (1879), the Court rejected the contention that death by firing squad was cruel and unusual. In so doing, it reviewed the various modes of execution catalogued by Blackstone, repeating his observation that "in very atrocious crimes other circumstances of terror, pain, or disgrace were sometimes superadded." The Court found it "safe to affirm that punishments of torture, such as those mentioned by [Blackstone], and all others in the same line of unnecessary cruelty, are forbidden by [the Eighth Amendment]." The unanimous Court had no difficulty concluding that death by firing squad did not "fal[l] within that category."

Similarly, when the Court in *In re Kemmler,* 136 U.S. 436, 446 (1890), unanimously rejected a challenge to electrocution, it interpreted the Eighth Amendment to prohibit punishments that "were manifestly cruel and unusual, as burning at the stake, crucifixion, breaking on the wheel, or the like":

"Punishments are cruel when they involve torture or a lingering death; but the punishment of death is not cruel, within the meaning of that word as used in the Constitution. It implies there something inhuman and barbarous, something more than the mere extinguishment of life."

Finally, in *Louisiana ex rel. Francis v. Resweber,* 329 U.S. 459 (1947), the Court rejected the petitioner's contention that the Eighth Amendment prohibited Louisiana from subjecting him to a second attempt at electrocution, the first attempt having failed when "[t]he executioner threw the switch but, presumably because of some mechanical difficulty, death did not result." Characterizing the abortive attempt as "an accident, with no suggestion of malevolence," the plurality opinion concluded that "the fact that petitioner ha[d] already been subjected to a current of electricity [did] not make his subsequent execution any more cruel in the constitutional sense than any other execution":

"The cruelty against which the Constitution protects a convicted man is cruelty inherent in the method of punishment, not the necessary suffering involved in any method employed to extinguish life humanely. The fact that an unforeseeable accident prevented the prompt consummation of the sentence cannot, it seems to us, add an element of cruelty to a subsequent execution. There is no purpose to inflict unnecessary pain nor any unnecessary pain involved in the proposed execution."

III

In light of this consistent understanding of the Cruel and Unusual Punishments Clause as forbidding purposely torturous punishments, it is not surprising that even an ardent abolitionist was constrained to acknowledge in 1977 that "[a]n unbroken line of interpreters has held that it was the original understanding and intent of the framers of the Eighth Amendment . . . to proscribe as 'cruel and unusual' *only* such modes of execution as compound the simple infliction of death with added cruelties or indignities." H. Bedau, The Courts, the Constitution, and Capital Punishment 35. What is surprising is the plurality's willingness to discard this unbroken line of authority in favor of a standard that finds no support in the original understanding of the Eighth Amendment or in our method-of-execution cases and that, disclaimers notwithstanding, "threaten[s] to transform courts into boards of inquiry charged with determining 'best practices' for executions, with each ruling supplanted by another round of litigation touting a new and improved methodology."

We have never suggested that a method of execution is "cruel and unusual" within the meaning of the Eighth Amendment simply because it involves a risk of pain – whether "substantial," "unnecessary," or "untoward" – that could be reduced by adopting alternative procedures. And for good reason. It strains credulity to suggest that the defining characteristic of burning at the stake, disemboweling, drawing and quartering, beheading, and the like was that they involved risks of pain that could be eliminated by using alternative methods of execution. Quite plainly, what defined these punishments was that they were *designed* to inflict torture as a way of enhancing a death sentence; they were *intended* to produce a penalty worse than death, to accomplish something "more than the mere extinguishment of life." The evil the Eighth Amendment targets is intentional infliction of gratuitous pain, and that is the standard our method-of-execution cases have explicitly or implicitly invoked.

Thus, the Court did not find it necessary in *Wilkerson* to conduct a comparative analysis of death by firing squad as opposed to hanging or some other method of execution. Nor did the Court inquire into the precise procedures used to execute an individual by firing squad in order to determine whether they involved risks of pain that could be alleviated by adopting different procedures. It was enough that death by firing squad was well established in military practice, and plainly did not fall within the "same line of unnecessary cruelty" as the punishments described by Blackstone.

The same was true in *Kemmler*. One searches the opinion in vain for a comparative analysis of electrocution versus other methods of execution. The Court observed that the New York Legislature had adopted electrocution in order to replace hanging with "the most humane and practical method known to modern science of carrying into effect the sentence of death in capital cases." But there is no suggestion that the Court thought it necessary to sift through the "voluminous mass of evidence . . . taken [in the courts below] as to the effect of electricity as an agent of death," in order to confirm that electrocution in fact involved less substantial risks of pain or lingering death than hanging. The court below had rejected the challenge because the "act was passed in the effort to devise a more humane method of reaching the result," and "courts were bound to presume that the legislature was possessed of the facts upon which it took action." Treating the lower court's decision "as involving an adjudication that the statute was not repugnant to the Federal Constitution," the Court found that conclusion "so plainly right," that it had "no hesitation" in denying the writ of error.

Likewise in *Resweber,* the Court was confronted in dramatic fashion with the reality that the electric chair involved risks of error or malfunction that could result in excruciating pain. *See* 329 U.S., at 480, n. 2 (Burton, J., dissenting) (quoting affidavits from the petitioner's brief recounting that during the unsuccessful first attempt at electrocution, the petitioner's "lips puffed out and his body squirmed and tensed and he jumped so that the chair rocked on the floor"). But absent "malevolence" or a "purpose to inflict unnecessary pain," the Court concluded that the Constitution did not prohibit Louisiana from subjecting the petitioner to those very risks a second time in order to carry out his death sentence. No one suggested that Louisiana was required to implement additional safeguards or alternative procedures in order to reduce the risk of a second malfunction. And it was the *dissenters* in *Resweber* who insisted that the absence of an intent to inflict pain was irrelevant.

IV

Aside from lacking support in history or precedent, the various risk-based standards proposed in this case suffer from other flaws, not the least of which is that they cast substantial doubt on every method of execution other than lethal injection. It may well be that other methods of execution such as hanging, the firing squad, electrocution, and lethal gas involve risks of pain that could be eliminated by switching to lethal injection. Indeed, they have been attacked as unconstitutional for that very reason. *See, e.g., Gomez v. United States Dist. Court for Northern Dist. of Cal.,* 503 U.S. 653, 654, 656-657, (1992) (Stevens, J., dissenting) (arguing that lethal gas violates the Eighth Amendment because of "the availability of more humane and less violent methods of execution," namely, lethal injection); *Glass v. Louisiana,* 471 U.S. 1080, 1093 (1985) (Brennan, J., dissenting from denial of certiorari) (arguing that electrocution violates the Eighth Amendment because it poses risks of pain that could be alleviated by "other currently available means of execution," such as lethal injection); *Campbell v. Wood,* 18 F.3d 662, 715 (C.A.9 1994) (Reinhardt, J., concurring and dissenting) (arguing that hanging violates the Eighth Amendment because it involves risks of pain and mutilation not presented by lethal injection). But the notion that the Eighth Amendment permits only one mode of execution, or that it requires an anesthetized death, cannot be squared with the history of the Constitution.

It is not a little ironic – and telling – that lethal injection, hailed just a few years ago as *the* humane alternative in light of which every other method of execution was deemed an unconstitutional relic of the past, is the subject of today's challenge. It appears the Constitution is "evolving" even faster than I suspected. And it is obvious that, for some who oppose capital punishment on policy grounds, the only acceptable end point of the evolution is for this Court, in an exercise of raw judicial power unsupported by the text or history of the Constitution, or even by a contemporary moral consensus, to strike down the death penalty as cruel and unusual in all circumstances. In the meantime, though, the next best option for those seeking to abolish the death penalty is to embroil the States in never-ending litigation concerning the adequacy of their execution procedures. But far from putting an end to abusive litigation in this area, and thereby vindicating in some small measure the States' "significant interest in meting out a sentence of death in a timely fashion,"*Nelson v. Campbell,* 541 U.S. 637, 644 (2004), today's decision is sure to engender more litigation. At what point does a risk become "substantial"? Which alternative procedures are "feasible" and "readily implemented"? When is a reduction in risk "significant"? What penological justifications are "legitimate"? Such are the questions the lower courts will have to grapple with in the wake of today's decision. Needless to say, we have left the States with nothing resembling a bright-line rule.

Which brings me to yet a further problem with comparative-risk standards: They require courts to resolve medical and scientific controversies that are largely beyond judicial ken. Little need be said here, other than to refer to the various opinions filed by my colleagues today. Under the competing risk standards advanced by the plurality opinion and the dissent, for example, the difference between a lethal injection procedure that satisfies the Eighth Amendment and one that does not may well come down to one's judgment with respect to something as hairsplitting as whether an eyelash stroke is necessary to ensure that the inmate is unconscious, or whether instead other measures have already provided sufficient assurance of unconsciousness. Compare (Ginsburg, J., dissenting) (criticizing Kentucky's protocol because "[n]o one calls the inmate's name, shakes him, brushes his eyelashes to test for a reflex, or applies a noxious stimulus to gauge his response"), with [Roberts, C.J., majority opinion] (rejecting the dissent's criticisms because "an inmate cannot succeed on an Eighth Amendment claim simply by showing one more step the State could take as a failsafe for other, independently adequate measures"). We have neither the authority nor the expertise to micromanage the States' administration of the death penalty in this manner. There is simply no reason to believe that "unelected" judges without scientific, medical, or penological training are any better suited to resolve the delicate issues surrounding the administration of the death penalty than are state administrative personnel specifically charged with the task.

In short, I reject as both unprecedented and unworkable any standard that would require the courts to weigh the relative advantages and disadvantages of different methods of execution or of different procedures for implementing a given method of execution. To the extent that there is any comparative element to the inquiry, it should be limited to whether the challenged method inherently inflicts significantly more pain than traditional modes of execution such as hanging and the firing squad.

V

Judged under the proper standard, this is an easy case. It is undisputed that Kentucky adopted its lethal injection protocol in an effort to make capital punishment more humane, not to add elements of terror, pain, or disgrace to the death penalty. And it is undisputed that, if administered properly, Kentucky's lethal injection protocol will result in a swift and painless death. As the Sixth Circuit observed in rejecting a similar challenge to Tennessee's lethal injection protocol, we "do not have a situation where the State has any intent (or anything approaching intent) to inflict unnecessary pain; the complaint is that the State's *pain-avoidance procedure* may fail because the executioners may make a mistake in implementing it." *Workman v. Bredesen,* 486 F.3d 896, 907 (2007).   But "[t]he risk of negligence in implementing a death-penalty procedure ... does not establish a cognizable Eighth Amendment claim." Because Kentucky's lethal injection protocol is designed to eliminate pain rather than to inflict it, petitioners' challenge must fail. I accordingly concur in the Court's judgment affirming the decision below.

Justice GINSBURG, with whom Justice Souter joins, dissenting.

It is undisputed that the second and third drugs used in Kentucky's three-drug lethal injection protocol, pancuronium bromide and potassium chloride, would cause a conscious inmate to suffer excruciating pain. Pancuronium bromide paralyzes the lung muscles and results in slow asphyxiation. Potassium chloride causes burning and intense pain as it circulates throughout the body. Use of pancuronium bromide and potassium chloride on a conscious inmate, the plurality recognizes, would be "constitutionally unacceptable."

The constitutionality of Kentucky's protocol therefore turns on whether inmates are adequately anesthetized by the first drug in the protocol, sodium thiopental. Kentucky's system is constitutional, the plurality states, because "petitioners have not shown that the risk of an inadequate dose of the first drug is substantial." I would not dispose of the case so swiftly given the character of the risk at stake. Kentucky's protocol lacks basic safeguards used by other

States to confirm that an inmate is unconscious before injection of the second and third drugs. I would vacate and remand with instructions to consider whether Kentucky's omission of those safeguards poses an untoward, readily avoidable risk of inflicting severe and unnecessary pain.

I

The Court has considered the constitutionality of a specific method of execution on only three prior occasions. Those cases, and other decisions cited by the parties and *amici,* provide little guidance on the standard that should govern petitioners' challenge to Kentucky's lethal injection protocol.

In *Wilkerson v. Utah,* 99 U.S. 130 (1879), the Court held that death by firing squad did not rank among the "cruel and unusual punishments" banned by the Eighth Amendment. In so ruling, the Court did not endeavor "to define with exactness the extent of the constitutional provision which provides that cruel and unusual punishments shall not be inflicted." But it was "safe to affirm," the Court stated, that "punishments of torture . . ., and all others in the same line of unnecessary cruelty, are forbidden."

Next, in *In re Kemmler,* 136 U.S. 436 (1890), death by electrocution was the assailed method of execution.[1] The Court reiterated that the Eighth Amendment prohibits "torture" and "lingering death." The word "cruel," the Court further observed, "implies . . . something inhuman . . . something more than the mere extinguishment of life." Those statements, however, were made *en passant. Kemmler's* actual holding was that the Eighth Amendment does not apply to the States,[2] a proposition we have since repudiated, *see, e.g.,Robinson v. California,* 370 U.S. 660 (1962).

Finally, in *Louisiana ex rel. Francis v. Resweber,* 329 U.S. 459 (1947), the Court rejected Eighth and Fourteenth Amendment challenges to a reelectrocution following an earlier attempt that failed to cause death. The plurality opinion in that case first stated: "The traditional humanity of modern Anglo-American law forbids the infliction of unnecessary pain in the execution of the death sentence." But the very next sentence varied the formulation; it referred to the "[p]rohibition against the wanton infliction of pain."

No clear standard for determining the constitutionality of a method of execution emerges from these decisions. Moreover, the age of the opinions limits their utility as an aid to

---

[1]Hanging was the State's prior mode of execution. Electrocution, considered "less barbarous," indeed "the most humane" way to administer the death penalty, was believed at the time to "result in instantaneous, and consequently in painless, death." *In re Kemmler,* 136 U.S. 436, 443-444 (1890) (internal quotation marks omitted).

[2] The Court also ruled in *Kemmler* that the State's election to carry out the death penalty by electrocution in lieu of hanging encountered no Fourteenth Amendment shoal: No privilege or immunity of United States citizenship was entailed, nor did the Court discern any deprivation of due process.

resolution of the present controversy. The Eighth Amendment, we have held, " 'must draw its meaning from the evolving standards of decency that mark the progress of a maturing society.' " *Atkins v. Virginia,* 536 U.S. 304, 311-312 (2002) (quoting *Trop v. Dulles,* 356 U.S. 86, 101 (1958) (plurality opinion)). *Wilkerson* was decided 129 years ago, *Kemmler* 118 years ago, and *Resweber* 61 years ago. Whatever little light our prior method-of-execution cases might shed is thus dimmed by the passage of time.

Further phrases and tests can be drawn from more recent decisions, for example, *Gregg v. Georgia,* 428 U.S. 153 (1976). Speaking of capital punishment in the abstract, the lead opinion said that the Eighth Amendment prohibits "the unnecessary and wanton infliction of pain,"*id.,* at 173 (joint opinion of Stewart, Powell, and Stevens, JJ.); the same opinion also cautioned that a death sentence cannot "be imposed under sentencing procedures that creat[e] a substantial risk that it would be inflicted in an arbitrary and capricious manner," *id.,* at 188.

Relying on *Gregg* and our earlier decisions, the Kentucky Supreme Court stated that an execution procedure violates the Eighth Amendment if it "creates a substantial risk of wanton and unnecessary infliction of pain, torture or lingering death." Petitioners respond that courts should consider "(a) the severity of pain risked, (b) the likelihood of that pain occurring, *and* (c) the extent to which alternative means are feasible." The plurality settles somewhere in between, requiring a "substantial risk of serious harm" and considering whether a "feasible, readily implemented" alternative can "significantly reduce" that risk.

I agree with petitioners and the plurality that the degree of risk, magnitude of pain, and availability of alternatives must be considered. I part ways with the plurality, however, to the extent its "substantial risk" test sets a fixed threshold for the first factor. The three factors are interrelated; a strong showing on one reduces the importance of the others.

Lethal injection as a mode of execution can be expected, in most instances, to result in painless death. Rare though errors may be, the consequences of a mistake about the condemned inmate's consciousness are horrendous and effectively undetectable after injection of the second drug. Given the opposing tugs of the degree of risk and magnitude of pain, the critical question here, as I see it, is whether a feasible alternative exists. Proof of "a slightly or marginally safer alternative" is, as the plurality notes, insufficient. But if readily available measures can materially increase the likelihood that the protocol will cause no pain, a State fails to adhere to contemporary standards of decency if it declines to employ those measures.

II

Kentucky's Legislature adopted lethal injection as a method of execution in 1998. *See* 1998 Ky. Acts ch. 220, p. 777, Ky.Rev.Stat. Ann. § 431.220(1)(a) (West 2006). Lawmakers left the development of the lethal injection protocol to officials in the Department of Corrections. Those officials, the trial court found, were "given the task without the benefit of scientific aid or policy oversight." "Kentucky's protocol," that court observed, "was copied from other states and accepted without challenge." Kentucky "did not conduct any independent scientific or medical studies or consult any medical professionals concerning the drugs and dosage amounts to be injected into the condemned." Instead, the trial court noted, Kentucky followed the path taken in other States that "simply fell in line" behind the three-drug protocol first developed by Oklahoma in 1977.

Kentucky's protocol begins with a careful measure: Only medical professionals may perform the venipunctures and establish intravenous (IV) access. Members of the IV team must have at least one year's experience as a certified medical assistant, phlebotomist, emergency medical technician (EMT), paramedic, or military corpsman. Kentucky's IV team currently has two members: a phlebotomist with 8 years' experience and an EMT with 20 years' experience. Both members practice siting catheters at ten lethal injection training sessions held annually.

Other than using qualified and trained personnel to establish IV access, however, Kentucky does little to ensure that the inmate receives an effective dose of sodium thiopental. After siting the catheters, the IV team leaves the execution chamber. From that point forward, only the warden and deputy warden remain with the inmate. Neither the warden nor the deputy warden has any medical training.

The warden relies on visual observation to determine whether the inmate "appears" unconscious. In Kentucky's only previous execution by lethal injection, the warden's position allowed him to see the inmate best from the waist down, with only a peripheral view of the inmate's face. No other check for consciousness occurs before injection of pancuronium bromide. Kentucky's protocol does not include an automatic pause in the "rapid flow" of the drugs, or any of the most basic tests to determine whether the sodium thiopental has worked. No one calls the inmate's name, shakes him, brushes his eyelashes to test for a reflex, or applies a noxious stimulus to gauge his response.

Nor does Kentucky monitor the effectiveness of the sodium thiopental using readily available equipment, even though the inmate is already connected to an electrocardiogram (EKG). A drop in blood pressure or heart rate after injection of sodium thiopental would not prove that the inmate is unconscious, but would signal that the drug has entered the inmate's bloodstream. Kentucky's own expert testified that the sodium thiopental should "cause the inmate's blood pressure to become very, very low," and that a precipitous drop in blood pressure would "confir[m]" that the drug was having its expected effect. Use of a blood pressure cuff and EKG, the record shows, is the standard of care in surgery requiring anesthesia. [3]

---

[3] The plurality deems medical standards irrelevant in part because "drawn from a different context." Medical professionals monitor blood pressure and heart rate, however, not just to save lives, but also to reduce the risk of consciousness during otherwise painful procedures. Considering that the constitutionality of Kentucky's protocol depends on guarding against the same risk, the plurality's reluctance to consider medical practice is

A consciousness check supplementing the warden's visual observation before injection of the second drug is easily implemented and can reduce a risk of dreadful pain. Pancuronium bromide is a powerful paralytic that prevents all voluntary muscle movement. Once it is injected, further monitoring of the inmate's consciousness becomes impractical without sophisticated equipment and training. Even if the inmate were conscious and in excruciating pain, there would be no visible indication.[4]

Recognizing the importance of a window between the first and second drugs, other States have adopted safeguards not contained in Kentucky's protocol.[5] Florida pauses between injection of the first and second drugs so the warden can "determine, after consultation, that the inmate is indeed unconscious." *Lightbourne v. McCollum,* 969 So.2d 326, 346 (Fla.2007) (*per curiam*) (internal quotation marks omitted). The warden does so by touching the inmate's eyelashes, calling his name, and shaking him.[6] If the inmate's consciousness remains in doubt in Florida, "the medical team members will come out from the chemical room and consult in the assessment of the inmate." During the entire execution, the person who inserted the IV line monitors the IV access point and the inmate's face on closed circuit television.

In Missouri, "medical personnel must examine the prisoner physically to confirm that he is unconscious using standard clinical techniques and must inspect the catheter site again." *Taylor v. Crawford,* 487 F.3d 1072, 1083 (C.A.8 2007). "The second and third chemicals are injected only after confirmation that the prisoner is unconscious and after a period of at least three minutes has elapsed from the first injection of thiopental."

In California, a member of the IV team brushes the inmate's eyelashes, speaks to him, and shakes him at the halfway point and, again, at the completion of the sodium thiopental

---

puzzling. No one is advocating the wholesale incorporation of medical standards into the Eighth Amendment. But Kentucky could easily monitor the inmate's blood pressure and heart rate without physician involvement. That medical professionals consider such monitoring important enough to make it the standard of care in medical practice, I remain persuaded, is highly instructive.

[4] Petitioners' expert testified that a layperson could not tell from visual observation if a paralyzed inmate was conscious and that doing so would be difficult even for a professional. Kentucky's warden candidly admitted: "I honestly don't know what you'd look for."

[5] Because most death-penalty States keep their protocols secret, a comprehensive survey of other States' practices is not available.

[6] Florida's expert in *Lightbourne v. McCollum,* 969 So.2d 326 (Fla.2007) (*per curiam*), who also served as Kentucky's expert in this case, testified that the eyelash test is "probably the most common first assessment that we use in the operating room to determine . . . when a patient might have crossed the line from being conscious to unconscious." "A conscious person, if you touch their eyelashes very lightly, will blink; an unconscious person typically will not." The shaking and name-calling tests, he further testified, are similar to those taught in basic life support courses.

injection. *See* State of California, San Quentin Operational Procedure No. 0-770, Execution by Lethal Injection, § V(S)(4)(e) (2007), online at http://www.cdcr.ca.gov/News/docs/Revised Protocol. pdf.

In Alabama, a member of the execution team "begin[s] by saying the condemned inmate's name. If there is no response, the team member will gently stroke the condemned inmate's eyelashes. If there is no response, the team member will then pinch the condemned inmate's arm."

In Indiana, officials inspect the injection site after administration of sodium thiopental, say the inmate's name, touch him, and use ammonia tablets to test his response to a noxious nasal stimulus.[7]

These checks provide a degree of assurance – missing from Kentucky's protocol – that the first drug has been properly administered. They are simple and essentially costless to employ, yet work to lower the risk that the inmate will be subjected to the agony of conscious suffocation caused by pancuronium bromide and the searing pain caused by potassium chloride. The record contains no explanation why Kentucky does not take any of these elementary measures.

The risk that an error administering sodium thiopental would go undetected is minimal, Kentucky urges, because if the drug was mistakenly injected into the inmate's tissue, not a vein, he "would be awake and screaming." That argument ignores aspects of Kentucky's protocol that render passive reliance on obvious signs of consciousness, such as screaming, inadequate to determine whether the inmate is experiencing pain.

First, Kentucky's use of pancuronium bromide to paralyze the inmate means he will not be able to scream after the second drug is injected, no matter how much pain he is experiencing. Kentucky's argument, therefore, appears to rest on the assertion that sodium thiopental is itself painful when injected into tissue rather than a vein. The trial court made no finding on that point, and Kentucky cites no supporting evidence from executions in which it is known that sodium thiopental was injected into the inmate's soft tissue. *See, e.g., Lightbourne,* 969 So.2d, at 344 (describing execution of Angel Diaz).

Second, the inmate may receive enough sodium thiopental to mask the most obvious signs of consciousness without receiving a dose sufficient to achieve a surgical plane of anesthesia. If the drug is injected too quickly, the increase in blood pressure can cause the inmate's veins to burst after a small amount of sodium thiopental has been administered. Kentucky's protocol does not specify the rate at which sodium thiopental should be injected.

---

[7] In Indiana, a physician also examines the inmate after injection of the first drug.

The executioner, who does not have any medical training, pushes the drug "by feel" through five feet of tubing.[8] In practice sessions, unlike in an actual execution, there is no resistance on the catheter; thus the executioner's training may lead him to push the drugs too fast.

"The easiest and most obvious way to ensure that an inmate is unconscious during an execution," petitioners argued to the Kentucky Supreme Court, "is to check for consciousness prior to injecting pancuronium [bromide]." The court did not address petitioners' argument. I would therefore remand with instructions to consider whether the failure to include readily available safeguards to confirm that the inmate is unconscious after injection of sodium thiopental, in combination with the other elements of Kentucky's protocol, creates an untoward, readily avoidable risk of inflicting severe and unnecessary pain.

Page 133. Add following note 8:

Note on Baze v. Rees

9.   In a concurring opinion in *Baze v. Rees*, 128 S.Ct. 1520 (2008), Justice Alito discussed the ethical restraints imposed on physicians and medical professionals who participate in executions:

> "Prominent among the practical constraints that must be taken into account in considering the feasibility and availability of any suggested modification of a lethal injection protocol are the ethical restrictions applicable to medical professionals. The first step in the lethal injection protocols currently in use is the anesthetization of the prisoner. If this step is carried out properly, it is agreed, the prisoner will not experience pain during the remainder of the procedure. Every day, general anesthetics are administered to surgical patients in this country, and if the medical professionals who participate in these surgeries also participated in the anesthetization of prisoners facing execution by lethal injection, the risk of pain would be minimized. But the ethics rules of medical professionals-for reasons that I certainly do not question here-prohibit their participation in executions.
>
> Guidelines issued by the American Medical Association (AMA) state that "[a]n individual's opinion on capital punishment is the personal moral decision of the individual," but that "[a] physician, as a member of a profession

---

[8] The length of the tubing contributes to the risk that the inmate will receive an inadequate dose of sodium thiopental. The warden and deputy warden watch for obvious leaks in the execution chamber, but the line also snakes into the neighboring control room through a small hole in the wall.

dedicated to preserving life when there is hope of doing so, should not be a participant in a legally authorized execution." The guidelines explain:

> "Physician participation in an execution includes, but is not limited to, the following actions: prescribing or administering tranquilizers and other psychotropic agents and medications that are part of the execution procedure; monitoring vital signs on site or remotely (including monitoring electrocardiograms); attending or observing an execution as a physician; and rendering of technical advice regarding execution."

The head of ethics at the AMA has reportedly opined that "[e]ven helping to design a more humane protocol would disregard the AMA code." Harris, Will Medics' Qualms Kill the Death Penalty? 441 Nature 8-9 (May 4, 2006).

The American Nurses Association (ANA) takes the position that participation in an execution "is a breach of the ethical traditions of nursing, and the *Code for Nurses*." This means, the ANA explains, that a nurse must not "take part in assessment, supervision or monitoring of the procedure or the prisoner; procuring, prescribing or preparing medications or solutions; inserting the intravenous catheter; injecting the lethal solution; and attending or witnessing the execution as a nurse."

The National Association of Emergency Medical Technicians (NAEMT) holds that "[p]articipation in capital punishment is inconsistent with the ethical precepts and goals of the [Emergency Medical Services] profession." The NAEMT's Position Statement advises that emergency medical technicians and paramedics should refrain from the same activities outlined in the ANA statement.

Recent litigation in California has demonstrated the effect of such ethics rules. Michael Morales, who was convicted and sentenced to death for a 1981 murder, filed a federal civil rights action challenging California's lethal injection protocol, which, like Kentucky's, calls for the sequential administration of three drugs: sodium pentothal, pancuronium bromide, and potassium chloride. The District Court enjoined the State from proceeding with the execution unless it either (1) used only sodium pentothal or another barbiturate or (2) ensured that an anesthesiologist was present to ensure that Morales remained unconscious throughout the process. *Morales v. Hickman,* 415 F.Supp.2d 1037, 1047 (N.D.Cal.2006). The Ninth Circuit affirmed the District Court's order, *Morales v. Hickman,* 438 F.3d 926, 931 (2006), and the State arranged for two anesthesiologists to be present for the execution. However, they subsequently concluded that "they could not proceed for reasons of medical ethics,"*Morales v. Tilton,* 465 F.Supp.2d 972, 976 (N.D.Cal.2006), and neither Morales nor any other prisoner in California has since been executed.

Objections to features of a lethal injection protocol must be considered against the backdrop of the ethics rules of medical professionals and related practical constraints. Assuming, as previously discussed, that lethal injection is not unconstitutional *per se,* it follows that a suggested modification of a lethal injection protocol cannot be regarded as "feasible" or "readily" available if the modification would require participation-either in carrying out the execution or in training those who carry out the execution-by persons whose professional ethics rules or traditions impede their participation."

F.   Death Penalty Jurisdictions and Racial Characteristics of Death Row Populations

Page 134. Substitute for Note 2:

2. The following statistics report the racial characteristics of death row inmates in these jurisdictions as of January 1, 2008.

NAACP Legal Defense Fund Statistics
RACE OF DEATH ROW INMATES (as of January 1, 2008)

STATE	TOTAL	BLACK	WHITE	LATINO	NATIVE AM.	ASIAN	UNK.
ALABAMA	203	95	106	2	0	0	0
ARIZONA	126	13	91	19	3	0	0
ARKANSAS	40	25	15	0	0	0	0
CALIFORNIA	667	239	251	143	12	22	0
COLORADO	2	1	0	1	0	0	0
CONNECTICUT	9	5	3	1	0	0	0
DELAWARE	19	9	7	3	0	0	0
FLORIDA	397	137	222	36	1	1	0
GEORGIA	107	49	54	3	0	1	0
IDAHO	19	0	19	0	0	0	0
ILLINOIS	13	5	6	2	0	0	0
INDIANA	19	6	13	0	0	0	0
KANSAS	9	4	5	0	0	0	0
KENTUCKY	39	7	31	1	0	0	0
LOUISIANA	88	55	30	2	0	1	0
MARYLAND	6	4	2	0	0	0	0
MISSISSIPPI	64	33	30	0	0	1	0
MISSOURI	48	20	28	0	0	0	0
MONTANA	2	0	2	0	0	0	0
NEBRASKA	10	1	5	4	0	0	0
NEVADA	77	28	40	8	0	1	0
NEW MEXICO	2	0	2	0	0	0	0
N. CAROLINA	173	91	67	4	10	1	0
OHIO	188	96	85	3	2	2	0
OKLAHOMA	84	34	43	3	4	0	0
OREGON	35	3	28	2	1	0	1
PENNSYLVANIA	228	136	71	19	0	2	0
S. CAROLINA	63	36	27	0	0	0	0
SOUTH DAKOTA	3	0	3	0	0	0	0
TENNESSEE	102	42	55	1	2	2	0
TEXAS	373	153	111	104	0	5	0
UTAH	9	1	6	1	1	0	0
VIRGINIA	21	13	8	0	0	0	0
WASHINGTON	9	4	5	0	0	0	0
WYOMING	2	0	2	0	0	0	0
U.S. MILITARY	9	6	2	0	0	1	0
U.S. GOVM'T	51	28	20	2	1	0	0
TOTAL	3316	1379	1495	364	37	40	1
		42%	45%	11%	1%	1%	.03%

Note: 7 prisoners were sentenced to death in more than one state. They are included in the chart above for each state in which they were sentenced to death. The numbers of page 67, *infra*, were adjusted to reflect the total number of prisoners under sentence of death.

Distribution of Executions Throughout the Country Since 1976
(as of January 1, 2008)

STATE	TOTAL		STATE	TOTAL		STATE	TOTAL
Texas	405		Arizona	23		Nebraska	3
Virginia	98		Indiana	19		Pennsylvania.	3
Oklahoma	86		Delaware	14		US	3
Missouri	66		California	13		Kentucky	2
Florida	64		Illinois	12		Oregon	2
N. Carolina	43		Nevada	12		Colorado	1
Georgia	40		Mississippi	8		Connecticut	1
Alabama	38		Utah	6		Idaho	1
S. Carolina	37		Maryland	5		New Mexico	1
Arkansas	27		Tennessee	4		S. Dakota	1
Louisiana	27		Washington	4		Wyoming	1
Ohio	26		Montana	3			

CHAPTER 3 EARLY CONSTITUTIONAL CHALLENGES TO THE DEATH PENALTY

D. *Summary of the 1976 Supreme Court Cases*

Page 186. Insert before Walton v. Arizona:

Note on Justice John Paul Stevens' Death Penalty Conversion

In a concurring opinion in *Baze v. Rees,* 128 S.Ct. 1520 (2008), Justice Stevens expressed grave concerns regarding the continuing efficacy and constitutionality of the death penalty. An excerpt from Justice Stevens' opinion follows.

Baze v. Rees
128 S.Ct. 1520 (2008)

STEVENS, J., Concurring.

II

The thoughtful opinions written by the Chief Justice and by Justice Ginsburg have persuaded me that current decisions by state legislatures, by the Congress of the United States, and by this Court to retain the death penalty as a part of our law are the product of habit and inattention rather than an acceptable deliberative process that weighs the costs and risks of administering that penalty against its identifiable benefits, and rest in part on a faulty assumption about the retributive force of the death penalty.

In *Gregg v. Georgia,* 428 U.S. 153 (1976), we explained that unless a criminal sanction serves a legitimate penological function, it constitutes "gratuitous infliction of suffering" in violation of the Eighth Amendment. We then identified three societal purposes for death as a sanction: incapacitation, deterrence, and retribution. In the past three decades, however, each of these rationales has been called into question.

While incapacitation may have been a legitimate rationale in 1976, the recent rise in statutes providing for life imprisonment without the possibility of parole demonstrates that incapacitation is neither a necessary nor a sufficient justification for the death penalty.[10] Moreover, a recent poll indicates that support for the death penalty drops significantly when life without the possibility of parole is presented as an alternative option. And the available sociological evidence suggests that juries are less likely to impose the death penalty when life without parole is available as a sentence.

---

[10] Forty-eight states now have some form of life imprisonment without parole, with the majority of statutes enacted within the last two decades. *See* Note, A Matter of Life and Death: The Effect of Life-Without-Parole Statutes on Capital Punishment, 119 Harv. L.Rev. 1838, 1839, 1841-1844 (2006).

The legitimacy of deterrence as an acceptable justification for the death penalty is also questionable, at best. Despite 30 years of empirical research in the area, there remains no reliable statistical evidence that capital punishment in fact deters potential offenders.[13] In the absence of such evidence, deterrence cannot serve as a sufficient penological justification for this uniquely severe and irrevocable punishment.

We are left, then, with retribution as the primary rationale for imposing the death penalty. And indeed, it is the retribution rationale that animates much of the remaining enthusiasm for the death penalty.[14] As Lord Justice Denning argued in 1950, "some crimes are so outrageous that society insists on adequate punishment, because the wrong-doer deserves it, irrespective of whether it is a deterrent or not." Our Eighth Amendment jurisprudence has narrowed the class of offenders eligible for the death penalty to include only those who have committed outrageous crimes defined by specific aggravating factors. It is the cruel treatment of victims that provides the most persuasive arguments for prosecutors seeking the death penalty. A natural response to such heinous crimes is a thirst for vengeance.[15]

At the same time, however, as the thoughtful opinions by the Chief Justice and Justice Ginsburg make pellucidly clear, our society has moved away from public and painful retribution towards ever more humane forms of punishment. State-sanctioned killing is therefore becoming more and more anachronistic. In an attempt to bring executions in line with our evolving standards of decency, we have adopted increasingly less painful methods of execution, and then declared previous methods barbaric and archaic. But by requiring that an execution be relatively painless, we necessarily protect the inmate from enduring any

---

[13] Admittedly, there has been a recent surge in scholarship asserting the deterrent effect of the death penalty, *see, e.g.,* Mocan & Gittings, Getting Off Death Row: Commuted Sentences and the Deterrent Effect of Capital Punishment, 46 J. Law & Econ. 453 (2003); Adler & Summers, Capital Punishment Works, Wall Street Journal, Nov. 2, 2007, p. A13, but there has been an equal, if not greater, amount of scholarship criticizing the methodologies of those studies and questioning the results, *see, e.g.,* Fagan, Death and Deterrence Redux: Science, Law and Causal Reasoning on Capital Punishment, 4 Ohio St. J.Crim. L. 255 (2006); Donohue & Wolfers, Uses and Abuses of Empirical Evidence in the Death Penalty Debate, 58 Stan. L.Rev. 791 (2005).

[14] Retribution is the most common basis of support for the death penalty. A recent study found that 37% of death penalty supporters cited "an eye for an eye/they took a life/fits the crime" as their reason for supporting capital punishment. Another 13% cited "They deserve it." The next most common reasons – "sav[ing] taxpayers money/cost associated with prison" and deterrence – were each cited by 11% of supporters. *See* Dept. of Justice, Bureau of Justice Statistics, Sourcebook of Criminal Justice Statistics 147 (2003) (Table 2.55), online at http://www. albany. edu/ sourcebook/ pdf/ t 255. pdf.

[15] For example, family members of victims of the Oklahoma City bombing called for the Government to " 'put [Timothy McVeigh] inside a bomb and blow it up.' " Walsh, One Arraigned, Two Undergo Questioning, Washington Post, Apr. 22, 1995, pp. A1, A13. Commentators at the time noted that an overwhelming percentage of Americans felt that executing McVeigh was not enough. Linder, A Political Verdict: McVeigh: When Death Is Not Enough, L.A. Times, June 8, 1997, p. M1.

punishment that is comparable to the suffering inflicted on his victim.[16] This trend, while appropriate and required by the Eighth Amendment's prohibition on cruel and unusual punishment, actually undermines the very premise on which public approval of the retribution rationale is based. *See, e.g.,* Kaufman-Osborn, Regulating Death: Capital Punishment and the Late Liberal State, 111 Yale L.J. 681, 704 (2001) (explaining that there is "a tension between our desire to realize the claims of retribution by killing those who kill, and . . . a method [of execution] that, because it seems to do no harm other than killing, cannot satisfy the intuitive sense of equivalence that informs this conception of justice"); A. Sarat, When the State Kills: Capital Punishment and the American Condition 60-84 (2001).

Full recognition of the diminishing force of the principal rationales for retaining the death penalty should lead this Court and legislatures to reexamine the question recently posed by Professor Salinas, a former Texas prosecutor and judge: "Is it time to Kill the Death Penalty?" *See* Salinas, 34 Am. J.Crim. L. 39 (2006). The time for a dispassionate, impartial comparison of the enormous costs that death penalty litigation imposes on society with the benefits that it produces has surely arrived.[17]

Thus, they conclude that "we are left in limbo, with machinery that is immensely expensive, that chokes our legal institutions so they are impeded from doing all the other things a society expects from its courts, [and] that visits repeated trauma on victims' families . . . ." *See also* Block, A Slow Death, N.Y. Times, Mar. 15, 2007, p. A27 (discussing the "enormous costs and burdens to the judicial system" resulting from the death penalty).

Some argue that these costs are the consequence of judicial insistence on unnecessarily

---

[16] For example, one survivor of the Oklahoma City bombing expressed a belief that " 'death by [lethal] injection [was] "too good" for McVeigh.' " A. Sarat, When the State kills: Capital Punishment and the American Condition 64 (2001). Similarly, one mother, when told that her child's killer would die by lethal injection, asked: "Do they feel anything? Do they hurt? Is there any pain? Very humane compared to what they've done to our children. The torture they've put our kids through. I think sometimes it's too easy. They ought to feel something. If it's fire burning all the way through their body or whatever. There ought to be some little sense of pain to it." *Id.,* at 60 (emphasis deleted).

[17] For a discussion of the financial costs as well as some of the less tangible costs of the death penalty, *see* Kozinski & Gallagher, Death: The Ultimate Run-On Sentence, 46 Case W. Res. L.Rev. 1 (1995) (discussing, *inter alia,* the burden on the courts and the lack of finality for victim's families). Although a lack of finality in death cases may seem counterintuitive, Kozinski and Gallagher explain:

"Death cases raise many more issues, and far more complex issues, than other criminal cases, and they are attacked with more gusto and reviewed with more vigor in the courts. This means there is a strong possibility that the conviction or sentence will be reconsidered-seriously reconsidered-five, ten, twenty years after the trial. . . . One has to wonder and worry about the effect this has on the families of the victims, who have to live with the possibility – and often the reality – of retrials, evidentiary hearings, and last-minute stays of execution for decades after the crime." *Id.,* at 17-18 (footnotes omitted).

elaborate and lengthy appellate procedures. To the contrary, they result "in large part from the States' failure to apply constitutionally sufficient procedures at the time of initial [conviction or] sentencing." *Knight v. Florida,* 528 U.S. 990, 998 (1999) (Breyer, J., dissenting from denial of certiorari). They may also result from a general reluctance by States to put large numbers of defendants to death, even after a sentence of death is imposed. Cf. Tempest, Death Row Often Means a Long Life; California condemns many murderers, but few are ever executed, L.A. Times, Mar. 6, 2006, p. B1 (noting that California death row inmates account for about 20% of the Nation's total death row population, but that the State accounts for only 1% of the Nation's executions). In any event, they are most certainly not the fault of judges who do nothing more than ensure compliance with constitutional guarantees prior to imposing the irrevocable punishment of death.

III

"[A] penalty may be cruel and unusual because it is excessive and serves no valid legislative purpose." *Furman v. Georgia,* 408 U.S. 238, 331 (1972) (Marshall, J., concurring); *see also id.,* at 332 ("The entire thrust of the Eighth Amendment is, in short, against 'that which is excessive' "). Our cases holding that certain sanctions are "excessive," and therefore prohibited by the Eighth Amendment, have relied heavily on "objective criteria," such as legislative enactments. *See, e.g.,Solem v. Helm,* 463 U.S. 277, 292 (1983); *Harmelin v. Michigan,* 501 U.S. 957 (1991); *United States v. Bajakajian,* 524 U.S. 321 (1998). In our recent decision in *Atkins v. Virginia,* 536 U.S. 304 (2002), holding that death is an excessive sanction for a mentally retarded defendant, we also relied heavily on opinions written by Justice White holding that the death penalty is an excessive punishment for the crime of raping a 16-year-old woman, *Coker v. Georgia,* 433 U.S. 584 (1977), and for a murderer who did not intend to kill, *Enmund v. Florida,* 458 U.S. 782 (1982). In those opinions we acknowledged that "objective evidence, though of great importance, did not 'wholly determine' the controversy, 'for the Constitution contemplates that in the end our own judgment will be brought to bear on the question of the acceptability of the death penalty under the Eighth Amendment.' " *Atkins,* 536 U.S., at 312 (quoting *Coker,* 433 U.S., at 597 (plurality opinion)).

Justice White was exercising his own judgment in 1972 when he provided the decisive vote in *Furman,* the case that led to a nationwide reexamination of the death penalty. His conclusion that death amounted to "cruel and unusual punishment in the constitutional sense" as well as the "dictionary sense," rested on both an uncontroversial legal premise and on a factual premise that he admittedly could not "prove" on the basis of objective criteria. As a matter of law, he correctly stated that the "needless extinction of life with only marginal contributions to any discernible social or public purposes . . . would be patently excessive" and violative of the Eighth Amendment. As a matter of fact, he stated, "like my Brethren, I must arrive at judgment; and I can do no more than state a conclusion based on 10 years of almost daily exposure to the facts and circumstances of hundreds and hundreds of federal and state criminal cases involving crimes for which death is the authorized penalty." I agree with Justice White that there are occasions when a Member of this Court has a duty to make judgments on the basis of data that falls short of absolute proof.

Our decisions in 1976 upholding the constitutionality of the death penalty relied heavily on our belief that adequate procedures were in place that would avoid the danger of discriminatory application identified by Justice Douglas' opinion in *Furman,* of arbitrary application identified by Justice Stewart, and of excessiveness identified by Justices Brennan and Marshall. In subsequent years a number of our decisions relied on the premise that "death is different" from every other form of punishment to justify rules minimizing the risk of error in capital cases. *See, e.g., Gardner v. Florida,* 430 U.S. 349, 357-358 (1977) (plurality opinion). Ironically, however, more recent cases have endorsed procedures that provide less protections to capital defendants than to ordinary offenders.

Of special concern to me are rules that deprive the defendant of a trial by jurors representing a fair cross section of the community. Litigation involving both challenges for cause and peremptory challenges has persuaded me that the process of obtaining a "death qualified jury" is really a procedure that has the purpose and effect of obtaining a jury that is biased in favor of conviction. The prosecutorial concern that death verdicts would rarely be returned by 12 randomly selected jurors should be viewed as objective evidence supporting the conclusion that the penalty is excessive.

Another serious concern is that the risk of error in capital cases may be greater than in other cases because the facts are often so disturbing that the interest in making sure the crime does not go unpunished may overcome residual doubt concerning the identity of the offender. Our former emphasis on the importance of ensuring that decisions in death cases be adequately supported by reason rather than emotion, *Gardner,* 430 U.S. 349, has been undercut by more recent decisions placing a thumb on the prosecutor's side of the scales. Thus, in *Kansas v. Marsh,* 548 U.S. 163 (2006), the Court upheld a state statute that requires imposition of the death penalty when the jury finds that the aggravating and mitigating factors are in equipoise. And in *Payne v. Tennessee,* 501 U.S. 808 (1991), the Court overruled earlier cases and held that "victim impact" evidence relating to the personal characteristics of the victim and the emotional impact of the crime on the victim's family is admissible despite the fact that it sheds no light on the question of guilt or innocence or on the moral culpability of the defendant, and thus serves no purpose other than to encourage jurors to make life or death decisions on the basis of emotion rather than reason.

A third significant concern is the risk of discriminatory application of the death penalty. While that risk has been dramatically reduced, the Court has allowed it to continue to play an unacceptable role in capital cases. Thus, in *McCleskey v. Kemp,* 481 U.S. 279 (1987), the Court upheld a death sentence despite the "strong probability that [the defendant's] sentencing jury . . . was influenced by the fact that [he was] black and his victim was white." *Id.,* at 366 (Stevens, J., dissenting); *see also Evans v. State,* 396 Md. 256, 323, 914 A.2d 25, 64 (2006), (affirming a death sentence despite the existence of a study showing that "the death penalty is *statistically* more likely to be pursued against a black person who murders a white victim than against a defendant in any other racial combination").

Finally, given the real risk of error in this class of cases, the irrevocable nature of the consequences is of decisive importance to me. Whether or not any innocent defendants have actually been executed, abundant evidence accumulated in recent years has resulted in the exoneration of an unacceptable number of defendants found guilty of capital offenses. *See* Garrett, Judging Innocence, 108 Colum. L.Rev. 55 (2008); Risinger, Innocents Convicted: An Empirically Justified Factual Wrongful Conviction Rate, 97 J.Crim. L. & C. 761 (2007). The risk of executing innocent defendants can be entirely eliminated by treating any penalty more severe than life imprisonment without the possibility of parole as constitutionally excessive.

In sum, just as Justice White ultimately based his conclusion in *Furman* on his extensive exposure to countless cases for which death is the authorized penalty, I have relied on my own experience in reaching the conclusion that the imposition of the death penalty represents "the pointless and needless extinction of life with only marginal contributions to any discernible social or public purposes. A penalty with such negligible returns to the State [is] patently excessive and cruel and unusual punishment violative of the Eighth Amendment." *Furman,* 408 U.S., at 312 (White, J., concurring).[19]

IV

The conclusion that I have reached with regard to the constitutionality of the death penalty itself makes my decision in this case particularly difficult. It does not, however, justify a refusal to respect precedents that remain a part of our law. This Court has held that the death penalty is constitutional, and has established a framework for evaluating the constitutionality of particular methods of execution. Under those precedents, whether as interpreted by the Chief Justice or Justice Ginsburg, I am persuaded that the evidence adduced by petitioners fails to prove that Kentucky's lethal injection protocol violates the Eighth Amendment. Accordingly, I join the Court's judgment.

---

[19] Not a single Justice in *Furman* concluded that the mention of deprivation of "life" in the Fifth and Fourteenth Amendments insulated the death penalty from constitutional challenge. The five Justices who concurred in the judgment necessarily rejected this argument, and even the four dissenters, who explicitly acknowledged that the death penalty was not considered impermissibly cruel at the time of the framing, proceeded to evaluate whether anything had changed in the intervening 181 years that nevertheless rendered capital punishment unconstitutional. *Furman,* 408 U.S., at 380-384 (Burger, C.J., joined by Blackmun, Powell, and Rehnquist, JJ., dissenting); *see also id.,* at 420 ("Nor are 'cruel and unusual punishments' and 'due process of law' static concepts whose meaning and scope were sealed at the time of their writing") (Powell, J., joined by Burger, C.J., and Blackmun and Rehnquist, JJ., dissenting). And indeed, the guarantees of procedural fairness contained in the Fifth and Fourteenth Amendments do not resolve the substantive questions relating to the separate limitations imposed by the Eighth Amendment.

CHAPTER 4 RACE, GENDER AND SEXUAL ORIENTATION

B.   The Effects of Race

Page 226. Add to Note 14:

NAACP Legal Defense Fund Statistics

TOTAL NUMBER OF DEATH ROW INMATES KNOWN TO LDF:
3,309 (as of January 1, 2008)

Race of defendant

White	1489	(45.00%)
Black	1379	(41.67%)
Latino/Latina	364	(11.00%)
Asian	40	(1.21%)
Native American	36	(1.09%)
Unknown	1	(.03%)

According to LDF's Death Row, U.S.A., and the Death Penalty Information Center, as of January 1, 2008, 1099 inmates are known to have been executed since the 1976 reinstatement of capital punishment. Statistics on the race of the inmates executed and their victims are as follows:

Race of defendants executed

White	626	(56.96%)
Black	376	(34.21%)
Latino/Latina	75	(6.82%)
Native American	15	(1.36%)
Asian	7	(0.64%)

Race of victims

White	1295	(79.16%)
Black	226	(13.81%)
Latino/Latina	81	(4.95%)
Native American	5	(0.31%)
Asian	29	(1.77%)

Defendant-Victim Racial Combinations

	White Victim	Black Victim	Latino/Latina Victim	Asian Victim	Native American Victim
White Defendant	586 (53.32%)	15 (1.36%)	13 (1.18%)	3 (0.27%)	0 (0%)
Black Defendant	228 (20.75%)	117 (10.65%)	15 (1.36%)	9 (0.82%)	0 (0%)
Latino/Latina Defendant	36 (3.28%)	2 (0.18%)	32 (2.91%)	2 (0.18%)	0 (0%)
Asian Defendant	2 (0.18%)	0 (0%)	0 (0%)	5 (0.45%)	0 (0%)
Native American Defendant	13 (1.18%)	0 (0%)	0 (0%)	0 (0%)	2 (0.18%)
TOTAL	865 (78.71%)	134 (12.19%)	60 (5.46%)	19 (1.73%)	2 (0.18%)

Note: In addition, there were 19 defendants executed for the murders of multiple victims of different races. Of those, 11 defendants were white, 5 black and 3 Latino. (1.73%)

C.   The Effects of Gender

Page 233. Insert before Death Penalty for Female Offenders:

NAACP Legal Defense Fund Statistics

1. Of the 3,309 inmates known to LDF as of January 1, 2008, 3,253 (98.31%) are men and 56 (1.69%) are women.

2. According to LDF, as of January 1, 2008, the gender of death row inmates executed and the gender of the victims of death row inmates are as follows:

Gender of defendants executed ....total number 1099	Female............ 11 (1.00%) Male............ 1088 (99.00%)
Gender of victims ....total number 1636	Female...........806 (49.27%) Male..............830 (50.73%)

CHAPTER 5 CONSTITUTIONAL LIMITATIONS ON DEATH ELIGIBILITY

C. Insanity

Page 287. Insert before Lowenfield v. Butler:

Panetti v. Quarterman
127 S.Ct. 2842 (2007)

KENNEDY, J., delivered the opinion of the Court, in which Stevens, Souter, Ginsburg, and Breyer, JJ., joined. Thomas, J., filed a dissenting opinion, in which Roberts, C. J., and Scalia and Alito, JJ., joined.

"[T]he Eighth Amendment prohibits a State from carrying out a sentence of death upon a prisoner who is insane." *Ford* v. *Wainwright*, 477 U. S. 399, 409-410 (1986). The prohibition applies despite a prisoner's earlier competency to be held responsible for committing a crime and to be tried for it. Prior findings of competency do not foreclose a prisoner from proving he is incompetent to be executed because of his present mental condition. Under *Ford*, once a prisoner makes the requisite preliminary showing that his current mental state would bar his execution, the Eighth Amendment, applicable to the States under the Due Process Clause of the Fourteenth Amendment, entitles him to an adjudication to determine his condition. These determinations are governed by the substantive federal baseline for competency set down in *Ford*.

Scott Louis Panetti, referred to here as petitioner, was convicted and sentenced to death in a Texas state court. After the state trial court set an execution date, petitioner made a substantial showing he was not competent to be executed. The state court rejected his claim of incompetency on the merits. Filing a petition for writ of habeas corpus in the United States District Court for the Western District of Texas, petitioner claimed again that his mental condition barred his execution; that the Eighth Amendment set forth a substantive standard for competency different from the one advanced by the State; and that prior state-court proceedings on the issue were insufficient to satisfy the procedural requirements mandated by *Ford*. The State denied these assertions and argued, in addition, that the federal courts lacked jurisdiction to hear petitioner's claims.

We conclude we have statutory authority to adjudicate the claims petitioner raises in his habeas application; we find the state court failed to provide the procedures to which petitioner was entitled under the Constitution; and we determine that the federal appellate court employed an improperly restrictive test when it considered petitioner's claim of incompetency on the merits. We therefore reverse the judgment of the Court of Appeals for the Fifth Circuit and remand the case for further consideration.

I

On a morning in 1992 petitioner awoke before dawn, dressed in camouflage, and drove to the home of his estranged wife's parents. Breaking the front-door lock, he entered the house and, in front of his wife and daughter, shot and killed his wife's mother and father. He took his wife and daughter hostage for the night before surrendering to police.

Tried for capital murder in 1995, petitioner sought to represent himself. The court ordered a psychiatric evaluation, which indicated that petitioner suffered from a fragmented personality, delusions, and hallucinations. The evaluation noted that petitioner had been hospitalized numerous times for these disorders. Evidence later revealed that doctors had prescribed medication for petitioner's mental disorders that, in the opinion of one expert, would be difficult for a person not suffering from extreme psychosis even to tolerate. Petitioner's wife described one psychotic episode in a petition she filed in 1986 seeking extraordinary relief from the Texas state courts. She explained that petitioner had become convinced the devil had possessed their home and that, in an effort to cleanse their surroundings, petitioner had buried a number of valuables next to the house and engaged in other rituals. Petitioner nevertheless was found competent to be tried and to waive counsel. At trial he claimed he was not guilty by reason of insanity.

During his trial petitioner engaged in behavior later described by his standby counsel as "bizarre," "scary," and "trance-like." According to the attorney, petitioner's behavior both in private and in front of the jury made it evident that he was suffering from "mental incompetence," and the net effect of this dynamic was to render the trial "truly a judicial farce, and a mockery of self-representation." There was evidence on the record, moreover, to indicate that petitioner had stopped taking his antipsychotic medication a few months before trial, a rejection of medical advice that, it appears, petitioner has continued to this day with one brief exception. According to expert testimony, failing to take this medication tends to exacerbate the underlying mental dysfunction. And it is uncontested that, less than two months after petitioner was sentenced to death, the state trial court found him incompetent to waive the appointment of state habeas counsel. It appears, therefore, that petitioner's condition has only worsened since the start of trial.

The jury found petitioner guilty of capital murder and sentenced him to death. Petitioner challenged his conviction and sentence both on direct appeal and through state habeas proceedings. The Texas courts denied his requests for relief. This Court twice denied a petition for certiorari.

Petitioner filed a petition for writ of habeas corpus pursuant to 28 U.S.C. §2254 in the United States District Court for the Western District of Texas. His claims were again rejected, both by the District Court, and the Court of Appeals for the Fifth Circuit, and we again denied a petition for certiorari. Among the issues petitioner raised in the course of these state and federal proceedings was his competency to stand trial and to waive counsel. Petitioner did not argue, however, that mental illness rendered him incompetent to be executed.

On October 31, 2003, Judge Stephen B. Ables of the 216th Judicial District Court in Gillespie County, Texas, set petitioner's execution date for February 5, 2004. On December 10, 2003, counsel for petitioner filed with Judge Ables a motion under Tex. Code Crim. Proc. Ann., Art. 46.05 (Vernon Supp. Pamphlet 2006). Petitioner claimed, for the first time, that due to mental illness he was incompetent to be executed. The judge denied the motion without a hearing. When petitioner attempted to challenge the ruling, the Texas Court of Criminal Appeals dismissed his appeal for lack of jurisdiction, indicating it has authority to review an Art. 46.05 determination only when a trial court has determined a prisoner is incompetent.

Petitioner returned to federal court, where he filed another petition for writ of habeas corpus pursuant to §2254 and a motion for stay of execution. On February 4, 2004, the District Court stayed petitioner's execution to "allow the state court a reasonable period of time to consider the evidence of [petitioner's] current mental state."

The state court had before it, at that time, petitioner's Renewed Motion To Determine Competency To Be Executed (hereinafter Renewed Motion To Determine Competency). Attached to the motion were a letter and a declaration from two individuals, a psychologist and a law professor, who had interviewed petitioner while on death row on February 3, 2004. The new evidence, according to counsel, demonstrated that petitioner did not understand the reasons he was about to be executed.

Due to the absence of a transcript, the state-court proceedings after this point are not altogether clear. The claims raised before this Court nevertheless make it necessary to recount the procedural history in some detail. Based on the docket entries and the parties' filings it appears the following occurred.

The state trial court ordered the parties to participate in a telephone conference on February 9, 2004, to discuss the status of the case. There followed a court directive instructing counsel to submit, by February 20, the names of mental health experts the court should consider appointing pursuant to Art. 46.05(f). The court also gave the parties until February 20 to submit any motions concerning the competency procedures and advised it would hold another status conference on that same date.

On February 19, 2004, petitioner filed 10 motions related to the Art. 46.05 proceedings. They included requests for transcription of the proceedings, a competency hearing comporting with the procedural due process requirements set forth in *Ford*, and funds to hire a mental health expert.

On February 20 the court failed to hold its scheduled status conference. Petitioner's counsel called the courthouse and was advised Judge Ables was out of the office for the day. Counsel then called the Gillespie County District Attorney, who explained that the judge had informed state attorneys earlier that week that he was cancelling the conference he had set and would appoint the mental health experts without input from the parties.

On February 23, 2004, counsel for petitioner received an order, dated February 20, advising that the court was appointing two mental health experts pursuant to Art. §46.05(f). On February 25, at an informal status conference, the court denied two of petitioner's motions, indicating it would consider the others when the court-appointed mental health experts completed their evaluations. On March 4, petitioner filed a motion explaining that a delayed ruling would render a number of the motions moot. There is no indication the court responded to this motion.

The court-appointed experts returned with their evaluation on April 28, 2004. Concluding that petitioner "knows that he is to be executed, and that his execution will result in his death," and, moreover, that he "has the ability to understand the reason he is to be executed," the experts alleged that petitioner's uncooperative and bizarre behavior was due to calculated design: "Mr. Panetti deliberately and persistently chose to control and manipulate our interview situation," they claimed. They maintained that petitioner "could answer questions about relevant legal issues … if he were willing to do so."

The judge sent a letter to counsel, including petitioner's attorney, Michael C. Gross, dated May 14, 2004. It said:

"Dear Counsel:

"It appears from the evaluations performed by [the court-appointed experts] that they are of the opinion that [petitioner] is competent to be executed in accordance with the standards set out in Art. 46.05 of the Code of Criminal Procedure.

"Mr. Gross, if you have any other matters you wish to have considered, please file them in the case papers and get me copies by 5:00 p.m. on May 21, 2004."

Petitioner responded with a filing entitled "Objections to Experts' Report, Renewed Motion for Funds To Hire Mental Health Expert and Investigator, Renewed Motion for Appointment of Counsel, and Motion for Competency Hearing" in Cause No. 3310 (May 24, 2004) (hereinafter Objections to Experts' Report). In this filing petitioner criticized the methodology and conclusions of the court-appointed experts; asserted his continued need for a mental health expert as his own criticisms of the report were "by necessity limited,"; again asked the court to rule on his outstanding motions for funds and appointment of counsel; and requested a competency hearing. Petitioner also argued, as a more general matter, that the process he had received thus far failed to comply with Art. 46.05 and the procedural mandates set by *Ford*.

The court, in response, closed the case. On May 26, it released a short order identifying the report submitted by the court-appointed experts and explaining that "[b]ased on the aforesaid doctors' reports, the Court finds that [petitioner] has failed to show, by a preponderance of the evidence, that he is incompetent to be executed." The order made no mention of petitioner's motions or other filings. Petitioner did not appeal the ruling to the Court of Criminal Appeals, and he did not petition this Court for certiorari.

This background leads to the matter now before us. Petitioner returned to federal court, seeking resolution of the §2254 petition he had filed on January 26. The District Court granted petitioner's motions to reconsider, to stay his execution, to appoint counsel, and to provide funds. The court, in addition, set the case for an evidentiary hearing, which included testimony by a psychiatrist, a professor, and two psychologists, all called by petitioner, as well as two psychologists and three correctional officers, called by respondent. We describe the substance of the experts' testimony in more detail later in our opinion.

On September 29, 2004, the District Court denied petitioner's habeas application on the merits. It concluded that the state trial court had failed to comply with Art. 46.05; found the state proceedings "constitutionally inadequate" in light of *Ford;* and reviewed petitioner's Eighth Amendment claim without deferring to the state court's finding of competency. The court nevertheless denied relief. It found petitioner had not shown incompetency as defined by Circuit precedent. "Ultimately," the court explained, "the Fifth Circuit test for competency to be executed requires the petitioner know no more than the fact of his impending execution and the factual predicate for the execution." The Court of Appeals affirmed, and we granted certiorari.

. . . .

III

A

Petitioner claims that the Eighth and Fourteenth Amendments of the Constitution, as elaborated by *Ford*, entitled him to certain procedures not provided in the state court; that the failure to provide these procedures constituted an unreasonable application of clearly established Supreme Court law; and that under §2254(d) this misapplication of *Ford* allows federal-court review of his incompetency claim without deference to the state court's decision.

We agree with petitioner that no deference is due. The state court's failure to provide the procedures mandated by *Ford* constituted an unreasonable application of clearly established law as determined by this Court. It is uncontested that petitioner made a substantial showing of incompetency. This showing entitled him to, among other things, an adequate means by which to submit expert psychiatric evidence in response to the evidence that had been solicited by the state court. And it is clear from the record that the state court reached its competency determination after failing to provide petitioner with this process, notwithstanding counsel's sustained effort, diligence, and compliance with court orders. As a result of this error, our review of petitioner's underlying incompetency claim is unencumbered by the deference AEDPA normally requires.

Ford identifies the measures a State must provide when a prisoner alleges incompetency to be executed. The four-Justice plurality in *Ford* concluded as follows:

"Although the condemned prisoner does not enjoy the same presumptions accorded a defendant who has yet to be convicted or sentenced, he has not lost the protection of the Constitution altogether; if the Constitution renders the fact or timing of his execution contingent upon establishment of a further fact, then that fact must be determined with the high regard for truth that befits a decision affecting the life or death of a human being. Thus, the ascertainment of a prisoner's sanity as a predicate to lawful execution calls for no less stringent standards than those demanded in any other aspect of a capital proceeding."

Justice Powell's concurrence, which also addressed the question of procedure, offered a more limited holding. When there is no majority opinion, the narrower holding controls. Under this rule Justice Powell's opinion constitutes "clearly established" law for purposes of §2254 and sets the minimum procedures a State must provide to a prisoner raising a *Ford*-based competency claim.

Justice Powell's opinion states the relevant standard as follows. Once a prisoner seeking a stay of execution has made "a substantial threshold showing of insanity," the protection afforded by procedural due process includes a "fair hearing" in accord with fundamental fairness. This protection means a prisoner must be accorded an "opportunity to be heard," though "a constitutionally acceptable procedure may be far less formal than a trial". As an example of why the state procedures on review in *Ford* were deficient, Justice Powell explained, the determination of sanity "appear[ed] to have been made *solely* on the basis of the examinations performed by state-appointed psychiatrists." "Such a procedure invites arbitrariness and error by preventing the affected parties from offering contrary medical evidence or even from explaining the inadequacies of the State's examinations."

Justice Powell did not set forth "the precise limits that due process imposes in this area." He observed that a State "should have substantial leeway to determine what process best balances the various interests at stake" once it has met the "basic requirements" required by due process. These basic requirements include an opportunity to submit "evidence and argument from the prisoner's counsel, including expert psychiatric evidence that may differ from the State's own psychiatric examination."

Petitioner was entitled to these protections once he had made a "substantial threshold showing of insanity." He made this showing when he filed his Renewed Motion To Determine Competency – a fact disputed by no party, confirmed by the trial court's appointment of mental health experts pursuant to Article 46.05(f), and verified by our independent review of the record. The Renewed Motion included pointed observations made by two experts the day before petitioner's scheduled execution; and it incorporated, through petitioner's first Motion To Determine Competency, references to the extensive evidence of mental dysfunction considered in earlier legal proceedings.

In light of this showing, the state court failed to provide petitioner with the minimum process required by *Ford*.

The state court refused to transcribe its proceedings, notwithstanding the multiple motions petitioner filed requesting this process. To the extent a more complete record may have put some of the court's actions in a more favorable light, this only constitutes further evidence of the inadequacy of the proceedings. Based on the materials available to this Court, it appears the state court on repeated occasions conveyed information to petitioner's counsel that turned out not to be true; provided at least one significant update to the State without providing the same notice to petitioner; and failed in general to keep petitioner informed as to the opportunity, if any, he would have to present his case. There is also a strong argument the court violated state law by failing to provide a competency hearing. If this did, in fact, constitute a violation of the procedural framework Texas has mandated for the adjudication of incompetency claims, the violation undermines any reliance the State might now place on Justice Powell's assertion that "the States should have substantial leeway to determine what process best balances the various interests at stake." What is more, the order issued by the state court implied that its determination of petitioner's competency was made solely on the basis of the examinations performed by the psychiatrists it had appointed – precisely the sort of adjudication Justice Powell warned would "invit[e] arbitrariness and error".

The state court made an additional error, one that *Ford* makes clear is impermissible under the Constitution: It failed to provide petitioner with an adequate opportunity to submit expert evidence in response to the report filed by the court-appointed experts. The court mailed the experts' report to both parties in the first week of May. The report, which rejected the factual basis for petitioner's claim, set forth new allegations suggesting that petitioner's bizarre behavior was due, at least in part, to deliberate design rather than mental illness. Petitioner's counsel reached the reasonable conclusion that these allegations warranted a response. On May 14 the court told petitioner's counsel, by letter, to file "any other matters you wish to have considered" within a week. Petitioner, in response, renewed his motions for an evidentiary hearing, funds to hire a mental health expert, and other relief. He did not submit at that time expert psychiatric evidence to challenge the court-appointed experts' report, a decision that in context made sense: The court had said it would rule on his outstanding motions, which included a request for funds to hire a mental-health expert and a request for an evidentiary hearing, once the court-appointed experts had completed their evaluation. Counsel was justified in relying on this representation by the court.

Texas law, moreover, provides that a court's finding of incompetency will be made on the basis of, *inter alia*, a "final competency hearing." Had the court advised counsel it would resolve the case without first ruling on petitioner's motions and without holding a competency hearing, petitioner's counsel might have managed to procure the assistance of experts, as he had been able to do on a *pro bono* basis the day before petitioner's previously scheduled execution. It was, in any event, reasonable for counsel to refrain from procuring and submitting expert psychiatric evidence while waiting for the court to rule on the timely filed motions, all in reliance on the court's assurances.

But at this point the court simply ended the matter.

The state court failed to provide petitioner with a constitutionally adequate opportunity to be heard. After a prisoner has made the requisite threshold showing, *Ford* requires, at a minimum, that a court allow a prisoner's counsel the opportunity to make an adequate response to evidence solicited by the state court. In petitioner's case this meant an opportunity to submit psychiatric evidence as a counterweight to the report filed by the court-appointed experts. Yet petitioner failed to receive even this rudimentary process.

In light of this error we need not address whether other procedures, such as the opportunity for discovery or for the cross-examination of witnesses, would in some cases be required under the Due Process Clause. As *Ford* makes clear, the procedural deficiencies already identified constituted a violation of petitioner's federal rights.

. . . .

IV

A

This brings us to the question petitioner asks the Court to resolve: whether the Eighth Amendment permits the execution of a prisoner whose mental illness deprives him of "the mental capacity to understand that [he] is being executed as a punishment for a crime."

A review of the expert testimony helps frame the issue. Four expert witnesses testified on petitioner's behalf in the District Court proceedings. One explained that petitioner's mental problems are indicative of "schizo-affective disorder," resulting in a "genuine delusion" involving his understanding of the reason for his execution. According to the expert, this delusion has recast petitioner's execution as "part of spiritual warfare … between the demons and the forces of the darkness and God and the angels and the forces of light." As a result, the expert explained, although petitioner claims to understand "that the state is saying that [it wishes] to execute him for [his] murder[s]," he believes in earnest that the stated reason is a "sham" and the State in truth wants to execute him "to stop him from preaching." Petitioner's other expert witnesses reached similar conclusions concerning the strength and sincerity of this "fixed delusion."

While the State's expert witnesses resisted the conclusion that petitioner's stated beliefs were necessarily indicative of incompetency, particularly in light of his perceived ability to understand certain concepts and, at times, to be "clear and lucid," they acknowledged evidence of mental problems. Petitioner's rebuttal witness attempted to reconcile the experts' testimony:

"Well, first, you have to understand that when somebody is schizophrenic, it doesn't diminish their cognitive ability…. . Instead, you have a situation where – and why we call schizophrenia thought disorder [–] the logical integration and reality connection of their thoughts are disrupted, so the stimulus comes in,

76

and instead of being analyzed and processed in a rational, logical, linear sort of way, it gets scrambled up and it comes out in a tangential, circumstantial, symbolic … not really relevant kind of way. That's the essence of somebody being schizophrenic.… . Now, it may be that if they're dealing with someone who's more familiar … [in] what may feel like a safer, more enclosed environment … those sorts of interactions may be reasonably lucid whereas a more extended conversation about more loaded material would reflect the severity of his mental illness."

There is, in short, much in the record to support the conclusion that petitioner suffers from severe delusions.

The legal inquiry concerns whether these delusions can be said to render him incompetent. The Court of Appeals held that they could not. That holding, we conclude, rests on a flawed interpretation of *Ford*.

The Court of Appeals stated that competency is determined by whether a prisoner is aware " 'that he [is] going to be executed and why he [is] going to be executed'". To this end, the Court of Appeals identified the relevant District Court findings as follows: first, petitioner is aware that he committed the murders; second, he is aware that he will be executed; and, third, he is aware that the reason the State has given for the execution is his commission of the crimes in question. Under Circuit precedent this ends the analysis as a matter of law; for the Court of Appeals regards these three factual findings as necessarily demonstrating that a prisoner is aware of the reason for his execution.

The Court of Appeals concluded that its standard foreclosed petitioner from establishing incompetency by the means he now seeks to employ: a showing that his mental illness obstructs a rational understanding of the State's reason for his execution. As the court explained, "[b]ecause we hold that 'awareness,' as that term is used in *Ford*, is not necessarily synonymous with 'rational understanding,' as argued by [petitioner,] we conclude that the district court's findings are sufficient to establish that [petitioner] is competent to be executed."

In our view the Court of Appeals' standard is too restrictive to afford a prisoner the protections granted by the Eighth Amendment. The opinions in *Ford*, it must be acknowledged, did not set forth a precise standard for competency. The four-Justice plurality discussed the substantive standard at a high level of generality; and Justice Powell wrote only for himself when he articulated more specific criteria. Yet in the portion of Justice Marshall's discussion constituting the opinion of the Court (the portion Justice Powell joined) the majority did reach the express conclusion that the Constitution "places a substantive restriction on the State's power to take the life of an insane prisoner." The Court stated the foundation for this principle as follows:

> "[T]oday, no less than before, we may seriously question the retributive value of executing a person who has no comprehension of why he has been singled out and stripped of his fundamental right to life.... . Similarly, the natural abhorrence civilized societies feel at killing one who has no capacity to come to grips with his own conscience or deity is still vivid today. And the intuition that such an execution simply offends humanity is evidently shared across this Nation. Faced with such widespread evidence of a restriction upon sovereign power, this Court is compelled to conclude that the Eighth Amendment prohibits a State from carrying out a sentence of death upon a prisoner who is insane."

Writing for four Justices, Justice Marshall concluded by indicating that the Eighth Amendment prohibits execution of "one whose mental illness prevents him from comprehending the reasons for the penalty or its implications." Justice Powell, in his separate opinion, asserted that the Eighth Amendment "forbids the execution only of those who are unaware of the punishment they are about to suffer and why they are to suffer it."

The Court of Appeals' standard treats a prisoner's delusional belief system as irrelevant if the prisoner knows that the State has identified his crimes as the reason for his execution. Yet the *Ford* opinions nowhere indicate that delusions are irrelevant to "comprehen[sion]" or "aware[ness]" if they so impair the prisoner's concept of reality that he cannot reach a rational understanding of the reason for the execution. If anything, the *Ford* majority suggests the opposite.

Explaining the prohibition against executing a prisoner who has lost his sanity, Justice Marshall in the controlling portion of his opinion set forth various rationales, including recognition that "the execution of an insane person simply offends humanity"; that it "provides no example to others"; that "it is uncharitable to dispatch an offender into another world, when he is not of a capacity to fit himself for it"; that "madness is its own punishment"; and that executing an insane person serves no retributive purpose.

Considering the last – whether retribution is served – it might be said that capital punishment is imposed because it has the potential to make the offender recognize at last the gravity of his crime and to allow the community as a whole, including the surviving family and friends of the victim, to affirm its own judgment that the culpability of the prisoner is so serious that the ultimate penalty must be sought and imposed. The potential for a prisoner's recognition of the severity of the offense and the objective of community vindication are called in question, however, if the prisoner's mental state is so distorted by a mental illness that his awareness of the crime and punishment has little or no relation to the understanding of those concepts shared by the community as a whole. This problem is not necessarily overcome once the test set forth by the Court of Appeals is met. And under a similar logic the other rationales set forth by *Ford* fail to align with the distinctions drawn by the Court of Appeals.

Whether *Ford*'s inquiry into competency is formulated as a question of the prisoner's ability to "comprehen[d] the reasons" for his punishment or as a determination into whether he is "unaware of … why [he is] to suffer it," then, the approach taken by the Court of Appeals is inconsistent with *Ford*. The principles set forth in *Ford* are put at risk by a rule that deems delusions relevant only with respect to the State's announced reason for a punishment or the fact of an imminent execution, as opposed to the real interests the State seeks to vindicate. We likewise find no support elsewhere in *Ford*, including in its discussions of the common law and the state standards, for the proposition that a prisoner is automatically foreclosed from demonstrating incompetency once a court has found he can identify the stated reason for his execution. A prisoner's awareness of the State's rationale for an execution is not the same as a rational understanding of it. *Ford* does not foreclose inquiry into the latter.

This is not to deny the fact that a concept like rational understanding is difficult to define. And we must not ignore the concern that some prisoners, whose cases are not implicated by this decision, will fail to understand why they are to be punished on account of reasons other than those stemming from a severe mental illness. The mental state requisite for competence to suffer capital punishment neither presumes nor requires a person who would be considered "normal," or even "rational," in a layperson's understanding of those terms. Someone who is condemned to death for an atrocious murder may be so callous as to be unrepentant; so self-centered and devoid of compassion as to lack all sense of guilt; so adept in transferring blame to others as to be considered, at least in the colloquial sense, to be out of touch with reality. Those states of mind, even if extreme compared to the criminal population at large, are not what petitioner contends lie at the threshold of a competence inquiry. The beginning of doubt about competence in a case like petitioner's is not a misanthropic personality or an amoral character. It is a psychotic disorder.

Petitioner's submission is that he suffers from a severe, documented mental illness that is the source of gross delusions preventing him from comprehending the meaning and purpose of the punishment to which he has been sentenced. This argument, we hold, should have been considered.

The flaws of the Court of Appeals' test are pronounced in petitioner's case. Circuit precedent required the District Court to disregard evidence of psychological dysfunction that, in the words of the judge, may have resulted in petitioner's "fundamental failure to appreciate the connection between the petitioner's crime and his execution." To refuse to consider evidence of this nature is to mistake *Ford*'s holding and its logic. Gross delusions stemming from a severe mental disorder may put an awareness of a link between a crime and its punishment in a context so far removed from reality that the punishment can serve no proper purpose. It is therefore error to derive from *Ford*, and the substantive standard for incompetency its opinions broadly identify, a strict test for competency that treats delusional beliefs as irrelevant once the prisoner is aware the State has identified the link between his crime and the punishment to be inflicted.

B

Although we reject the standard followed by the Court of Appeals, we do not attempt to set down a rule governing all competency determinations. The record is not as informative as it might be, even on the narrower issue of how a mental illness of the sort alleged by petitioner might affect this analysis. In overseeing the development of the record and in making its factual findings, the District Court found itself bound to analyze the question of competency in the terms set by Circuit precedent. It acknowledged, for example, the "difficult issue" posed by the delusions allegedly interfering with petitioner's understanding of the reason behind his execution, but it refrained from making definitive findings of fact with respect to these matters. *See also id.*, at 712 (identifying testimony by Dr. Mark Cunningham indicating that petitioner "believes the State is in league with the forces of evil that have conspired against him" and, as a result, "does not even understand that the State of Texas is a lawfully constituted authority," but refraining from setting forth definitive findings of fact concerning whether this was an accurate characterization of petitioner's mindset).

The District Court declined to consider the significance those findings might have on the ultimate question of competency under the Eighth Amendment. *See ibid.* (disregarding Dr. Cunningham's testimony in light of Circuit precedent). And notwithstanding the numerous questions the District Court asked of the witnesses, it did not press the experts on the difficult issue it identified in its opinion. The District Court, of course, was bound by Circuit precedent, and the record was developed pursuant to a standard we have found to be improper. As a result, we find it difficult to amplify our conclusions or to make them more precise. We are also hesitant to decide a question of this complexity before the District Court and the Court of Appeals have addressed, in a more definitive manner and in light of the expert evidence found to be probative, the nature and severity of petitioner's alleged mental problems.

The underpinnings of petitioner's claims should be explained and evaluated in further detail on remand. The conclusions of physicians, psychiatrists, and other experts in the field will bear upon the proper analysis. Expert evidence may clarify the extent to which severe delusions may render a subject's perception of reality so distorted that he should be deemed incompetent. And there is precedent to guide a court conducting Eighth Amendment analysis.

It is proper to allow the court charged with overseeing the development of the evidentiary record in this case the initial opportunity to resolve petitioner's constitutional claim. These issues may be resolved in the first instance by the District Court.

. . .The judgment of the Court of Appeals is reversed, and the case is remanded for further proceedings consistent with this opinion.

Page 311. Insert after Note and Questions on Singleton v. Norris:

For additional discussion on a medical doctor's views on this issue see Julie D. Cantor, *Of Pills and Needles: Involuntarily Medicating the Psychotic Inmate When Execution Looms*, 2 Ind. Health L. Rev. 119 (2005).

CHAPTER 6 SELECTING THE CAPITAL JURY

B.   Death Qualification

Page 344. Insert after Note 2:

Note on Uttecht v. Brown, 127 S.Ct. 2218 (2007)

The Supreme Court in *Uttecht v. Brown*, 127 S.Ct. 2218 (2007), by a five-to-four vote, found that the Ninth Circuit Court of Appeals erred in granting federal habeas corpus relief to a state capital defendant based on a *Witherspoon-Witt* error. The majority set out four principles it discerned from the *Witherspoon-Witt* line of cases:

> When considering the controlling precedents, *Witherspoon* is not the final word, but it is a necessary starting point. During the *voir dire* that preceded William Witherspoon's capital trial, the prosecution succeeded in removing a substantial number of jurors based on their general scruples against inflicting the death penalty. The State challenged, and the trial court excused for cause, 47 members of the 96-person venire, without significant examination of the individual prospective jurors. The Court held that the systematic removal of those in the venire opposed to the death penalty had led to a jury "uncommonly willing to condemn a man to die," and thus "woefully short of that impartiality to which the petitioner was entitled under the Sixth and Fourteenth Amendments." Because "[a] man who opposes the death penalty, no less than one who favors it, can make the discretionary judgment entrusted to him by the State," the Court held that "a sentence of death cannot be carried out if the jury that imposed or recommended it was chosen by excluding veniremen for cause simply because they voiced general objections to the death penalty." The Court also set forth, in dicta in a footnote, a strict standard for when an individual member of the venire may be removed for cause on account of his or her views on the death penalty.

E.   *Race-Based Peremptory Challenges*

Page 379. Insert before Gender-Based Peremptory Challenges:

2. In 2008, the Supreme Court considered another case in which a capital defendant alleged he was convicted by a jury empaneled by a process that violated the Supreme Court's prohibition on the use of race-based peremptory challenges. Below is an excerpt of *Snyder v. Louisiana*, 128 S.Ct. 1203 (2008), in which the Court by a seven-to-two vote once again found a *Batson* violation in a death-penalty case.

Snyder v. Louisiana
128 S.Ct. 1203 (2008)

Justice ALITO delivered the opinion of the Court.

Petitioner Allen Snyder was convicted of first-degree murder in a Louisiana court and was sentenced to death. He asks us to review a decision of the Louisiana Supreme Court rejecting his claim that the prosecution exercised some of its peremptory jury challenges based on race, in violation of *Batson v. Kentucky*, 476 U.S. 79 (1986). We hold that the trial court committed clear error in its ruling on a *Batson* objection, and we therefore reverse.

I

. . . The State charged petitioner with first-degree murder and sought the death penalty based on the aggravating circumstance that petitioner had knowingly created a risk of death or great bodily harm to more than one person.

Voir dire began on Tuesday, August 27, 1996, and proceeded as follows. During the first phase, the trial court screened the panel to identify jurors who did not meet Louisiana's requirements for jury service or claimed that service on the jury or sequestration for the duration of the trial would result in extreme hardship. More than 50 prospective jurors reported that they had work, family, or other commitments that would interfere with jury service. In each of those instances, the nature of the conflicting commitments was explored, and some of these jurors were dismissed.

In the next phase, the court randomly selected panels of 13 potential jurors for further questioning. The defense and prosecution addressed each panel and questioned the jurors both as a group and individually. At the conclusion of this questioning, the court ruled on challenges for cause. Then, the prosecution and the defense were given the opportunity to use peremptory challenges (each side had 12) to remove remaining jurors. The court continued this process of calling 13-person panels until the jury was filled. In accordance with Louisiana law, the parties were permitted to exercise "backstrikes." That is, they were allowed to use their peremptories up until the time when the final jury was sworn and thus were permitted to strike jurors whom they had initially accepted when the jurors' panels were called.

Eighty-five prospective jurors were questioned as members of a panel. Thirty-six of these survived challenges for cause; 5 of the 36 were black; and all 5 of the prospective black jurors were eliminated by the prosecution through the use of peremptory strikes. The jury found petitioner guilty of first-degree murder and determined that he should receive the death penalty.

. . . Petitioner petitioned this Court for a writ of certiorari, and while his petition was pending, this Court decided *Miller-El v. Dretke*, 545 U.S. 231 (2005). We then granted the petition, vacated the judgment, and remanded the case to the Louisiana Supreme Court for further consideration in light of *Miller-El*. On remand, the Louisiana Supreme Court again rejected Snyder's *Batson* claim, this time by a vote of 4 to 3. We again granted certiorari, and now reverse.

II

. . . The trial court has a pivotal role in evaluating *Batson* claims. Step three of the *Batson* inquiry involves an evaluation of the prosecutor's credibility, and "the best evidence [of discriminatory intent] often will be the demeanor of the attorney who exercises the challenge." In addition, race-neutral reasons for peremptory challenges often invoke a juror's demeanor (e.g., nervousness, inattention), making the trial court's first-hand observations of even greater importance. In this situation, the trial court must evaluate not only whether the prosecutor's demeanor belies a discriminatory intent, but also whether the juror's demeanor can credibly be said to have exhibited the basis for the strike attributed to the juror by the prosecutor. We have recognized that these determinations of credibility and demeanor lie " 'peculiarly within a trial judge's province,' " and we have stated that "in the absence of exceptional circumstances, we would defer to [the trial court]."

III

Petitioner centers his *Batson* claim on the prosecution's strikes of two black jurors, Jeffrey Brooks and Elaine Scott. Because we find that the trial court committed clear error in overruling petitioner's *Batson* objection with respect to Mr. Brooks, we have no need to consider petitioner's claim regarding Ms. Scott.

In *Miller-El v. Dretke*, the Court made it clear that in considering a *Batson* objection, or in reviewing a ruling claimed to be *Batson* error, all of the circumstances that bear upon the issue of racial animosity must be consulted. Here, as just one example, if there were persisting doubts as to the outcome, a court would be required to consider the strike of Ms. Scott for the bearing it might have upon the strike of Mr. Brooks. In this case, however, the explanation given for the strike of Mr. Brooks is by itself unconvincing and suffices for the determination that there was *Batson* error.

When defense counsel made a *Batson* objection concerning the strike of Mr. Brooks, a college senior who was attempting to fulfill his student-teaching obligation, the prosecution offered two race-neutral reasons for the strike. The prosecutor explained:

> "I thought about it last night. Number 1, the main reason is that he looked very nervous to me throughout the questioning. Number 2, he's one of the fellows that came up at the beginning [of voir dire] and said he was going to miss class. He's a student teacher. My main concern is for that reason, that being that he might, to go home quickly, come back with guilty of a lesser verdict so there wouldn't be a penalty phase. Those are my two reasons."

Defense counsel disputed both explanations, and the trial judge ruled as follows: "All right. I'm going to allow the challenge. I'm going to allow the challenge." We discuss the prosecution's two proffered grounds for striking Mr. Brooks in turn.

A

With respect to the first reason, the Louisiana Supreme Court was correct that "nervousness cannot be shown from a cold transcript, which is why . . . the [trial] judge's evaluation must be given much deference." As noted above, deference is especially appropriate where a trial judge has made a finding that an attorney credibly relied on demeanor in exercising a strike. Here, however, the record does not show that the trial judge actually made a determination concerning Mr. Brooks' demeanor. The trial judge was given two explanations for the strike. Rather than making a specific finding on the record concerning Mr. Brooks' demeanor, the trial judge simply allowed the challenge without explanation. It is possible that the judge did not have any impression one way or the other concerning Mr. Brooks' demeanor. Mr. Brooks was not challenged until the day after he was questioned, and by that time dozens of other jurors had been questioned. Thus, the trial judge may not have recalled Mr. Brooks' demeanor. Or, the trial judge may have found it unnecessary to consider Mr. Brooks' demeanor, instead basing his ruling completely on the second proffered justification for the strike. For these reasons, we cannot presume that the trial judge credited the prosecutor's assertion that Mr. Brooks was nervous.

B

The second reason proffered for the strike of Mr. Brooks – his student-teaching obligation – fails even under the highly deferential standard of review that is applicable here. At the beginning of voir dire, when the trial court asked the members of the venire whether jury service or sequestration would pose an extreme hardship, Mr. Brooks was 1 of more than 50 members of the venire who expressed concern that jury service or sequestration would interfere with work, school, family, or other obligations.

When Mr. Brooks came forward, the following exchange took place:

"MR. JEFFREY BROOKS: . . . I'm a student at Southern University, New Orleans. This is my last semester. My major requires me to student teach, and today I've already missed a half a day. That is part of my-it's required for me to graduate this semester.

"[DEFENSE COUNSEL]: Mr. Brooks, if you-how many days would you miss if you were sequestered on this jury? Do you teach every day?

"MR. JEFFREY BROOKS: Five days a week.

"[DEFENSE COUNSEL]: Five days a week.

"MR. JEFFREY BROOKS: And it's 8:30 through 3:00.

"[DEFENSE COUNSEL]: If you missed this week, is there any way that you could make it up this semester?

"MR. JEFFREY BROOKS: Well, the first two weeks I observe, the remaining I begin teaching, so there is something I'm missing right now that will better me towards my teaching career.

"[DEFENSE COUNSEL]: Is there any way that you could make up the observed observation [sic] that you're missing today, at another time?

"MR. JEFFREY BROOKS: It may be possible, I'm not sure.

"[DEFENSE COUNSEL]: Okay. So that-

"THE COURT: Is there anyone we could call, like a Dean or anything, that we could speak to?

"MR. JEFFREY BROOKS: Actually, I spoke to my Dean, Doctor Tillman, who's at the university probably right now.

"THE COURT: All right.

"MR. JEFFREY BROOKS: Would you like to speak to him?

"THE COURT: Yeah.

"MR. JEFFREY BROOKS: I don't have his card on me.

"THE COURT: Why don't you give [a law clerk] his number, give [a law clerk] his name and we'll call him and we'll see what we can do.

"(MR. JEFFREY BROOKS LEFT THE BENCH)."

Shortly thereafter, the court again spoke with Mr. Brooks:

"THE LAW CLERK: Jeffrey Brooks, the requirement for his teaching is a three hundred clock hour observation. Doctor Tillman at Southern University said that as long as it's just this week, he doesn't see that it would cause a problem with Mr. Brooks completing his observation time within this semester.

"(MR. BROOKS APPROACHED THE BENCH)

"THE COURT: We talked to Doctor Tillman and he says he doesn't see a problem as long as it's just this week, you know, he'll work with you on it. Okay?

"MR. JEFFREY BROOKS: Okay.

"(MR. JEFFREY BROOKS LEFT THE BENCH)."

Once Mr. Brooks heard the law clerk's report about the conversation with Doctor Tillman, Mr. Brooks did not express any further concern about serving on the jury, and the prosecution did not choose to question him more deeply about this matter.

The colloquy with Mr. Brooks and the law clerk's report took place on Tuesday, August 27; the prosecution struck Mr. Brooks the following day, Wednesday, August 28; the guilt phase of petitioner's trial ended the next day, Thursday, August 29; and the penalty phase was completed by the end of the week, on Friday, August 30.

The prosecutor's second proffered reason for striking Mr. Brooks must be evaluated in light of these circumstances. The prosecutor claimed to be apprehensive that Mr. Brooks, in order to minimize the student-teaching hours missed during jury service, might have been motivated to find petitioner guilty, not of first-degree murder, but of a lesser included offense because this would obviate the need for a penalty phase proceeding. But this scenario was highly speculative. Even if Mr. Brooks had favored a quick resolution, that would not have necessarily led him to reject a finding of first-degree murder. If the majority of jurors had initially favored a finding of first-degree murder, Mr. Brooks' purported inclination might have led him to agree in order to speed the deliberations. Only if all or most of the other jurors had favored the lesser verdict would Mr. Brooks have been in a position to shorten the trial by favoring such a verdict.

Perhaps most telling, the brevity of petitioner's trial – something that the prosecutor anticipated on the record during voir dire – meant that serving on the jury would not have seriously interfered with Mr. Brooks' ability to complete his required student teaching. As noted, petitioner's trial was completed by Friday, August 30. If Mr. Brooks, who reported to court and was peremptorily challenged on Wednesday, August 28, had been permitted to serve, he would have missed only two additional days of student teaching, Thursday, August 29, and Friday, August 30. Mr. Brooks' dean promised to "work with" Mr. Brooks to see that he was able to make up any student-teaching time that he missed due to jury service; the dean stated that he did not think that this would be a problem; and the record contains no suggestion that Mr. Brooks remained troubled after hearing the report of the dean's remarks. In addition, although the record does not include the academic calendar of Mr. Brooks' university, it is apparent that the trial occurred relatively early in the fall semester. With many weeks remaining in the term, Mr. Brooks would have needed to make up no more than an hour or two per week in order to compensate for the time that he would have lost due to jury service. When all of these considerations are taken into account, the prosecutor's second proffered justification for striking Mr. Brooks is suspicious.

The implausibility of this explanation is reinforced by the prosecutor's acceptance of white jurors who disclosed conflicting obligations that appear to have been at least as serious as Mr. Brooks'. We recognize that a retrospective comparison of jurors based on a cold appellate record may be very misleading when alleged similarities were not raised at trial. In that situation, an appellate court must be mindful that an exploration of the alleged similarities at the time of trial might have shown that the jurors in question were not really comparable. In this case, however, the shared characteristic, i.e., concern about serving on the jury due to conflicting obligations, was thoroughly explored by the trial court when the relevant jurors asked to be excused for cause.

A comparison between Mr. Brooks and Roland Laws, a white juror, is particularly striking. During the initial stage of voir dire, Mr. Laws approached the court and offered strong reasons why serving on the sequestered jury would cause him hardship. Mr. Laws stated that he was "a self-employed general contractor," with "two houses that are nearing completion, one [with the occupants] . . . moving in this weekend." He explained that, if he served on the jury, "the people won't [be able to] move in." Mr. Laws also had demanding family obligations:

> "[M]y wife just had a hysterectomy, so I'm running the kids back and forth to school, and we're not originally from here, so I have no family in the area, so between the two things, it's kind of bad timing for me."

Although these obligations seem substantially more pressing than Mr. Brooks', the prosecution questioned Mr. Laws and attempted to elicit assurances that he would be able to serve despite his work and family obligations. *See ibid* (prosecutor asking Mr. Laws "[i]f you got stuck on jury duty anyway . . . would you try to make other arrangements as best you could?"). And the prosecution declined the opportunity to use a peremptory strike on Mr. Laws. If the prosecution had been sincerely concerned that Mr. Brooks would favor a lesser verdict than first-degree murder in order to shorten the trial, it is hard to see why the prosecution would not have had at least as much concern regarding Mr. Laws.

The situation regarding another white juror, John Donnes, although less fully developed, is also significant. At the end of the first day of voir dire, Mr. Donnes approached the court and raised the possibility that he would have an important work commitment later that week. Because Mr. Donnes stated that he would know the next morning whether he would actually have a problem, the court suggested that Mr. Donnes raise the matter again at that time. The next day, Mr. Donnes again expressed concern about serving, stating that, in order to serve, "I'd have to cancel too many things," including an urgent appointment at which his presence was essential. Despite Mr. Donnes' concern, the prosecution did not strike him.

As previously noted, the question presented at the third stage of the *Batson* inquiry is "whether the defendant has shown purposeful discrimination." *Miller-El v. Dretke*, 545 U.S., at 277. The prosecution's proffer of this pretextual explanation naturally gives rise to an inference of discriminatory intent.

In other circumstances, we have held that, once it is shown that a discriminatory intent was a substantial or motivating factor in an action taken by a state actor, the burden shifts to the party defending the action to show that this factor was not determinative. We have not previously applied this rule in a *Batson* case, and we need not decide here whether that standard governs in this context. For present purposes, it is enough to recognize that a peremptory strike shown to have been motivated in substantial part by discriminatory intent could not be sustained based on any lesser showing by the prosecution. And in light of the circumstances here-including absence of anything in the record showing that the trial judge credited the claim that Mr. Brooks was nervous, the prosecution's description of both of its proffered explanations as "main concern[s]," and the adverse inference noted above-the record does not show that the prosecution would have pre-emptively challenged Mr. Brooks based on his nervousness alone. Nor is there any realistic possibility that this subtle question of causation could be profitably explored further on remand at this late date, more than a decade after petitioner's trial.

. . .We therefore reverse the judgment of the Louisiana Supreme Court and remand the case for further proceedings not inconsistent with this opinion.

CHAPTER 8 THE ROLE OF MITIGATING CIRCUMSTANCES

A.   General Principles of Mitigation

8.   The Requirement that Jurors Give Effect to Mitigating Evidence

Page 493. Insert before B. Balancing Aggravating and Mitigating Circumstances:

In *Smith v. Texas*, 543 U.S. 37 (2004), the Supreme Court remanded to the Texas courts for reconsideration based on the *Penry I* and *Penry II* errors that had occurred during the sentencing proceedings in Smith's capital murder trial. The Texas courts again denied Smith relief, holding that (1) Smith's failure to adequately raise a *Penry II* error required him to show that the error caused egregious harm and (2) he failed to meet this burden. The Supreme Court again granted Smith relief. A portion of this decision is excerpted below.

Smith v. Texas
127 S.Ct. 1686 (2007)

Justice KENNEDY delivered the opinion of the Court.

The jury in a Texas state court convicted petitioner LaRoyce Lathair Smith of first-degree murder and determined he should receive a death sentence. This Court now reviews a challenge to the sentencing proceeding for a second time.

The sentencing took place in the interim between our decisions in *Penry v. Lynaugh,* 492 U.S. 302 (1989) *(Penry I),* and *Penry v. Johnson,* 532 U.S. 782 (2001) *(Penry II).* In *Penry I* the Court addressed the special-issue questions then submitted to Texas juries to guide their sentencing determinations in capital cases. The decision held that the Texas special issues were insufficient to allow proper consideration of some forms of mitigating evidence. Following a pretrial challenge to the special issues by Smith, the trial court issued a charge instructing the jury to nullify the special issues if the mitigating evidence, taken as a whole, convinced the jury Smith did not deserve the death penalty. After Smith's trial, *Penry II* held a similar nullification charge insufficient to cure the flawed special issues. Smith, on state collateral review, continued to seek relief based on the inadequacy of the special issues, arguing that the nullification charge had not remedied the problem identified in his pretrial objection. The Texas Court of Criminal Appeals affirmed the denial of relief, distinguishing Smith's case from the *Penry* precedents.

This Court, by summary disposition, reversed. *Smith v. Texas,* 543 U.S. 37 (2004) *(per curiam) (Smith I).* On remand the Court of Criminal Appeals again denied Smith relief. It held, for the first time, that Smith's pretrial objections did not preserve the claim of constitutional error he asserts. Under the Texas framework for determining whether an instructional error merits reversal, the state court explained, this procedural default required Smith to show egregious harm – a burden the court held he did not meet. The requirement that Smith show egregious harm was predicated, we hold, on a misunderstanding of the federal right Smith asserts; and we therefore reverse.

II

B

Under [Texas case law], once Smith established the existence of instructional error that was preserved by a proper objection, he needed only to show he suffered "*some harm*" from that error. In other words relief should be granted so long as the error was not harmless. It would appear this lower standard applies to Smith's preserved challenge to the special issues.

The Court of Criminal Appeals explained in its recent decision in *Penry v. State,* 178 S.W.3d 782 (2005), that once a state habeas petitioner establishes "a reasonable likelihood that the jury believed that it was not permitted to consider" some mitigating evidence, he has shown that the error was not harmless and therefore is grounds for reversal. We note that the Court of Criminal Appeals stated in dicta in this case that even assuming Smith had established that there was a reasonable probability of error, he had not shown "actual harm," and therefore would not even satisfy the lower *Almanza* standard. We must assume that this departure from the clear rule of *Penry v. State* resulted from the state court's confusion over our decision in *Smith I.*

The Court of Criminal Appeals is, of course, required to defer to our finding of *Penry* error, which is to say our finding that Smith has shown there was a reasonable likelihood that the jury interpreted the special issues to foreclose adequate consideration of his mitigating evidence. Accordingly, it appears Smith is entitled to relief under the state harmless-error framework.

In light of our resolution of this case, we need not reach the question whether the nullification charge resulted in a separate jury-confusion error, and if so whether that error is subject to harmless-error review.

For the reasons we have stated, the judgment of the Court of Criminal Appeals is reversed, and the case is remanded for further proceedings not inconsistent with this opinion.

Note

The same day the Court decided *Smith v. Texas,* it also granted relief in two other Texas cases where the capital defendants had complained of *Penry I* and *Penry II* errors. In *Abdul-Kabir v. Quarterman,* 127 S.Ct.1654 (2007), the Court determined that Abdul-Kabir was entitled to federal habeas relief based on his claim that there was a reasonable likelihood that the jury instructions failed to provide meaningful consideration of relevant mitigating evidence. The mitigating evidence at issue in *Abdul-Kabir* included (1) "testimony from his mother and his aunt, who described his unhappy childhood," and (2) testimony from two expert witnesses "who discussed the consequences of Cole's [Abdul-Kabir's] childhood neglect and abandonment." The Supreme Court set out the instructions at issue as follows:

> "Was the conduct of the defendant, TED CALVIN COLE, that caused the death of the deceased, RAYMOND C. RICHARDSON, committed deliberately and with the reasonable expectation that the death of the deceased or another would result?
>
> "Is there a probability that the defendant, TED CALVIN COLE, would commit criminal acts of violence that would constitute a continuing threat to society?"[2]
>
> The trial judge instructed the jury to take into consideration evidence presented at the guilt phase as well as the sentencing phase of the trial but made no reference to mitigating evidence. Under the provisions of the Texas criminal code, the jury's affirmative answers to these two special issues required the judge to impose a death sentence.

The Court ultimately found that these instructions constitutionally inadequate. The portion of the Court's opinion discussing the constitutional deficiency of the instructions is excerpted below:

Abdul-Kabir v. Quarterman
127 S.Ct. 1654 (2007)

Justice STEVENS delivered the opinion of the Court.

V

In recommending denial of Cole's application for collateral relief, the Texas trial judge did not analyze *Penry I* itself. Under the framework set forth in *Penry I,* the testimony of Cole's mother and aunt, as well as the portions of the expert testimony suggesting that his dangerous character may have been the result of his rough childhood and possible neurological damage, were not relevant to either of the special verdict questions, except, possibly, as evidence supporting the State's argument that Cole would be dangerous in the future. This would not satisfy the requirement of *Penry I,* however, that the evidence be permitted its mitigating force beyond the scope of the special issues. Therefore, it would have followed that those questions

---

[2] These were the two standard Texas special issues in place at the time of Cole's sentencing. In 1991, the Texas Legislature amended the special issues in response to this Court's decision in *Penry v. Lynaugh,* 492 U.S. 302 (1989) (*Penry I*), to include language instructing the jury to decide "[w]hether, taking into consideration all of the evidence, including the circumstances of the offense, the defendant's character and background, and the personal moral culpability of the defendant, there is a sufficient mitigating circumstance or circumstances to warrant that a sentence of life imprisonment without parole rather than a death sentence be imposed."

failed to provide the jury with a vehicle for expressing its "reasoned moral response" to that evidence.

The lynchpin of the Chief Justice's dissent is his assumption that Justice O'Connor's opinions in *Franklin* and *Penry I* merely described two ad hoc judgments – rather than her understanding of the governing rule of law announced in *Lockett, Eddings,* and *Hitchcock v. Dugger,* 481 U.S. 393 (1987). In his view, our line of cases in this area has flip-flopped, depending on the composition of the majority, rather than slowly defining core principles by eliminating those interpretations of the rule that are unsupportable. The fact that Justice O'Connor's understanding of the law was confirmed by the Court in *Penry I* in 1989 – well before AEDPA was enacted – is a sufficient response to most of the rhetoric in the dissent. Neither Justice O'Connor's opinion for the Court in *Penry I,* nor any other opinion she joined, ever endorsed the "'*some* arguable relevance'" position described by the Chief Justice, which mistakenly interprets our opinion as adopting the rule that the dissenters in *Franklin* and *Saffle* would have chosen. The fact that the Court never endorsed that broader standard is fully consistent with our conclusion that the narrower rule applied in *Penry I* itself is "clearly established." Arguments advanced in later dissenting opinions do not affect that conclusion.

Instead of relying on *Penry I,* the trial judge relied on three later Texas cases and on our opinion in *Graham v. Collins,* 506 U.S. 461 (1993), as having held that nine different categories of mitigating evidence – including a troubled family background, bipolar disorder, low IQ, substance abuse, paranoid personality disorder, and child abuse – were sufficiently considered under the Texas special issues. Applying those cases, the judge defined the legal issue "whether the mitigating evidence can be sufficiently considered" as one that "must be determined on a case by case basis, depending on the nature of the mitigating evidence offered and whether there exists other testimony in the record that would allow consideration to be given." As we have noted, in endorsing this formulation of the issue, neither the trial judge nor the CCA had the benefit of any input from counsel representing petitioner. In our view, denying relief on the basis of that formulation of the issue, while ignoring the fundamental principles established by our most relevant precedents, resulted in a decision that was both "contrary to" and "involved an unreasonable application of, clearly established Federal law, as determined by the Supreme Court of the United States." 28 U.S.C. § 2254(d).

The state court's primary reliance on *Graham,* to the exclusion of our other cases in this line of jurisprudence, was misguided. In *Graham,* we held that granting collateral relief to a defendant who had been sentenced to death in 1984 would require the announcement of a new rule of constitutional law in contravention of *Teague v. Lane,* 489 U.S. 288 (1989). In reaching that conclusion we relied heavily on the fact that in 1984 it was reasonable for judges to rely on the interpretation of *Jurek* that the plurality had espoused in *Franklin.* But as we have explained, in both *Franklin* and *Penry I,* a majority of the Court ultimately rejected the plurality's interpretation of *Jurek.* Neither *Franklin* nor *Penry I* was inconsistent with *Graham's* narrow holding, but they do suggest that our later decisions – including *Johnson v. Texas,* 509

U.S. 350 (1993), in which we refused to adopt the rule that Graham sought – are of more relevance to Cole's case than *Graham*. The relevance of those cases lies not in their results – in several instances, we concluded, after applying the relevant law, that the special issues provided for adequate consideration of the defendant's mitigating evidence – but in their failure to disturb the basic legal principle that continues to govern such cases: The jury must have a "meaningful basis to consider the relevant mitigating qualities" of the defendant's proffered evidence.

Before turning to those more recent cases, it is appropriate to identify the reasons why the CCA's ruling was not a reasonable application of *Penry I* itself. First, the ruling ignored the fact that even though Cole's mitigating evidence may not have been as persuasive as Penry's, it was relevant to the question of Cole's moral culpability for precisely the same reason as Penry's. Like Penry's evidence, Cole's evidence of childhood deprivation and lack of self-control did not rebut either deliberateness or future dangerousness but was intended to provide the jury with an entirely different reason for not imposing a death sentence. Second, the judge's assumption that it would be appropriate to look at "other testimony in the record" to determine whether the jury could give mitigating effect to the testimony of Cole's mother and aunt is neither reasonable nor supported by the *Penry* opinion. Third, the fact that the jury could give mitigating effect to some of the experts' testimony, namely, their predictions that Cole could be expected to become less dangerous as he aged, provides no support for the conclusion that the jury understood it could give such effect to other portions of the experts' testimony or that of other witnesses. In sum, the judge ignored our entire line of cases establishing the importance of allowing juries to give meaningful effect to any mitigating evidence providing a basis for a sentence of life rather than death. His recommendation to the CCA was therefore unsupported by either the text or the reasoning in *Penry I*.

VI

The same principles originally set forth in earlier cases such as *Lockett* and *Eddings* have been articulated explicitly by our later cases, which explained that the jury must be permitted to "consider fully" such mitigating evidence and that such consideration "would be meaningless" unless the jury not only had such evidence available to it, but also was permitted to give that evidence meaningful, mitigating effect in imposing the ultimate sentence.

Four of our more recent cases lend support to the conclusion that the CCA's decision was unsupported by either the text or the reasoning of *Penry I*. In *Johnson v. Texas,* we held that the Texas special issues allowed adequate consideration of petitioner's youth as a mitigating circumstance. Indeed, we thought it "strain[ed] credulity to suppose that the jury would have viewed the evidence of petitioner's youth as outside its effective reach" because its relevance was so obvious. There is of course a vast difference between youth – a universally applicable mitigating circumstance that every juror has experienced and which necessarily is transient – and the particularized childhood experiences of abuse and neglect that *Penry I* and *Cole* described – which presumably most jurors have never experienced and which affect each individual in a distinct manner.

Evidence of youth, moreover, has special relevance to the question of future dangerousness. A critical assumption motivating the Court's decision in *Johnson* was that juries would in fact be able to give mitigating effect to the evidence, albeit within the confines of the special issues. Prosecutors in some subsequent cases, however, have undermined this assumption, taking pains to convince jurors that the law compels them to disregard the force of evidence offered in mitigation. Cole's prosecution is illustrative: the State made jurors "promise" they would look only at the questions posed by the special issues, which, according to the prosecutor, required a juror to "put . . . out of [his] mind" Cole's mitigating evidence and "just go by the facts." Arguments like these are at odds with the Court's understanding in *Johnson* that juries could and would reach mitigating evidence proffered by a defendant. Nothing in *Johnson* forecloses relief in these circumstances.

This conclusion derives further support from the fact that, in *Johnson,* the Court understood that the defendant's evidence of youth – including testimony from his father that "his son's actions were due in large part to his youth," and counsel's corresponding arguments that the defendant could change as he grew older – was "readily comprehended as a mitigating factor," in the context of the special issues. The evidence offered in this case, however, as well as that offered by the petitioner in *Brewer, –* U.S. at – , and n.1, 2007 WL 1201609, is closer in nature to that offered by the defendant in *Penry I* than that at issue in *Johnson*. While the consideration of the defendant's mitigating evidence of youth in *Johnson* could easily have directed jurors towards a "no" answer with regard to the question of future dangerousness, a juror considering Cole's evidence of childhood neglect and abandonment and possible neurological damage or Brewer's evidence of mental illness, substance abuse, and a troubled childhood could feel compelled to provide a "yes" answer to the same question, finding himself without a means for giving *meaningful* effect to the mitigating qualities of such evidence. In such a case, there is a reasonable likelihood that the special issues would preclude that juror from giving meaningful consideration to such mitigating evidence, as required by *Penry I.*

In three later cases, we gave *Penry I* the "fair reading" required by *Johnson* and repudiated several Fifth Circuit precedents providing the basis for its narrow reading of that case. First, in our review of Penry's resentencing, at which the judge had supplemented the special issues with a nullification instruction, we again concluded that the jury had not been provided with an adequate "vehicle for expressing its reasoned moral response" to his mitigating evidence. *Penry v. Johnson,* 532 U.S. 782, 797 (2001) (*Penry II*). Indeed, given that the resentencing occurred after the enactment of AEDPA, we concluded (contrary to the views of the Fifth Circuit, which had denied Penry a [Certificate of Appealability]) that the CCA's judgment affirming the death sentence was objectively unreasonable. Second, and as we have already noted, in *Tennard* we held that the Fifth Circuit's test for identifying relevant mitigating evidence was incorrect. Most recently, in *Smith v. Texas,* 543 U.S. 37 (2004) (*per curiam*), and again contrary to the views of the Fifth Circuit, we held that a nullification instruction that was different from the one used in Penry's second sentencing hearing did not foreclose the defendant's claim that the special issues had precluded the jury from "expressing a 'reasoned moral response' to *all* of the evidence relevant to the defendant's culpability."

VII

Our line of cases in this area has long recognized that before a jury can undertake the grave task of imposing a death sentence, it must be allowed to consider a defendant's moral culpability and decide whether death is an appropriate punishment for that individual in light of his personal history and characteristics and the circumstances of the offense. As Chief Justice Burger wrote in *Lockett:*

> "There is no perfect procedure for deciding in which cases governmental authority should be used to impose death. But a statute that prevents the sentencer in all capital cases from giving independent mitigating weight to aspects of the defendant's character and record and to circumstances of the offense proffered in mitigation creates the risk that the death penalty will be imposed in spite of factors which may call for a less severe penalty. When the choice is between life and death, that risk is unacceptable and incompatible with the commands of the Eighth and Fourteenth Amendments."

Our cases following *Lockett* have made clear that when the jury is not permitted to give meaningful effect or a "reasoned moral response" to a defendant's mitigating evidence – because it is forbidden from doing so by statute or a judicial interpretation of a statute – the sentencing process is fatally flawed. For that reason, our post-*Penry* cases are fully consistent with our conclusion that the judgment of the Court of Appeals in this case must be reversed. The case is remanded for further proceedings consistent with this opinion.

Note on Brewer v. Quarterman, 127 S.Ct. 1706 (2007)

In *Brewer v. Quarterman*, 127 S.Ct.1706 (2007), the companion case to *Abdul-Kabir*, Justice Stevens writing for the Court again laid out its view of how Texas courts should apply *Penry I* and *Penry II*:

III

Under the narrowest possible reading of our opinion in *Penry I,* the Texas special issues do not provide for adequate consideration of a defendant's mitigating evidence when that evidence functions as a "two-edged sword."

. . . For reasons not supported by our prior precedents, but instead dictated by what until quite recently has been the Fifth Circuit's difficult *Penry* jurisprudence, the Court of Appeals concluded that Brewer's evidence of mental illness and substance abuse could not constitute a *Penry* violation. It further concluded that "evidence of a troubled childhood may, as a result of its temporary character, fall sufficiently within the ambit of" the special issues. For the reasons explained above, as well as in our opinion in *Abdul-Kabir,* these conclusions fail to heed the warnings that have repeatedly issued from this Court regarding the extent to which the jury must be allowed not only to consider such evidence, or to have such evidence before it, but to respond to it in a reasoned, moral manner and to weigh such evidence in its calculus of deciding whether a defendant is truly deserving of death. Accordingly, the judgment of the Court of Appeals is reversed.

B.   Balancing Aggravating and Mitigating Circumstances

Page 513. Insert at the end of the page:

4.   Aggravating and Mitigating Circumstances in Equipoise

Kansas v. Marsh
548 U.S. 163 (2006)

Justice THOMAS delivered the opinion of the Court.

Kansas law provides that if a unanimous jury finds that aggravating circumstances are not outweighed by mitigating circumstances, the death penalty shall be imposed. Kan. Stat. Ann. § 21-4624(e) (1995). We must decide whether this statute, which requires the imposition of the death penalty when the sentencing jury determines that aggravating evidence and mitigating evidence are in equipoise, violates the Constitution. We hold that it does not.

I

Respondent Michael Lee Marsh II broke into the home of Marry Ane Pusch and lay in wait for her to return. When Marry Ane entered her home with her 19-month-old daughter, M. P., Marsh repeatedly shot Marry Ane, stabbed her, and slashed her throat. The home was set on fire with the toddler inside, and M.P. burned to death.

The jury convicted Marsh of the capital murder of M. P., the first-degree premeditated murder of Marry Ane, aggravated arson, and aggravated burglary. The jury found beyond a reasonable doubt the existence of three aggravating circumstances, and that those circumstances were not outweighed by any mitigating circumstances. On the basis of those findings, the jury sentenced Marsh to death for the capital murder of M.P. The jury also sentenced Marsh to life imprisonment without possibility of parole for 40 years for the first-degree murder of Marry Ane, and consecutive sentences of 51 months' imprisonment for aggravated arson and 34 months' imprisonment for aggravated burglary.

On direct appeal, Marsh challenged § 21-4624(e), which reads:

> "If, by unanimous vote, the jury finds beyond a reasonable doubt that one or more of the aggravating circumstances enumerated in K.S.A. 21-4625 . . . exist and, further, that the existence of such aggravating circumstances is not outweighed by any mitigating circumstances which are found to exist, the defendant shall be sentenced to death; otherwise the defendant shall be sentenced as provided by law."

Focusing on the phrase "shall be sentenced to death," Marsh argued that § 21-4624(e) establishes an unconstitutional presumption in favor of death because it directs imposition of the death penalty when aggravating and mitigating circumstances are in equipoise.

The Kansas Supreme Court agreed, and held that the Kansas death penalty statute, § 21-4624(e), is facially unconstitutional. The court concluded that the statute's weighing equation violated the Eighth and Fourteenth Amendments of the United States Constitution because, "[i]n the event of equipoise, *i.e.,* the jury's determination that the balance of any aggravating circumstances and any mitigating circumstances weighed equal, the death penalty would be required." The Kansas Supreme Court affirmed Marsh's conviction and sentence for aggravated burglary and premeditated murder of Marry Ane, and reversed and remanded for new trial Marsh's convictions for capital murder of M.P. and aggravated arson. We granted certiorari, and now reverse the Kansas Supreme Court's judgment that Kansas' capital sentencing statute, Kan. Stat. Ann. § 21-4624(e), is facially unconstitutional. . . .

III

This case is controlled by *Walton v. Arizona,* 497 U.S. 639 (1990), overruled on other grounds, *Ring v. Arizona,* 536 U.S. 584 (2002). In that case, a jury had convicted Walton of a capital offense. At sentencing, the trial judge found the existence of two aggravating circumstances and that the mitigating circumstances did not call for leniency, and sentenced Walton to death. The Arizona Supreme Court affirmed, and this Court granted certiorari to resolve the conflict between the Arizona Supreme Court's decision in *State v. Walton,* 159 Ariz. 571, 769 P.2d 1017 (1989) (en banc) (holding the Arizona death penalty statute constitutional), and the Ninth Circuit's decision in *Adamson v. Ricketts,* 865 F.2d 1011, 1043-1044 (1988) (en banc) (finding the Arizona death penalty statute unconstitutional because, "in situations where the mitigating and aggravating circumstances are in balance, or, where the mitigating circumstances give the court reservation but still fall below the weight of the aggravating circumstances, the statute bars the court from imposing a sentence less than death").

Consistent with the Ninth Circuit's conclusion in *Adamson,* Walton argued to this Court that the Arizona capital sentencing system created an unconstitutional presumption in favor of death because it "tells an Arizona sentencing judge who finds even a single aggravating factor, that death must be imposed, unless – as the Arizona Supreme Court put it in Petitioner's case

– there are 'utweighing mitigating factors.'" Rejecting Walton's argument, this Court stated:

> "So long as a State's method of allocating the burdens of proof does not lessen the State's burden to prove every element of the offense charged, or in this case to prove the existence of aggravating circumstances, a defendant's constitutional rights are not violated by placing on him the burden of proving mitigating circumstances sufficiently substantial to call for leniency."

This Court noted that, as a requirement of individualized sentencing, a jury must have the opportunity to consider all evidence relevant to mitigation, and that a state statute that permits a jury to consider any mitigating evidence comports with that requirement. The Court also pointedly observed that while the Constitution requires that a sentencing jury have discretion, it does not mandate that discretion be unfettered; the States are free to determine the manner in which a jury may consider mitigating evidence. So long as the sentencer is not precluded from considering relevant mitigating evidence, a capital sentencing statute cannot be said to impermissibly, much less automatically, impose death. Indeed, *Walton* suggested that the only capital sentencing systems that would be impermissibly mandatory were those that would "automatically impose death upon conviction for certain types of murder."

Contrary to Marsh's contentions and the Kansas Supreme Court's conclusions, the question presented in the instant case was squarely before this Court in *Walton*. Though, as Marsh notes, the *Walton* Court did not employ the term "equipoise," that issue undeniably gave rise to the question this Court sought to resolve, and it was necessarily included in Walton's argument that the Arizona system was unconstitutional because it required the death penalty unless the mitigating circumstances *outweighed* the aggravating circumstances. Moreover, the dissent in *Walton* reinforces what is evident from the opinion and the judgment of the Court – that the equipoise issue was before the Court, and that the Court resolved the issue in favor of the State. Indeed, the "equipoise" issue was, in large measure, the basis of the *Walton* dissent.

Our conclusion that *Walton* controls here is reinforced by the fact that the Arizona and Kansas statutes are comparable in important respects. Similar to the express language of the Kansas statute, the Arizona statute at issue in *Walton* has been consistently construed to mean that the death penalty will be imposed upon a finding that aggravating circumstances are not outweighed by mitigating circumstances. Like the Kansas statute, the Arizona statute places the burden of proving the existence of aggravating circumstances on the State, and both statutes require the defendant to proffer mitigating evidence.

The statutes are distinct in one respect. The Arizona statute, once the State has met its burden, tasks the defendant with the burden of proving sufficient mitigating circumstances to overcome the aggravating circumstances and that a sentence less than death is therefore warranted. In contrast, the Kansas statute requires the State to bear the burden of proving to the jury, beyond a reasonable doubt, that aggravators are not outweighed by mitigators and that a sentence of death is therefore appropriate; it places no additional evidentiary burden on the capital defendant. This distinction operates in favor of Kansas capital defendants. Otherwise the statutes function in substantially the same manner and are sufficiently analogous for our purposes. Thus, *Walton* is not distinguishable from the instant case.

Accordingly, the reasoning of *Walton* requires approval of the Kansas death penalty statute. At bottom, in *Walton,* the Court held that a state death penalty statute may place the burden on the defendant to prove that mitigating circumstances outweigh aggravating circumstances. *A fortiori,* Kansas' death penalty statute, consistent with the Constitution, may direct imposition of the death penalty when the State has proved beyond a reasonable doubt that mitigators do not outweigh aggravators, including where the aggravating circumstances and mitigating circumstances are in equipoise.

IV
A

Even if, as Marsh contends, *Walton* does not directly control, the general principles set forth in our death penalty jurisprudence would lead us to conclude that the Kansas capital sentencing system is constitutionally permissible. Together, our decisions in *Furman v. Georgia,* 408 U.S. 238 (1972) *(per curiam),* and *Gregg v. Georgia,* 428 U.S. 153 (1976) (joint opinion of Stewart, Powell, and Stevens, JJ.), establish that a state capital sentencing system must: (1) rationally narrow the class of death-eligible defendants; and (2) permit a jury to render a reasoned, individualized sentencing determination based on a death-eligible defendant's record, personal characteristics, and the circumstances of his crime. So long as a state system satisfies these requirements, our precedents establish that a State enjoys a range of discretion in imposing the death penalty, including the manner in which aggravating and mitigating circumstances are to be weighed.

The use of mitigation evidence is a product of the requirement of individualized sentencing. In *Lockett v. Ohio,* 438 U.S. 586, 604 (1978), a plurality of this Court held that "the Eighth and Fourteenth Amendments require that the sentencer . . . not be precluded from considering, *as a mitigating factor,* any aspect of a defendant's character or record and any of the circumstances of the offense that the defendant proffers as a basis for a sentence less than death." (Emphasis in original.) The Court has held that the sentencer must have full access to this "'highly relevant'" information. Thus, in *Lockett,* the Court struck down the Ohio death penalty statute as unconstitutional because, by limiting a jury's consideration of mitigation to three factors specified in the statute, it prevented sentencers in capital cases from giving independent weight to mitigating evidence militating in favor of a sentence other than death. Following *Lockett*, in *Eddings v. Oklahoma,* 455 U.S. 104 (1982), a majority of the Court held that a sentencer may not categorically refuse to consider any relevant mitigating evidence.

In aggregate, our precedents confer upon defendants the right to present sentencers with information relevant to the sentencing decision and oblige sentencers to consider that information in determining the appropriate sentence. The thrust of our mitigation jurisprudence ends here. "[W]e have never held that a specific method for balancing mitigating and aggravating factors in a capital sentencing proceeding is constitutionally required." Rather, this Court has held that the States enjoy "a constitutionally permissible range of discretion in imposing the death penalty."

B

The Kansas death penalty statute satisfies the constitutional mandates of *Furman* and its progeny because it rationally narrows the class of death-eligible defendants and permits a jury to consider any mitigating evidence relevant to its sentencing determination. It does not interfere, in a constitutionally significant way, with a jury's ability to give independent weight to evidence offered in mitigation.

Kansas' procedure narrows the universe of death-eligible defendants consistent with Eighth Amendment requirements. Under Kansas law, imposition of the death penalty is an *option* only after a defendant is convicted of capital murder, which requires that one or more specific elements beyond intentional premeditated murder be found. Once convicted of capital murder, a defendant becomes *eligible* for the death penalty only if the State seeks a separate sentencing hearing, and proves beyond a reasonable doubt the existence of one or more statutorily enumerated aggravating circumstances. Kan. Stat. Ann. §§ 21-4624(c), (e), and 21-462.

Consonant with the individualized sentencing requirement, a Kansas jury is permitted to consider *any* evidence relating to *any* mitigating circumstance in determining the appropriate sentence for a capital defendant, so long as that evidence is relevant. § 21-4624(c). Specifically, jurors are instructed:

> "A mitigating circumstance is that which in fairness or mercy may be considered as extenuating or reducing the degree of moral culpability or blame or which justify a sentence of less than death, although it does not justify or excuse the offense. The determination of what are mitigating circumstances is for you as jurors to resolve under the facts and circumstances of this case.

> "The appropriateness of the exercise of mercy can itself be a mitigating factor you may consider in determining whether the State has proved beyond a reasonable doubt that the death penalty is warranted."

Jurors are then apprised of, but not limited to, the factors that the defendant contends are mitigating. They are then instructed that "[e]ach juror must consider every mitigating factor that he or she individually finds to exist."

Kansas' weighing equation, merely channels a jury's discretion by providing it with criteria by which it may determine whether a sentence of life or death is appropriate. The system in Kansas provides the type of "guided discretion," we have sanctioned in *Walton, Boyde,* and *Blystone.*

Indeed, in *Boyde,* this Court sanctioned a weighing jury instruction that is analytically indistinguishable from the Kansas jury instruction under review today. The *Boyde* jury instruction read:

> "'If you conclude that the aggravating circumstances outweigh the mitigating circumstances, you *shall impose* a sentence of death. However, if you determine that the mitigating circumstances outweigh the aggravating circumstances, you *shall impose* a sentence of confinement in the state prison for life without the possibility of parole.'"

Boyde argued that the mandatory language of the instruction prevented the jury from rendering an individualized sentencing determination. This Court rejected that argument, concluding that it was foreclosed by *Blystone,* where the Court rejected a nearly identical challenge to the Pennsylvania death penalty statute. In so holding, this Court noted that the mandatory language of the statute did not prevent the jury from *considering* all relevant mitigating evidence. Similarly here, § 21-4624(e) does not prevent a Kansas jury from considering mitigating evidence. Marsh's argument that the Kansas provision is impermissibly mandatory is likewise foreclosed.

Contrary to Marsh's argument, § 21-4624(e) does not create a general presumption in favor of the death penalty in the State of Kansas. Rather, the Kansas capital sentencing system is dominated by the presumption that life imprisonment is the appropriate sentence for a capital conviction. If the State fails to meet its burden to demonstrate the existence of an aggravating circumstance(s) beyond a reasonable doubt, a sentence of life imprisonment must be imposed. § 21-4624(e). If the State overcomes this hurdle, then it bears the additional burden of proving beyond a reasonable doubt that aggravating circumstances are not outweighed by mitigating circumstances. Significantly, although the defendant appropriately bears the burden of proffering mitigating circumstances – a burden of production – he never bears the burden of demonstrating that mitigating circumstances outweigh aggravating circumstances. Instead, the State always has the burden of demonstrating that mitigating evidence does not outweigh aggravating evidence. Absent the State's ability to meet that burden, the default is life imprisonment. Moreover, if the jury is unable to reach a unanimous decision – in any respect – a sentence of life must be imposed. This system does not create a presumption that death is the appropriate sentence for capital murder.

Nor is there any force behind Marsh's contention that an equipoise determination reflects juror confusion or inability to decide between life and death, or that a jury may use equipoise as a loophole to shirk its constitutional duty to render a reasoned, moral decision, see

California v. Brown, 479 U.S. 538, 545 (1987) (O'Connor, J., concurring), regarding whether death is an appropriate sentence for a particular defendant. Such an argument rests on an implausible characterization of the Kansas statute – that a jury's determination that aggravators and mitigators are in equipoise is not a *decision,* much less a decision *for death* – and thus misses the mark. Weighing is not an end; it is merely a means to reaching a decision. The decision the jury must reach is whether life or death is the appropriate punishment. The Kansas jury instructions clearly inform the jury that a determination that the evidence is in equipoise is a decision for – not a presumption in favor of – death. Kansas jurors, presumed to follow their instructions, are made aware that: a determination that mitigators outweigh aggravators is a decision that a life sentence is appropriate; a determination that aggravators outweigh mitigators *or* a determination that mitigators do not outweigh aggravators – including a finding that aggravators and mitigators are in balance – is a decision that death is the appropriate sentence; and an inability to reach a unanimous decision will result in a sentence of life imprisonment. So informed, far from the abdication of duty or the inability to select an appropriate sentence depicted by Marsh and Justice Souter, a jury's conclusion that aggravating evidence and mitigating evidence are in equipoise is a *decision for death* and is indicative of the type of measured, normative process in which a jury is constitutionally tasked to engage when deciding the appropriate sentence for a capital defendant.

V

Justice Souter argues (hereinafter the dissent) that the advent of DNA testing has resulted in the "exoneratio[n]" of "innocent" persons "in numbers never imagined before the development of DNA tests." Based upon this "new empirical demonstration of how 'death is different,'" the dissent concludes that Kansas' sentencing system permits the imposition of the death penalty in the absence of reasoned moral judgment.

But the availability of DNA testing, and the questions it might raise about the accuracy of guilt-phase determinations in capital cases, is simply irrelevant to the question before the Court today, namely, the constitutionality of Kansas' capital *sentencing* system. Accordingly, the accuracy of the dissent's factual claim that DNA testing has established the "innocence" of numerous convicted persons under death sentences – and the incendiary debate it invokes – is beyond the scope of this opinion.

The dissent's general criticisms against the death penalty are ultimately a call for resolving all legal disputes in capital cases by adopting the outcome that makes the death penalty more difficult to impose. While such a bright-line rule may be easily applied, it has no basis in law. Indeed, the logical consequence of the dissent's argument is that the death penalty can only be just in a system that does not permit error. Because the criminal justice system does not operate perfectly, abolition of the death penalty is the only answer to the moral dilemma the dissent poses. This Court, however, does not sit as a moral authority. Our precedents do not prohibit the States from authorizing the death penalty, even in our imperfect system. And those precedents do not empower this Court to chip away at the States' prerogatives to do so on the grounds the dissent invokes today. . . .

We hold that the Kansas capital sentencing system, which directs imposition of the death penalty when a jury finds that aggravating and mitigating circumstances are in equipoise, is constitutional. Accordingly, we reverse the judgment of the Kansas Supreme Court, and remand the case for further proceedings not inconsistent with this opinion.

CHAPTER 9 THE SENTENCING PHASE OF CAPITAL TRIALS

D.   *The "Truly Awesome Responsibility" of Capital Jurors*

Notes and Questions on Juror Confusion

Page 537. Insert at the end of Note 2:

Note on Ayers v. Belmontes, 549 U.S. 7 (2006)

In *Ayers v. Belmonte*s, 549 U.S. 7 (2006), the Court considered whether the California catch-all instruction allowed the jury to adequately consider the defendant's forward-looking mitigation evidence as a basis for returning a sentence other than death. This catch-all instruction, which is based on factor (k) in the California death penalty statute, instructs a jury "to consider '[a]ny other circumstance which extenuates the gravity of the crime even though it is not a legal excuse for the crime.'" The Court found that the instruction was constitutionally sufficient to allow jury consideration of the forward-looking mitigation evidence that the defendant would likely lead a constructive life if he were incarcerated.

E.   *Closing Arguments and Fundamental Fairness*

Page 551. Insert before Allocution:

Carey v. Musladin
549 U.S. 70 (2006)

Justice Thomas delivered the opinion of the Court.

This Court has recognized that certain courtroom practices are so inherently prejudicial that they deprive the defendant of a fair trial. *Estelle v. Williams,* 425 U.S. 501, 503-506 (1976); *Holbrook v. Flynn,* 475 U.S. 560, 568 (1986). In this case, a state court held that buttons displaying the victim's image worn by the victim's family during respondent's trial did not deny respondent his right to a fair trial. We must decide whether that holding was contrary to or an unreasonable application of clearly established federal law, as determined by this Court. 28 U.S.C. § 2254(d)(1). We hold that it was not. . . .

II
A

In *Estelle v. Williams* and *Flynn,* this Court addressed the effect of courtroom practices on defendants' fair-trial rights. In *Williams,* the Court considered "whether an accused who is compelled to wear identifiable prison clothing at his trial by a jury is denied due process or equal protection of the laws." The Court stated that "the State cannot, consistently with the Fourteenth Amendment, compel an accused to stand trial before a jury while dressed in identifiable prison clothes," but held that the defendant in that case had waived any objection to being tried in prison clothes by failing to object at trial.

In *Flynn,* the Court addressed whether seating "four uniformed state troopers" in the row of spectators' seats immediately behind the defendant at trial denied the defendant his right to a fair trial. The Court held that the presence of the troopers was not so inherently prejudicial that it denied the defendant a fair trial. In reaching that holding, the Court stated that "the question must be . . . whether 'an unacceptable risk is presented of impermissible factors coming into play.'"

Both *Williams* and *Flynn* dealt with government-sponsored practices: In *Williams,* the State compelled the defendant to stand trial in prison clothes, and in *Flynn,* the State seated the troopers immediately behind the defendant. Moreover, in both cases, this Court noted that some practices are so inherently prejudicial that they must be justified by an "essential state" policy or interest.

B

In contrast to state-sponsored courtroom practices, the effect on a defendant's fair-trial rights of the spectator conduct to which Musladin objects is an open question in our jurisprudence. This Court has never addressed a claim that such private-actor courtroom conduct was so inherently prejudicial that it deprived a defendant of a fair trial. And although the Court articulated the test for inherent prejudice that applies to state conduct in *Williams* and *Flynn,* we have never applied that test to spectators' conduct. Indeed, part of the legal test of *Williams* and *Flynn* – asking whether the practices furthered an essential *state* interest – suggests that those cases apply only to state-sponsored practices. . . .

Given the lack of holdings from this Court regarding the potentially prejudicial effect of spectators' courtroom conduct of the kind involved here, it cannot be said that the state court "unreasonabl[y] appli[ed] clearly established Federal law." § 2254(d)(1). No holding of this Court required the California Court of Appeal to apply the test of *Williams* and *Flynn* to the spectators' conduct here. Therefore, the state court's decision was not contrary to or an unreasonable application of clearly established federal law.

III

The Court of Appeals improperly concluded that the California Court of Appeal's decision was contrary to or an unreasonable application of clearly established federal law as determined by this Court. For these reasons, the judgment of the Court of Appeals is vacated, and the case is remanded for further proceedings consistent with this opinion.

CHAPTER 12 STAYS OF EXECUTION AND STATE POST-CONVICTION RELIEF PROCEEDINGS

A. *Stays of Execution*

1. *Introduction*

Page 717. Add at the end of Note on Supreme Court's Internal Rules Governing Stays:

Emmett v. Kelly
128 S.Ct. 1 (2007)

The petition for a writ of certiorari is denied.

Statement of Justice STEVENS, with whom Justice Ginsburg joins, respecting the denial of certiorari.

The petition for certiorari seeking review of the Court of Appeals judgment upholding petitioner's death sentence was filed on June 1, 2007, well in advance of its June 27 due date. Under our normal practice, that timely petition would have been reviewed at our Conference on September 24, 2007. Nevertheless, Virginia set an execution date of June 13, 2007, making it impossible for us to consider the merits of the petition in the normal course, and making it necessary for the Court to rule on petitioner's last-minute application for a stay of execution. Although only four Members of the Court voted to grant that application, the Governor of Virginia, recognizing that basic fairness demands that capital defendants be given the opportunity to complete the legal appeals process prior to execution, granted petitioner a reprieve to afford us the opportunity to give the petition the careful consideration that it clearly merited.

As the majority opinion filed by Judge Traxler and the dissenting opinion filed by Judge Gregory demonstrate, reasonable judges can and do disagree about the merits of petitioner's challenge to the adequacy of his counsel's representation at the penalty phase of his trial. Moreover, those opinions also make it clear that a thorough examination of the trial record, as well as the evidence that he claims his lawyers should have discovered, is essential for a correct appraisal of the merits. Having conducted that review, I do not dissent from the Court's decision to deny certiorari. I do, however, remain firmly convinced that no State should be allowed to foreshorten this Court's orderly review of federal constitutional claims of first-time habeas petitioners by executing prisoners before that review can be completed.

Both the interest in avoiding irreversible error in capital cases, and the interest in the efficient management of our docket, would be served by a routine practice of staying all executions scheduled in advance of the completion of our review of the denial of a capital defendant's first application for a federal writ of habeas corpus. Such a practice would be faithful to the distinction between first and successive habeas petitions recognized by Congress in the Antiterrorism and Effective Death Penalty Act (AEDPA) and would accord death row inmates the same, rather than lesser, procedural safeguards as ordinary litigants. It is a practice that Justice Ginsburg and I have followed in the past and one that I hope a majority of the Court will eventually endorse.

CHAPTER 13 INTRODUCTION TO FEDERAL HABEAS CORPUS REVIEW

A.   Historical Overview

Page 757. Insert after Note:

Note on Availability of Habeas to Guantanamo Detainees

The right of prisoners to challenge the legal basis of their detention – the centuries-old right known as habeas corpus – provides a basic check against the abuses inherent in unfettered executive power.   The June 12, 2008 ruling in *Boumediene v. Bush,* 128 S.Ct. 2229, undermines the Bush administration's practice of holding terrorism suspects – including those who face capital charges – in indefinite detention at the U.S. naval base at Guantanamo. The Supreme Court's 5-4 decision, written by Justice Anthony Kennedy, rejects the Bush administration's argument that prisoners can be held for years without a fair process for assessing the evidence against them. It means that the federal courts   which are equipped with the procedures necessary to protect sensitive national security information – will now be able to examine the basis for detainees' claims that they are wrongly held.

In reaching its decision, the Court rejected the administration's assertion that the procedures established in the Detainee Treatment Act of 2005 and the Military Commissions Act of 2006 were an adequate substitute for habeas. Unlike the Court's decision in *Rasul v. Bush*, 540 U.S. 466 (2004), *Boumediene* is based on the U.S. Constitution, making it more difficult for Congress to legislatively overturn. *Boumediene* firmly rejects the Bush administration's view of Guantanamo as a "law-free zone," which provided the original impetus for transferring hundreds of men for detention there.

In *Boumediene* the Supreme Court found that the Suspension Clause of the Constitution applied to the enemy combatants held at the United States Naval Station at Guantanamo Bay and that the detainees held there were entitled to pursue the writ of habeas corpus to challenge the legality of their detention. Because the Military Commission Act denied the writ to the detainees held at Guantanamo, the Court had to decide whether Congress set up an adequate substitute for the writ in the procedures it provided to the detainees in the Detainee Treatment Act (DTA).

The Court expressed serious concern that the DTA procedures did not allow the detainees to present reasonably available exculpatory evidence, lacked an explicit release remedy, failed to provide expressly that detainees could fully challenge the President's authority to hold them indefinitely, and constricted the ability of federal courts to make factual findings. Due to these deficiencies in the DTA process, the Court concluded that Congress had improperly suspended the writ as to the detainees. Further, due to the delays of the combatant status review tribunals (CSRTs, the process established for determining whether detainees qualified as "enemy combatants"), the Court concluded that the detainees did not have to

111

exhaust the CSRT process before seeking habeas review. As Justice Kennedy's majority opinion stated:

> Our decision today holds only that the petitioners before us are entitled to seek the writ; that the DTA review procedures are an inadequate substitute for habeas corpus; and that the petitioners in these cases need not exhaust the review procedures in the Court of Appeals before proceeding with their habeas actions in the District Court. The only law we identify as unconstitutional is MCA § 7, 28 U.S.C.A. § 2241(e) (Supp.2007). Accordingly, both the DTA and the CSRT process remain intact. Our holding with regard to exhaustion should not be read to imply that a habeas court should intervene the moment an enemy combatant steps foot in a territory where the writ runs. The Executive is entitled to a reasonable period of time to determine a detainee's status before a court entertains that detainee's habeas corpus petition. The CSRT process is the mechanism Congress and the President set up to deal with these issues. Except in cases of undue delay, federal courts should refrain from entertaining an enemy combatant's habeas corpus petition at least until after the Department, acting via the CSRT, has had a chance to review his status.
>
> . . . It bears repeating that our opinion does not address the content of the law that governs petitioners' detention. That is a matter yet to be determined. We hold that petitioners may invoke the fundamental procedural protections of habeas corpus. The laws and Constitution are designed to survive, and remain in force, in extraordinary times. Liberty and security can be reconciled; and in our system they are reconciled within the framework of the law. The Framers decided that habeas corpus, a right of first importance, must be a part of that framework, a part of that law.
>
> The determination by the Court of Appeals that the Suspension Clause and its protections are inapplicable to petitioners was in error. The judgment of the Court of Appeals is reversed. The cases are remanded to the Court of Appeals with instructions that it remand the cases to the District Court for proceedings consistent with this opinion.

128 S.Ct. at 2275-2277.

C.   The Antiterrorism and Effective Death Penalty Act of 1996

Page 770. Insert after Note 5:

6. In the following case, the Supreme Court considered the application of the one-year statute of limitations for filing a petition for federal habeas corpus relief.

Lawrence v. Florida
127 S.Ct. 1079 (2007)

Justice THOMAS delivered the opinion of the Court.

Congress established a 1-year statute of limitations for seeking federal habeas corpus relief from a state-court judgment, 28 U.S.C. § 2244(d), and further provided that the limitations period is tolled while an "application for State post-conviction or other collateral review" "is pending," § 2244(d)(2). We must decide whether a state application is still "pending" when the state courts have entered a final judgment on the matter but a petition for certiorari has been filed in this Court. We hold that it is not.

I

Petitioner Gary Lawrence and his wife used a pipe and baseball bat to kill Michael Finken. A Florida jury convicted Lawrence of first-degree murder, conspiracy to commit murder, auto theft, and petty theft. The trial court sentenced Lawrence to death. The Florida Supreme Court affirmed Lawrence's conviction and sentence on appeal, and this Court denied certiorari on January 20, 1998.

On January 19, 1999, 364 days later, Lawrence filed an application for state postconviction relief in a Florida trial court. The court denied relief, and the Florida Supreme Court affirmed, issuing its mandate on November 18, 2002. Lawrence sought review of the denial of state postconviction relief in this Court. We denied certiorari on March 24, 2003.

While Lawrence's petition for certiorari was pending, he filed the present federal habeas application. The Federal District Court dismissed it as untimely under § 2244(d)'s 1-year limitations period. All but one day of the limitations period had lapsed during the 364 days between the time Lawrence's conviction became final and when he filed for state postconviction relief. The limitations period was then tolled while the Florida courts entertained his state application. After the Florida Supreme Court issued its mandate, Lawrence waited another 113 days – well beyond the one day that remained in the limitations period – to file his federal habeas application. As a consequence, his federal application could be considered timely only if the limitations period continued to be tolled during this Court's consideration of his petition for certiorari. Then-applicable Eleventh Circuit precedent foreclosed any argument that § 2244's statute of limitations was tolled by the pendency of a petition for certiorari seeking review of a state postconviction proceeding. Accordingly, the District Court concluded that Lawrence had only one day to file a federal habeas application after the Florida Supreme Court issued its mandate. The Eleventh Circuit affirmed. We granted certiorari and now affirm.

II

The Antiterrorism and Effective Death Penalty Act of 1996 (AEDPA), sets a one-year statute of limitations for seeking federal habeas corpus relief from a state-court judgment. 28 U.S.C. § 2244(d)(1). This limitations period is tolled while a state prisoner seeks postconviction relief in state court:

> "The time during which a properly filed application for State post-conviction or other collateral review with respect to the pertinent judgment or claim is pending shall not be counted toward any period of limitation under this subsection."

Based on this provision, the parties agree that AEDPA's limitations period was tolled from the filing of Lawrence's petition for state postconviction relief until the Florida Supreme Court issued its mandate affirming the denial of that petition. At issue here is whether the limitations period was also tolled during the pendency of Lawrence's petition for certiorari to this Court seeking review of the denial of state postconviction relief. If it was tolled, Lawrence's federal habeas application was timely. So we must decide whether, according to § 2244(d)(2), an "application for State post-conviction or other collateral review" "is pending" while this Court considers a certiorari petition.

Read naturally, the text of the statute must mean that the statute of limitations is tolled only while state courts review the application. As we stated in *Carey v. Saffold,* 536 U.S. 214, 220 (2002) (internal quotation marks omitted), a state postconviction application "remains pending" "until the application has achieved final resolution through the State's postconviction procedures." This Court is not a part of a "State's post-conviction procedures." State review ends when the state courts have finally resolved an application for state postconviction relief. After the State's highest court has issued its mandate or denied review, no other state avenues for relief remain open. And an application for state postconviction review no longer exists. All that remains is a separate certiorari petition pending before a *federal* court. The application for state postconviction review is therefore not "pending" after the state court's postconviction review is complete, and § 2244(d)(2) does not toll the 1-year limitations period during the pendency of a petition for certiorari.

If an application for state postconviction review were "pending" during the pendency of a certiorari petition in this Court, it is difficult to understand how a state prisoner could exhaust state postconviction remedies without filing a petition for certiorari. Indeed, AEDPA's exhaustion provision and tolling provision work together:

> "The tolling provision of § 2244(d)(2) balances the interests served by the exhaustion requirement and the limitation period. . . . Section 2244(d)(1)'s limitation period and § 2244(d)(2)'s tolling provision, together with § 2254(b)'s exhaustion requirement, encourage litigants *first* to exhaust all state remedies

114

and *then* to file their federal habeas petitions *as soon as possible.*" *Duncan v. Walker,* 533 U.S. 167, 179 (2001) (final emphasis added).

Yet we have said that state prisoners need not petition for certiorari to exhaust state remedies. State remedies are exhausted at the end of state-court review.

Lawrence argues that § 2244(d)(2) should be construed to have the same meaning as § 2244(d)(1)(A), the trigger provision that determines when AEDPA's statute of limitations begins to run. But § 2244(d)(1)(A) uses much different language from § 2244(d)(2), referring to "the date on which the judgment became final by *the conclusion of direct review* or the expiration of the time for seeking such review." § 2244(d)(1)(A) (emphasis added). When interpreting similar language in § 2255, we explained that "direct review" has long included review by this Court. *Clay v. United States,* 537 U.S. 522, 527-528 (2003). Indeed, we noted that "[t]he Courts of Appeals have uniformly interpreted 'direct review' in § 2244(d)(1)(A) to encompass review of a state conviction by this Court." By contrast, § 2244(d)(2) refers exclusively to "*State* post-conviction or other collateral review," language not easily interpreted to include participation by a federal court.

Furthermore, § 2244(d)(1)(A) refers to the "time for seeking" direct review, which includes review by this Court under *Clay.* By parity of reasoning, the "time for seeking" review of a state postconviction judgment arguably would include the period for filing a certiorari petition before this Court. However, § 2244(d)(2) makes no reference to the "time for seeking" review of a state postconviction court's judgment. Instead, it seeks to know when an application for "State . . . review" is pending. The linguistic difference is not insignificant: When the state courts have issued a final judgment on a state application, it is no longer pending even if a prisoner has additional time for seeking review of that judgment through a petition for certiorari.

A more analogous statutory provision is § 2263(b)(2), which is part of AEDPA's "opt-in" provisions for States that comply with specific requirements relating to the provision of postconviction counsel. Under § 2263, the limitations period is tolled "from the date on which the first petition for post-conviction review or other collateral relief is filed until the final State court disposition of such petition." § 2263(b)(2). Lawrence concedes that under this language there would be no tolling for certiorari petitions seeking review of state postconviction applications. And although he correctly notes that the language in § 2263 differs from the language of § 2244(d)(2), it is clear that the language used in both sections provides that tolling hinges on the pendency of state review. Given Congress' clear intent in § 2263 to provide tolling for certiorari petitions on direct review but not for certiorari petitions following state postconviction review, it is not surprising that Congress would make the same distinction in § 2244.

Lawrence also argues that our interpretation would result in awkward situations in which state prisoners have to file federal habeas applications while they have certiorari petitions from state postconviction proceedings pending before this Court. But these situations will also arise under the express terms of § 2263, and Lawrence admits that Congress intended that provision to preclude tolling for certiorari petitions. Because Congress was not concerned by this potential for awkwardness in § 2263, there is no reason for us to construe the statute to avoid it in § 2244(d)(2).

Contrary to Lawrence's suggestion, our interpretation of § 2244(d)(2) results in few practical problems. As Justice Stevens has noted, "this Court rarely grants review at this stage of the litigation even when the application for state collateral relief is supported by arguably meritorious federal constitutional claims," choosing instead to wait for "federal habeas proceedings." *Kyles v. Whitley,* 498 U.S. 931, 932 (1990) (opinion concurring in denial of stay of execution). Thus, the likelihood that the District Court will duplicate work or analysis that might be done by this Court if we granted certiorari to review the state postconviction proceeding is quite small. And in any event, a district court concerned about duplicative work can stay the habeas application until this Court resolves the case or, more likely, denies the petition for certiorari.

Lawrence argues that even greater anomalies result from our interpretation when the state court grants relief to a prisoner and the state petitions for certiorari. In that hypothetical, Lawrence maintains that the prisoner would arguably lack standing to file a federal habeas application immediately after the state court's judgment (because the state court granted him relief) but would later be time barred from filing a federal habeas application if we granted certiorari and the State prevailed. Again, this particular procedural posture is extremely rare. Even so, equitable tolling may be available, in light of the arguably extraordinary circumstances and the prisoner's diligence. We cannot base our interpretation of the statute on an exceedingly rare inequity that Congress almost certainly was not contemplating and that may well be cured by equitable tolling.

In contrast to the hypothetical problems identified by Lawrence, allowing the statute of limitations to be tolled by certiorari petitions would provide incentives for state prisoners to file certiorari petitions as a delay tactic. By filing a petition for certiorari, the prisoner would push back § 2254's deadline while we resolved the petition for certiorari. This tolling rule would provide an incentive for prisoners to file certiorari petitions – regardless of the merit of the claims asserted – so that they receive additional time to file their habeas applications. . . .

IV

The Court of Appeals correctly determined that the filing of a petition for certiorari before this Court does not toll the statute of limitations under § 2244(d)(2). It also correctly declined to equitably toll the limitations period in the factual circumstances of Lawrence's case. For these reasons, the judgment of the Court of Appeals is affirmed.

Justice GINSBURG with whom Justice Stevens, Justice Souter, and Justice Breyer join, dissenting.

The Court today concludes that an application for state postconviction review "no longer exists" – and therefore is not "pending" – once it has been decided by a State's highest court. What remains, the majority reasons, is a "separate" certiorari proceeding pending before this Court. But petitions for certiorari do not exist in a vacuum; they arise from actions instituted in lower courts. When we are asked to review a state court's denial of habeas relief, we consider an application for that relief – not an application for federal habeas relief. Until we have disposed of the petition for certiorari, the application remains live as one for state postconviction relief; it is not transformed into a federal application simply because the state-court applicant petitions for this Court's review.

I would therefore hold that 28 U.S.C. § 2244(d)'s statute of limitations is tolled during the pendency of a petition for certiorari. Congress instructed that the one-year limitation period for filing a habeas petition in the appropriate federal district court does not include "[t]he time during which a properly filed application for State post-conviction or other collateral review . . . is pending." § 2244(d)(2). That provision can and should be read to continue statutory tolling until this Court has either decided or denied a petition for certiorari addressed to the state court's disposition of an application for postconviction relief. The majority's contrary reading of § 2244(d)(2) cuts short the tolling period before this Court has had an opportunity to consider an application for state postconviction relief. That reading, I conclude, is neither a necessary nor a proper interpretation of the statute.

II

Not only is the majority's reading of § 2244(d)(2) unwarranted, it will also spark the simultaneous filing of two pleadings seeking essentially the same relief. A petitioner denied relief by a State's highest court will now have to file, contemporaneously, a petition for certiorari in this Court and a habeas petition in federal district court. Only by expeditiously filing for federal habeas relief will a prisoner ensure that the limitation period does not run before we have disposed of his or her petition for certiorari. Protective petitions will be essential, too, when we grant review of a state court's ruling on a state habeas petition, for many months can elapse between the date we agree to hear a case and the date we issue an opinion. Consequently, the same claims will be pending in two courts at once, and the duplication will occasion administrative problems; for example, no decision, law, or rule tells us in which court the record in the case should be lodged. There is no indication that Congress intended to burden the court system or litigants with such premature filings.

The anticipatory filing in a federal district court will be all the more anomalous when a habeas petitioner prevails in state court and the State petitions for certiorari. Under the majority's decision, it appears, the petitioner will be obliged to file a protective petition in federal court even though he gained relief from the state tribunal. Lawrence questions whether the federal courts would even have jurisdiction over such a bizarre petition. While I incline to the view that a prisoner in such a position would have standing, Lawrence's concerns are at least plausible and raise the specter of a habeas petitioner prevailing in state court, yet losing the right to pursue constitutional claims in federal court altogether: By the time we have ruled on the State's petition, the statute of limitations likely would have run.

Though recognizing this problem, the majority suggests that equitable tolling may provide a solution. But in the next breath, the majority hastens to clarify that the Court does *not* hold that equitable tolling is available under AEDPA.

By contrast, no similar problems, practical or jurisdictional, would result from a determination that an application for state postconviction review remains "pending" while a petition for certiorari from the state court's decision is before this Court. Nor would such a determination create an untoward opportunity for abuse of the writ. The majority's suggestion that prisoners would have an incentive to petition for certiorari as a delay tactic has no basis in reality in the mine run of cases. Most prisoners want to be released from custody as soon as possible, not to prolong their incarceration. They are therefore interested in the expeditious resolution of their claims.

As earlier indicated, under the majority's rule, a petitioner could achieve the equivalent of tolling by filing a protective petition in federal court and seeking a stay while a certiorari petition is pending. In that event, today's decision does nothing to promote the finality of state-court determinations or the expeditious resolution of claims. Rather, it imposes an unnecessary administrative burden on federal district judges who must determine whether to grant a requested stay, and it sets a trap for those *pro se* litigants unaware of the need to file duplicative petitions.

In sum, the majority's reading is neither compelled by the text of § 2244(d)(2) nor practically sound. By cutting off tolling before this Court has had an opportunity to consider a pending petition for certiorari, the Court's holding will unnecessarily encumber the federal courts with anticipatory filings and deprive unwitting litigants of the opportunity to pursue their constitutional claims – all without furthering the purposes of AEDPA.

Note on Roper v. Weaver, 127 S.Ct. 2022 (2007)

In *Roper v. Weaver*, 127 S.Ct. 2022 (2007) (per curiam), the Supreme Court held that it was error for a federal court to dismiss a habeas petition as premature where the defendant had exhausted his state post-conviction proceedings in the state court system, but had not yet filed a petition for certiorari review of the state denial of relief.

D.   Other Limitations on Federal Habeas Review

Page 790. Insert at the end of Notes and Questions:

Note on Fry v. Plilier, 127 S.Ct. 2321 (2007)

3.   In *Fry v. Plilier*, 127 S.Ct. 2321 (2007), the Court held that "in § 2254 proceedings a court must assess the prejudicial impact of constitutional error in a state-court criminal trial under the 'substantial and injurious effect' standard set forth in *Brecht* [*v. Abrahamson*], 507 U.S. 619, whether or not the state appellate court recognized the error and reviewed it for harmlessness under the 'harmless beyond a reasonable doubt' standard set forth in *Chapman* [*v. California*], 386 U.S. 18."

CHAPTER 14 STATE BARRIERS TO FEDERAL HABEAS REVIEW

A.   Exhaustion of State Remedies

Page 812. Add after Note 3:

4. The AEDPA provides that the one-year statute of limitations may be tolled during the pendency of "a properly filed application for State post-conviction or other collateral review." 28 U.S.C. § 2244(d)(2). The Court considered that tolling provision in the following death penalty case.

Allen v. Siebert
128 S.Ct. 2 (2007)

PER CURIAM.

Daniel Siebert was convicted and sentenced to death in the State of Alabama for the murder of Linda Jarman. Siebert's conviction and sentence were affirmed on direct appeal, and the certificate of judgment issued on May 22, 1990. This Court denied certiorari on November 5, 1990. On August 25, 1992, Siebert filed a petition for postconviction relief in Alabama state court. The state courts denied the petition as untimely, however, because it was filed approximately three months after the expiration of the then-applicable 2-year statute of limitations, which began to run from the date the certificate of judgment issued. The Alabama Supreme Court denied certiorari on September 15, 2000. Siebert did not seek review in this Court. On September 14, 2001, Siebert filed a petition for a federal writ of habeas corpus, in the District Court for the Northern District of Alabama.

The Antiterrorism and Effective Death Penalty Act of 1996 (AEDPA) established a 1-year statute of limitations for filing a federal habeas petition. § 2244(d)(1). The limitations period is tolled, however, while "a properly filed application for State post-conviction or other collateral review with respect to the pertinent judgment or claim is pending." § 2244(d)(2). Because Siebert's direct appeal became final before AEDPA became effective, the 1-year limitations period began to run from April 24, 1996, AEDPA's effective date. Thus, absent tolling, Siebert's federal habeas petition would be untimely by over four years.

The District Court dismissed Siebert's habeas petition as untimely, reasoning that an application for state postconviction relief is not "properly filed" if it was rejected by the state court on statute-of-limitations grounds. The Court of Appeals reversed, however, holding that Siebert's state postconviction petition was "properly filed" within the meaning of § 2244(d)(2), because the state time bar was not jurisdictional and the Alabama courts therefore had discretion in enforcing it. The Court of Appeals accordingly remanded to the District Court to consider the merits of Siebert's petition.

While Siebert's habeas petition was pending on remand in the District Court, we decided *Pace v. DiGuglielmo*, 544 U.S. 408 (2005). In *Pace*, we held that a state postconviction petition rejected by the state court as untimely is not "properly filed" within the meaning of § 2244(d)(2). Relying on *Pace*, the District Court again found that Siebert's state postconviction petition was not "properly filed," and dismissed his federal habeas petition as untimely. The Court of Appeals, however, reversed and remanded. In a one-paragraph opinion, the court distinguished *Pace* on the ground that Rule 32.2(c), unlike the statute of limitations at issue in *Pace*, "operate[s] as an affirmative defense." Thus, the court found its prior holding-that Siebert's state postconviction petition was "properly filed" because the state court rejected it on a nonjurisdictional ground-stood as the law of the case.

The Court of Appeals' carve-out of time limits that operate as affirmative defenses is inconsistent with our holding in *Pace*. Although the Pennsylvania statute of limitations at issue in *Pace* happens to have been a jurisdictional time bar under state law, the jurisdictional nature of the time limit was not the basis for our decision. Rather, we built upon a distinction that we had earlier articulated in *Artuz v. Bennett*, 531 U.S. 4 (2000), between postconviction petitions rejected on the basis of "filing" conditions, which are not "properly filed" under § 2244(d)(2), and those rejected on the basis of "procedural bars [that] go to the ability to obtain relief," which are. We found that statutes of limitations are "filing" conditions because they "go to the very initiation of a petition and a court's ability to consider that petition." Thus, we held "that time limits, no matter their form, are 'filing' conditions," and that a state postconviction petition is therefore not "properly filed" if it was rejected by the state court as untimely.

In short, our holding in *Pace* turned not on the nature of the particular time limit relied upon by the state court, but rather on the fact that time limits generally establish "conditions to filing" a petition for state postconviction relief. Whether a time limit is jurisdictional, an affirmative defense, or something in between, it is a "condition to filing," it places a limit on how long a prisoner can wait before filing a postconviction petition. The fact that Alabama's Rule 32.2(c) is an affirmative defense that can be waived (or is subject to equitable tolling) renders it no less a "filing" requirement than a jurisdictional time bar would be; it only makes it a less stringent one. Indeed, in *Pace* we cited the very statute at issue in this case as an example of such a "filing" requirement.

Excluding from *Pace*'s scope those time limits that operate as affirmative defenses would leave a gaping hole in what we plainly meant to be a general rule, as statutes of limitations are often affirmative defenses. What is more, whether a time limit is jurisdictional or an affirmative defense is often a disputed question, as the interpretive history of Rule 32.2(c) itself illustrates. Under the Court of Appeals' approach, federal habeas courts would have to delve into the intricacies of state procedural law in deciding whether a postconviction petition rejected by the state courts as untimely was nonetheless "properly filed" under § 2244(d)(2). Our decision in Pace precludes such an approach.

We therefore reiterate now what we held in *Pace*: "When a postconviction petition is untimely under state law, 'that [is] the end of the matter' for purposes of § 2244(d)(2)." Because Siebert's petition for state postconviction relief was rejected as untimely by the Alabama courts, it was not "properly filed" under § 2244(d)(2). Accordingly, he was not entitled to tolling of AEDPA's 1-year statute of limitations.

Justice STEVENS, with whom Justice Ginsburg joins, dissenting.

There is an obvious distinction between time limits that go to the very initiation of a petition, and time limits that create an affirmative defense that can be waived. The time limit under consideration in *Pace v. DiGuglielmo*, 544 U.S. 408 (2005), was of the former kind – as the Court's opinion expressly noted. The time limit at issue in this case is of the latter, distinguishable kind – as the Court of Appeals correctly stated.

It is true that there is language in the majority opinion in *Pace* that is broad enough to cover both kinds of limitations provisions, but only the former (those that do not operate as affirmative defenses) can even arguably provide a reasonable basis for concluding that an untimely petition has not been "properly filed" within the meaning of the Antiterrorism and Effective Death Penalty Act of 1996, 110 Stat. 1214 (AEDPA).[*] I therefore respectfully dissent.

I. *Evidentiary Hearing under the AEDPA - Section 2254(e)*

Page 867. Add after Michael Williams v. Taylor:

Schriro v. Landrigan
127 S.Ct. 1933 (2007)

Justice THOMAS delivered the opinion of the Court.

In cases where an applicant for federal habeas relief is not barred from obtaining an evidentiary hearing by 28 U.S.C. § 2254(e)(2), the decision to grant such a hearing rests in the discretion of the district court. Here, the District Court determined that respondent could not make out a colorable claim of ineffective assistance of counsel and therefore was not entitled

---

[*] I continue to believe, as stated in my dissent in *Pace*, 544 U.S., at 427, that state timeliness bars that operate like procedural bars (for example, those that require the courts to consider enumerated exceptions) should not determine whether a state postconviction petition is "properly filed" under AEDPA. Even accepting *Pace*, however, this case is distinguishable and should not be summarily reversed.

to an evidentiary hearing. It did so after reviewing the state-court record and expanding the record to include additional evidence offered by the respondent. The Court of Appeals held that the District Court abused its discretion in refusing to grant the hearing. We hold that it did not.

I

Respondent Jeffrey Landrigan was convicted in Oklahoma of second-degree murder in 1982. In 1986, while in custody for that murder, Landrigan repeatedly stabbed another inmate and was subsequently convicted of assault and battery with a deadly weapon. Three years later, Landrigan escaped from prison and murdered Chester Dean Dyer in Arizona.

An Arizona jury found Landrigan guilty of theft, second-degree burglary, and felony murder for having caused the victim's death in the course of a burglary. At sentencing, Landrigan's counsel attempted to present the testimony of Landrigan's ex-wife and birth mother as mitigating evidence. But at Landrigan's request, both women refused to testify. When the trial judge asked why the witnesses refused, Landrigan's counsel responded that "it's at my client's wishes." Counsel explained that he had "advised [Landrigan] very strongly that I think it's very much against his interests to take that particular position." The court then questioned Landrigan:

> "THE COURT: Mr. Landrigan, have you instructed your lawyer that you do not wish for him to bring any mitigating circumstances to my attention?
>
> "THE DEFENDANT: Yeah.
>
> "THE COURT: Do you know what that means?
>
> "THE DEFENDANT: Yeah.
>
> "THE COURT: Mr. Landrigan, are there mitigating circumstances I should be aware of?
>
> "THE DEFENDANT: Not as far as I'm concerned."

Still not satisfied, the trial judge directly asked the witnesses to testify. Both refused. The judge then asked counsel to make a proffer of the witnesses' testimony. Counsel attempted to explain that the witnesses would testify that Landrigan's birth mother used drugs and alcohol (including while she was pregnant with Landrigan), that Landrigan abused drugs and alcohol, and that Landrigan had been a good father.

But Landrigan would have none of it. When counsel tried to explain that Landrigan had worked in a legitimate job to provide for his family, Landrigan interrupted and stated "[i]f I wanted this to be heard, I'd have my wife say it." Landrigan then explained that he was not only working but also "doing robberies supporting my family." When counsel characterized Landrigan's first murder as having elements of self-defense, Landrigan interrupted and clarified: "He didn't grab me. I stabbed him." Responding to counsel's statement implying that the prison stabbing involved self-defense because the assaulted inmate knew Landrigan's first murder victim, Landrigan interrupted to clarify that the inmate was not acquainted with his first victim, but just "a guy I got in an argument with. I stabbed him 14 times. It was lucky he lived."

At the conclusion of the sentencing hearing, the judge asked Landrigan if he had anything to say. Landrigan made a brief statement that concluded, "I think if you want to give me the death penalty, just bring it right on. I'm ready for it."

The trial judge found two statutory aggravating circumstances: that Landrigan murdered Dyer in expectation of pecuniary gain and that Landrigan was previously convicted of two felonies involving the use or threat of violence on another person. In addition, the judge found two nonstatutory mitigating circumstances: that Landrigan's family loved him and an absence of premeditation. Finally, the trial judge stated that she considered Landrigan "a person who has no scruples and no regard for human life and human beings." Based on these findings, the court sentenced Landrigan to death. On direct appeal, the Arizona Supreme Court unanimously affirmed Landrigan's sentence and conviction. In addressing an ineffective-assistance-of-counsel claim not relevant here, the court noted that Landrigan had stated his "desire not to have mitigating evidence presented in his behalf."

On January 31, 1995, Landrigan filed a petition for state postconviction relief and alleged his counsel's "fail[ure] to explore additional grounds for arguing mitigation evidence." Specifically, Landrigan maintained that his counsel should have investigated the "biological component" of his violent behavior by interviewing his biological father and other relatives. In addition, Landrigan stated that his biological father could confirm that his biological mother used drugs and alcohol while pregnant with Landrigan.

The Arizona postconviction court, presided over by the same judge who tried and sentenced Landrigan, rejected Landrigan's claim. The court found that "[Landrigan] instructed his attorney not to present any evidence at the sentencing hearing, [so] it is difficult to comprehend how [Landrigan] can claim counsel should have presented other evidence at sentencing." Noting Landrigan's contention that he "'would have cooperated'" had other mitigating evidence been presented, the court concluded that Landrigan's "statements at sentencing belie his new-found sense of cooperation." Describing Landrigan's claim as "frivolous," the court declined to hold an evidentiary hearing and dismissed Landrigan's petition. The Arizona Supreme Court denied Landrigan's petition for review on June 19, 1996.

Landrigan then filed a federal habeas application under § 2254. The District Court determined, after "expand[ing] the record to include . . . evidence of [Landrigan's] troubled background, his history of drug and alcohol abuse, and his family's history of criminal behavior," that Landrigan could not demonstrate that he was prejudiced by any error his counsel may have made. Because Landrigan could not make out even a "colorable" ineffective-assistance-of-counsel claim, the District Court refused to grant him an evidentiary hearing.

On appeal, a unanimous panel of the Court of Appeals for the Ninth Circuit affirmed, but the full court granted rehearing en banc, and reversed. The en banc Court of Appeals held that Landrigan was entitled to an evidentiary hearing because he raised a "colorable claim" that his counsel's performance fell below the standard required by *Strickland v. Washington,* 466 U.S. 668 (1984). With respect to counsel's performance, the Ninth Circuit found that he "did little to prepare for the sentencing aspect of the case," and that investigation would have revealed a wealth of mitigating evidence, including the family's history of drug and alcohol abuse and propensity for violence.

Turning to prejudice, the court held the Arizona postconviction court's determination that Landrigan refused to permit his counsel to present any mitigating evidence was "an 'unreasonable determination of the facts.'" The Court of Appeals found that when Landrigan stated that he did not want his counsel to present any mitigating evidence, he was clearly referring only to the evidence his attorney was about to introduce – that of his ex-wife and birth mother. The court further held that, even if Landrigan intended to forgo the presentation of all mitigation evidence, such a "last-minute decision cannot excuse his counsel's failure to conduct an adequate investigation *prior* to the sentencing." In conclusion, the court found "a reasonable probability that, if Landrigan's allegations are true, the sentencing judge would have reached a different conclusion." The court therefore remanded the case for an evidentiary hearing.

We granted certiorari and now reverse.

II

Prior to the Antiterrorism and Effective Death Penalty Act of 1996 (AEDPA), the decision to grant an evidentiary hearing was generally left to the sound discretion of district courts. *Brown v. Allen,* 344 U.S. 443, 463-464 (1953); see also *Townsend v. Sain,* 372 U.S. 293, 313 (1963). That basic rule has not changed. See 28 U.S.C. § 2254, Rule 8(a) ("[T]he judge must review the answer [and] any transcripts and records of state-court proceedings. . . to determine whether an evidentiary hearing is warranted").

AEDPA, however, changed the standards for granting federal habeas relief. Under AEDPA, Congress prohibited federal courts from granting habeas relief unless a state court's adjudication of a claim "resulted in a decision that was contrary to, or involved an unreasonable application of, clearly established Federal law, as determined by the Supreme Court of the United States," § 2254(d)(1), or the relevant state-court decision "was based on an unreasonable determination of the facts in light of the evidence presented in the State court proceeding." § 2254(d)(2). The question under AEDPA is not whether a federal court believes the state court's determination was incorrect but whether that determination was unreasonable – a substantially higher threshold. See *Williams v. Taylor,* 529 U.S. 362, 410 (2000). AEDPA also requires federal habeas courts to presume the correctness of state courts' factual findings unless applicants rebut this presumption with "clear and convincing evidence." § 2254(e)(1).

In deciding whether to grant an evidentiary hearing, a federal court must consider whether such a hearing could enable an applicant to prove the petition's factual allegations, which, if true, would entitle the applicant to federal habeas relief. Because the deferential standards prescribed by § 2254 control whether to grant habeas relief, a federal court must take into account those standards in deciding whether an evidentiary hearing is appropriate.

It follows that if the record refutes the applicant's factual allegations or otherwise precludes habeas relief, a district court is not required to hold an evidentiary hearing. The Ninth Circuit has recognized this point in other cases, holding that "an evidentiary hearing is not required on issues that can be resolved by reference to the state court record." This approach is not unique to the Ninth Circuit.

This principle accords with AEDPA's acknowledged purpose of "reduc[ing] delays in the execution of state and federal criminal sentences." If district courts were required to allow federal habeas applicants to develop even the most insubstantial factual allegations in evidentiary hearings, district courts would be forced to reopen factual disputes that were conclusively resolved in the state courts. With these standards in mind, we turn to the facts of this case.

III

For several reasons, the Court of Appeals believed that Landrigan might be entitled to federal habeas relief and that the District Court, therefore, abused its discretion by denying Landrigan an evidentiary hearing. To the contrary, the District Court was well within its discretion to determine that, even with the benefit of an evidentiary hearing, Landrigan could not develop a factual record that would entitle him to habeas relief.

A

The Court of Appeals first addressed the State's contention that Landrigan instructed his counsel not to offer any mitigating evidence. If Landrigan issued such an instruction, counsel's failure to investigate further could not have been prejudicial under *Strickland*. The Court of Appeals rejected the findings of "the Arizona Supreme Court (on direct appeal) and the Arizona Superior Court (on habeas review)" that Landrigan instructed his counsel not to introduce any mitigating evidence. According to the Ninth Circuit, those findings took Landrigan's colloquy with the sentencing court out of context in a manner that "amounts to an 'unreasonable determination of the facts.' "

Upon review of record material and the transcripts from the state courts, we disagree. As a threshold matter, the language of the colloquy plainly indicates that Landrigan informed his counsel not to present any mitigating evidence. When the Arizona trial judge asked Landrigan if he had instructed his lawyer not to present mitigating evidence, Landrigan responded affirmatively. Likewise, when asked if there was any relevant mitigating evidence, Landrigan answered, "Not as far as I'm concerned." These statements establish that the Arizona postconviction court's determination of the facts was reasonable. And it is worth noting, again, that the judge presiding on postconviction review was ideally situated to make this assessment because she is the same judge that sentenced Landrigan and discussed these issues with him.

Notwithstanding the plainness of these statements, the Court of Appeals concluded that they referred to only the specific testimony that counsel planned to offer – that of Landrigan's ex-wife and birth mother. The Court of Appeals further concluded that Landrigan, due to counsel's failure to investigate, could not have known about the mitigating evidence he now wants to explore. The record conclusively dispels that interpretation. First, Landrigan's birth mother would have offered testimony that overlaps with the evidence Landrigan now wants to present. For example, Landrigan wants to present evidence from his biological father that would "confirm [his biological mother's] alcohol and drug use during her pregnancy." But the record shows that counsel planned to call Landrigan's birth mother to testify about her "drug us[e] during her pregnancy," and the possible effects of such drug use. Second, Landrigan interrupted repeatedly when counsel tried to proffer anything that could have been considered mitigating. He even refused to allow his attorney to proffer that he had worked a regular job at one point. This behavior confirms what is plain from the transcript of the colloquy: that Landrigan would have undermined the presentation of any mitigating evidence that his attorney might have uncovered.

On the record before us, the Arizona court's determination that Landrigan refused to allow the presentation of any mitigating evidence was a reasonable determination of the facts. In this regard, we agree with the initial Court of Appeals panel that reviewed this case:

> "In the constellation of refusals to have mitigating evidence presented . . . this case is surely a bright star. No other case could illuminate the state of the client's mind and the nature of counsel's dilemma quite as brightly as this one. No flashes of insight could be more fulgurous than those which this record supplies." *Landrigan v. Stewart,* 272 F.3d 1221, 1226 (C.A.9 2001).

Because the Arizona postconviction court reasonably determined that Landrigan "instructed his attorney not to bring any mitigation to the attention of the [sentencing] court," it was not an abuse of discretion for the District Court to conclude that Landrigan could not overcome § 2254(d)(2)'s bar to granting federal habeas relief. The District Court was entitled to conclude that regardless of what information counsel might have uncovered in his investigation, Landrigan would have interrupted and refused to allow his counsel to present any such evidence. Accordingly, the District Court could conclude that because of his established recalcitrance, Landrigan could not demonstrate prejudice under *Strickland* even if granted an evidentiary hearing. . . .

IV

Finally, the Court of Appeals erred in rejecting the District Court's finding that the poor quality of Landrigan's alleged mitigating evidence prevented him from making "a colorable claim" of prejudice. As summarized by the Court of Appeals, Landrigan wanted to introduce as mitigation evidence:

> "[that] he was exposed to alcohol and drugs *in utero,* which may have resulted in cognitive and behavioral deficiencies consistent with fetal alcohol syndrome. He was abandoned by his birth mother and suffered abandonment and attachment issues, as well as other behavioral problems throughout his childhood.

> "His adoptive mother was also an alcoholic, and Landrigan's own alcohol and substance abuse began at an early age. Based on his biological family's history of violence, Landrigan claims he may also have been genetically predisposed to violence."

As explained above, all but the last sentence refer to information that Landrigan's birth mother and ex-wife could have offered if Landrigan had allowed them to testify. Indeed, the state postconviction court had much of this evidence before it by way of counsel's proffer. The District Court could reasonably conclude that any additional evidence would have made no difference in the sentencing.

In sum, the District Court did not abuse its discretion in finding that Landrigan could not establish prejudice based on his counsel's failure to present the evidence he now wishes to offer. Landrigan's mitigation evidence was weak, and the postconviction court was well acquainted with Landrigan's exceedingly violent past and had seen first hand his belligerent behavior. Again, it is difficult to improve upon the initial Court of Appeals panel's conclusion:

> "The prospect was chilling; before he was 30 years of age, Landrigan had murdered one man, repeatedly stabbed another one, escaped from prison, and within two months murdered still another man. As the Arizona Supreme Court so aptly put it when dealing with one of Landrigan's other claims, '[i]n his comments [to the sentencing judge], defendant not only failed to show remorse or offer mitigating evidence, but he flaunted his menacing behavior.' On this record, assuring the court that genetics made him the way he is could not have been very helpful. There was no prejudice."

V

The Court of Appeals erred in holding that the District Court abused its discretion in declining to grant Landrigan an evidentiary hearing. Even assuming the truth of all the facts Landrigan sought to prove at the evidentiary hearing, he still could not be granted federal habeas relief because the state courts' factual determination that Landrigan would not have allowed counsel to present any mitigating evidence at sentencing is not an unreasonable determination of the facts under § 2254(d)(2) and the mitigating evidence he seeks to introduce would not have changed the result. In such circumstances, a District Court has discretion to deny an evidentiary hearing. The judgment of the Court of Appeals for the Ninth Circuit is reversed, and the case is remanded for further proceedings consistent with this opinion.

Justice STEVENS, with whom Justice Souter, Justice Ginsburg, and Justice Breyer join, dissenting.

Significant mitigating evidence – evidence that may well have explained respondent's criminal conduct and unruly behavior at his capital sentencing hearing – was unknown at the time of sentencing. Only years later did respondent learn that he suffers from a serious psychological condition that sheds important light on his earlier actions. The reason why this and other mitigating evidence was unavailable is that respondent's counsel failed to conduct a constitutionally adequate investigation. In spite of this, the Court holds that respondent is not entitled to an evidentiary hearing to explore the prejudicial impact of his counsel's inadequate representation. It reasons that respondent "would have" waived his right to introduce any mitigating evidence that counsel might have uncovered, and that such evidence "would have" made no difference in the sentencing anyway. Without the benefit of an evidentiary hearing, this is pure guesswork.

The Court's decision rests on a parsimonious appraisal of a capital defendant's constitutional right to have the sentencing decision reflect meaningful consideration of all relevant mitigating evidence, a begrudging appreciation of the need for a knowing and intelligent waiver of constitutionally protected trial rights, and a cramped reading of the record. Unlike this Court, the en banc Court of Appeals properly accounted for these important constitutional and factual considerations. Its narrow holding that the District Court abused its discretion in denying respondent an evidentiary hearing should be affirmed.

I

No one, not even the Court, seriously contends that counsel's investigation of possible mitigating evidence was constitutionally sufficient. Indeed, both the majority and dissenting judges on the en banc Court of Appeals agreed that "counsel's limited investigation of Landrigan's background fell below the standards of professional representation prevailing" at the time of his sentencing hearing. The list of evidence that counsel failed to investigate is long. For instance, counsel did not complete a psychological evaluation of respondent, which we now know would have uncovered a serious organic brain disorder. He failed to consult an expert to explore the effects of respondent's birth mother's drinking and drug use during pregnancy. And he never developed a history of respondent's troubled childhood with his adoptive family – a childhood marked by physical and emotional abuse, neglect by his adoptive parents, his own serious substance abuse problems (including an overdose in his eighth or ninth grade classroom), a stunted education, and recurrent placement in substance abuse rehabilitation facilities, a psychiatric ward, and police custody. Counsel's failure to develop this background evidence was so glaring that even the sentencing judge noted that she had "received very little information concerning the defendant's difficult family history." At the time of sentencing, counsel was only prepared to put on the testimony by respondent's ex-wife and birth mother. By any measure, and especially for a capital case, this meager investigation "fell below an objective standard of reasonableness."

Given this deficient performance, the only issue is whether counsel's inadequate investigation prejudiced the outcome of sentencing. The bulk of the Court's opinion argues that the District Court reasonably found that respondent waived his right to present any and all mitigating evidence. As I shall explain, this argument finds no support in the Constitution or the record of this case.

II

. . .[R]espondent's purported waiver can only be appreciated in light of his counsel's deficient performance. To take just one example, respondent's counsel asked a psychologist, Dr. Mickey McMahon, to conduct an initial interview with respondent. But Dr. McMahon has submitted an affidavit stating that his experience was "quite different from the working relationship [he] had with counsel on other death penalty cases in which the psychological study went through a series of steps." In this case, Dr. McMahon was "not authorized to conduct the next step in psychological testing that would have told [him] if . . . there were any cognitive or neuropsychological deficits not observed during just an interview." Even though Dr. McMahon told respondent's counsel that "much more work was needed to provide an appropriate psychological study for a death penalty case," counsel refused to let him investigate any further.

A more thorough investigation would have revealed that respondent suffers from an organic brain disorder. Years after Dr. McMahon's aborted examination, another psychologist, Dr. Thomas C. Thompson, conducted a complete analysis of respondent. Based on extensive interviews with respondent and several of his family members, a review of his family history, and multiple clinical tests, Dr. Thompson diagnosed respondent with Antisocial Personality Disorder. See Declaration by Thomas C. Thompson. Dr. Thompson filed an affidavit in the District Court describing his diagnosis:

"[Respondent's] actions did not constitute a lifestyle choice in the sense of an individual operating with a large degree of freedom, as we have come to define free will. The inherited, prenatal, and early developmental factors severely impaired Mr. Landrigan's ability to function in a society that expects individuals to operate in an organized and adaptive manner, taking into account the actions and consequences of their behaviors and their impact on society and its individual members. Based on evaluation and investigation along with other relevant data, this type of responsible functioning is simply beyond Mr. Landrigan and, as far back as one can go, there is no indication that he ever had these capacities."

On the day of the sentencing hearing, the only mitigating evidence that respondent's counsel had investigated was the testimony of respondent's birth mother and ex-wife. None of this neuropsychological information was available to respondent at the time of his purported waiver. Yet the Court conspicuously avoids any mention of respondent's organic brain disorder. It instead provides an incomplete list of other mitigating evidence that respondent would have presented and incorrectly assumes that respondent's birth mother and ex-wife would have covered it all. Unless I missed the portion of the record indicating that respondent's ex-wife and birth mother were trained psychologists, neither could have offered expert testimony about respondent's organic brain disorder.

It is of course true that respondent was aware of many of the individual pieces of mitigating evidence that contributed to Dr. Thompson's subsequent diagnosis. He knew that his birth mother abandoned him at the age of six months; that his biological family had an extensive criminal history; that his adoptive mother had "affective disturbances and chronic alcoholism"; that she routinely drank vodka until she passed out; that she would frequently strike him, once even "hit[ting him] with a frying pan hard enough to leave a dent"; that his childhood was difficult and he exhibited abandonment and attachment problems at an early age; that he had a bad temper and often threw violent tantrums as a child; and that he "began getting into trouble and using alcohol and drugs at an early age and, by adolescence, he had begun a series of placements in juvenile detention facilities, a psychiatric ward, and twice in drug abuse rehabilitation programs". Perhaps respondent also knew that his biological mother abused alcohol and amphetamines during her pregnancy, and that *in utero* exposure to drugs and alcohol has deleterious effects on the child.

But even if respondent knew all these things, we cannot assume that he could understand their consequences the way an expert psychologist could. Without years of advanced education and a battery of complicated testing, respondent could not know that these experiences resulted in a serious organic brain disorder or what effect such a disorder might have on his behavior. And precisely because his counsel failed to conduct a proper investigation, he did not know that this important evidence was available to him when he purportedly waived the right to present mitigating evidence. It is hard to see how respondent's claim of *Strickland* prejudice can be prejudiced by counsel's *Strickland* error. . . .

IV

Almost as an afterthought, the Court holds in the alternative that "the District Court did not abuse its discretion in finding that Landrigan could not establish prejudice based on his counsel's failure to present the evidence he now wishes to offer." It of course does this on a cold and incomplete factual record. Describing respondent's mitigation case as "weak," and emphasizing his "exceedingly violent past" and "belligerent behavior" at sentencing, the Court concludes that there is no way that respondent can establish prejudice with the evidence he seeks to introduce. This reasoning is flawed in several respects.

First, as has been discussed above but bears repeating, the Court thoroughly misrepresents respondent's mitigating evidence. It is all too easy to view respondent's mitigation case as "weak" when you assume away his most powerful evidence. The Court ignores respondent's organic brain disorder, which would have explained not only his criminal history but also the repeated outbursts at sentencing. It mistakenly assumes that respondent's birth mother and ex-wife could have testified about the medical consequences of fetal alcohol syndrome. And it inaccurately states that these women could have described his turbulent childhood with his adoptive family. We have repeatedly said that evidence of this kind can influence a sentencer's decision as to whether death is the proper punishment.

Second, the aggravating circumstances relied on by the sentencing judge are not as strong as the Court makes them out to be. To be sure, respondent had already committed two violent offenses. But so had Terry Williams, and this Court still concluded that he suffered prejudice when his attorney failed to investigate and present mitigating evidence. The only other aggravating factor was that Landrigan committed his crime for pecuniary gain but there are serious doubts about that. As the en banc Court of Appeals explained, "[t]here was limited evidence regarding the pecuniary gain aggravator. The judge noted that the victim's apartment had been ransacked as if the perpetrator were looking for something, and that this demonstrated an expectation of pecuniary gain, *even though Landrigan did not actually steal anything of value*." Thus, while we should not ignore respondent's violent past, it is certainly possible – even likely – that evidence of his neurological disorder, fetal alcohol syndrome, and abusive upbringing would have influenced the sentencing judge's assessment of his moral blameworthiness and altered the outcome of his sentencing. As such, respondent has plainly alleged facts that, if substantiated at an evidentiary hearing, would entitle him to relief.

V

In the end, the Court's decision can only be explained by its increasingly familiar effort to guard the floodgates of litigation. Immediately before turning to the facts of this case, it states that "[i]f district courts were required to allow federal habeas applicants to develop even the most insubstantial factual allegations in evidentiary hearings, district courts would be forced to reopen factual disputes that were conclusively resolved in the state courts." However, habeas cases requiring evidentiary hearings have been "few in number," and "there is no clear evidence that this particular classification of habeas proceedings has burdened the dockets of the federal courts." Even prior to the passage of the Antiterrorism and Effective Death Act of 1996, district courts held evidentiary hearings in only *1.17%* of all federal habeas cases. This figure makes it abundantly clear that doing justice does not always cause the heavens to fall. The Court would therefore do well to heed Justice Kennedy's just reminder that "[w]e ought not take steps which diminish the likelihood that [federal] courts will base their legal decision on an accurate assessment of the facts."

It may well be true that respondent would have completely waived his right to present mitigating evidence if that evidence had been adequately investigated at the time of sentencing. It may also be true that respondent's mitigating evidence could not outweigh his violent past. What is certainly true, however, is that an evidentiary hearing would provide answers to these questions. I emphatically agree with the majority of judges on the en banc Court of Appeals that it was an abuse of discretion to refuse to conduct such a hearing in this capital case.

Accordingly, I respectfully dissent.

CHAPTER 15 RETROACTIVITY

Page 880. Insert following Note 9:

Note on Danforth v. Minnesota, 128 S.Ct. 1029 (2008)

10. In *Danforth v. Minnesota*, 128 S.Ct. 1029 (2008), the Supreme Court in a non-capital case considered whether state courts were obligated to enforce the retroactivity restrictions of *Teague* in their state post-conviction proceedings. The Court held that *Teague* does not constrain the power of state courts to give broader retroactive application to new rules in its state post-conviction proceedings than the federal courts give in federal habeas proceedings. Specifically, the Court stated:

> Our subsequent cases, which characterize the *Teague* rule as a standard limiting only the scope of federal habeas relief, confirm that *Teague* speaks only to the context of federal habeas. *See, e.g., Beard v. Banks*, 542 U.S. 406, 412 (2004) ("*Teague*'s nonretroactivity principle acts as a limitation on the power of federal courts to grant habeas corpus relief to state prisoners" (internal quotation marks, ellipsis, and brackets omitted)); *Caspari*, 510 U.S., at 389 ("The [*Teague*] nonretroactivity principle prevents a federal court from granting habeas corpus relief to a state prisoner based on a rule announced after his conviction and sentence became final").

> It is also noteworthy that for many years following *Teague*, state courts almost universally understood the *Teague* rule as binding only federal habeas courts, not state courts. *See, e.g., Cowell v. Leapley*, 458 N.W.2d 514 (S.D.1990); *Preciose*, 129 N.J. 451, 609 A.2d 1280; *State ex rel. Schmelzer v. Murphy*, 548 N.W.2d 45, 49 (1996) (choosing of its own volition to adopt the *Teague* rule); *but see State v. Egelhoff*, 900 P.2d 260 (1995).[17] Commentators were similarly confident that *Teague*'s "restrictions appl[ied] only to federal habeas cases," leaving States free to "determine whether to follow the federal courts' rulings on retroactivity or to fashion rules which respond to the unique concerns of that state." Hutton, *Retroactivity in the States: The Impact of Teague v. Lane on State Postconviction Remedies*, 44 Ala. L.Rev. 421, 423-424, 422-423 (1993).

> In sum, the *Teague* decision limits the kinds of constitutional violations that will entitle an individual to relief on federal habeas, but does not in any way limit the authority of a state court, when reviewing its own state criminal convictions, to provide a remedy for a violation that is deemed "nonretroactive" under *Teague*.

---

[17]   Today, the majority of state courts still read *Teague* this way. As far as we can tell, only three States – Minnesota, Oregon, and Montana – have adopted a contrary view. See *Page*, 84 P.3d 133; *Egelhoff*, 900 P.2d 260.

128 S.Ct. at 1041-1042.

Page 897. Insert after Note 2:

Note on Whorton v. Bockting, 127 S.Ct. 1173 (2007)

3. In *Whorton v. Bockting*, 127 S.Ct. 1173 (2007), the Supreme Court in a non-capital case considered whether to give retroactive effect to its decision in *Crawford v. Washington*, 541 U.S. 36 (2004). In *Crawford*, the Court overturned prior Supreme Court caselaw on the admission of hearsay evidence under the Confrontation Clause of the Constitution. Writing for the Court, Justice Alito found that *Crawford* established a new procedural rule that would not apply retroactively unless it fit within an exception to *Teague*. The exception at issue was the exception allowing retroactive application of a watershed, bedrock rule of law that is necessary to prevent an "impermissibly large risk" of an inaccurate conviction. The Court found that *Crawford* did not fit within this exception. In fact, the Court noted that it had yet to find any decision, other than possibly *Gideon v. Wainwright*, 372 U.S. 335 (1963) (providing the right to appointed counsel to indigent criminal defendants), to fall within this exception.

CHAPTER 19 INTERNATIONAL LAW AND THE DEATH PENALTY

B.   Selected Cases

*Page 1091. **Insert before Note on the Aftermath of the** Avena **Decision:***

Sanchez-Llamas v. Oregon
548 U.S. 331 (2006)

Chief Justice ROBERTS delivered the opinion of the Court.

Article 36 of the Vienna Convention on Consular Relations (Vienna Convention or Convention), Apr. 24, 1963, addresses communication between an individual and his consular officers when the individual is detained by authorities in a foreign country. These consolidated cases concern the availability of judicial relief for violations of Article 36. We are confronted with three questions. *First,* does Article 36 create rights that defendants may invoke against the detaining authorities in a criminal trial or in a postconviction proceeding? *Second,* does a violation of Article 36 require suppression of a defendant's statements to police? *Third,* may a State, in a postconviction proceeding, treat a defendant's Article 36 claim as defaulted because he failed to raise the claim at trial? We conclude, even assuming the Convention creates judicially enforceable rights, that suppression is not an appropriate remedy for a violation of Article 36, and that a State may apply its regular rules of procedural default to Article 36 claims. We therefore affirm the decisions below.

I
A

The Vienna Convention was drafted in 1963 with the purpose, evident in its preamble, of "contribut[ing] to the development of friendly relations among nations, irrespective of their differing constitutional and social systems." The Convention consists of 79 articles regulating various aspects of consular activities. At present, 170 countries are party to the Convention. The United States, upon the advice and consent of the Senate, ratified the Convention in 1969.

Article 36 of the Convention concerns consular officers' access to their nationals detained by authorities in a foreign country. The article provides that "if he so requests, the competent authorities of the receiving State shall, without delay, inform the consular post of the sending State if, within its consular district, a national of that State is arrested or committed to prison or to custody pending trial or is detained in any other manner." Art. 36(1)(b).[1], In

---

[1] In its entirety, Article 36 of the Vienna Convention states:

"1. With a view to facilitating the exercise of consular functions relating to nationals of the sending State:

"(a) consular officers shall be free to communicate with nationals of the sending State and to have access to them. Nationals of the sending State shall have the same freedom with respect to communication with and access to consular officers of the sending State;

other words, when a national of one country is detained by authorities in another, the authorities must notify the consular officers of the detainee's home country if the detainee so requests. Article 36(1)(b) further states that "[t]he said authorities shall inform the person concerned [*i.e.,* the detainee] without delay of his rights under this sub-paragraph." The Convention also provides guidance regarding how these requirements, and the other requirements of Article 36, are to be implemented:

> "The rights referred to in paragraph 1 of this Article shall be exercised in conformity with the laws and regulations of the receiving State, subject to the proviso, however, that the said laws and regulations must enable full effect to be given to the purposes for which the rights accorded under this Article are intended." Art. 36(2.

Along with the Vienna Convention, the United States ratified the Optional Protocol Concerning the Compulsory Settlement of Disputes (Optional Protocol or Protocol), Apr. 24, 1963, [1970] 21 U.S.T. 325, T.I.A.S. No. 6820. The Optional Protocol provides that "[d]isputes arising out of the interpretation or application of the Convention shall lie within the compulsory jurisdiction of the International Court of Justice [(ICJ)]," and allows parties to the Protocol to bring such disputes before the ICJ. The United States gave notice of its withdrawal from the Optional Protocol on March 7, 2005.

B

Petitioner Moises Sanchez-Llamas is a Mexican national. In December 1999, he was involved in an exchange of gunfire with police in which one officer suffered a gunshot wound in the leg. Police arrested Sanchez-Llamas and gave him warnings under *Miranda v. Arizona*, 384 U.S. 436 (1966), in both English and Spanish. At no time, however, did they inform him that he could ask to have the Mexican Consulate notified of his detention.

"(b) if he so requests, the competent authorities of the receiving State shall, without delay, inform the consular post of the sending State if, within its consular district, a national of that State is arrested or committed to prison or to custody pending trial or is detained in any other manner. Any communication addressed to the consular post by the person arrested, in prison, custody or detention shall also be forwarded by the said authorities without delay. The said authorities shall inform the person concerned without delay of his rights under this sub-paragraph;

"(c) consular officers shall have the right to visit a national of the sending State who is in prison, custody or detention, to converse and correspond with him and to arrange for his legal representation. They shall also have the right to visit any national of the sending State who is in prison, custody or detention in their district in pursuance of a judgment. Nevertheless, consular officers shall refrain from taking action on behalf of a national who is in prison, custody or detention if he expressly opposes such action.

"2. The rights referred to in paragraph 1 of this Article shall be exercised in conformity with the laws and regulations of the receiving State, subject to the proviso, however, that the said laws and regulations must enable full effect to be given to the purposes for which the rights accorded under this Article are intended."

Shortly after the arrest and *Miranda* warnings, police interrogated Sanchez-Llamas with the assistance of an interpreter. In the course of the interrogation, Sanchez-Llamas made several incriminating statements regarding the shootout with police. He was charged with attempted aggravated murder, attempted murder, and several other offenses. Before trial, Sanchez-Llamas moved to suppress the statements he made to police. He argued that suppression was warranted because the statements were made involuntarily and because the authorities had failed to comply with Article 36 of the Vienna Convention. The trial court denied the motion. The case proceeded to trial, and Sanchez-Llamas was convicted and sentenced to 20 1/2 years in prison.

He appealed, again arguing that the Vienna Convention violation required suppression of his statements. The Oregon Court of Appeals affirmed. The Oregon Supreme Court also affirmed, concluding that Article 36 "does not create rights to consular access or notification that are enforceable by detained individuals in a judicial proceeding." We granted certiorari.

C

Petitioner Mario Bustillo, a Honduran national, was with several other men at a restaurant in Springfield, Virginia, on the night of December 10, 1997. That evening, outside the restaurant, James Merry was struck in the head with a baseball bat as he stood smoking a cigarette. He died several days later. Several witnesses at the scene identified Bustillo as the assailant. Police arrested Bustillo the morning after the attack and eventually charged him with murder. Authorities never informed him that he could request to have the Honduran Consulate notified of his detention.

At trial, the defense pursued a theory that another man, known as "Sirena," was responsible for the attack. Two defense witnesses testified that Bustillo was not the killer. One of the witnesses specifically identified the attacker as Sirena. In addition, a third defense witness stated that she had seen Sirena on a flight to Honduras the day after the victim died. In its closing argument before the jury, the prosecution dismissed the defense theory about Sirena. A jury convicted Bustillo of first-degree murder, and he was sentenced to 30 years in prison. His conviction and sentence were affirmed on appeal.

After his conviction became final, Bustillo filed a petition for a writ of habeas corpus in state court. There, for the first time, he argued that authorities had violated his right to consular notification under Article 36 of the Vienna Convention. He claimed that if he had been advised of his right to confer with the Honduran Consulate, he "would have done so without delay." Moreover, the Honduran Consulate executed an affidavit stating that "it would have endeavoured to help Mr. Bustillo in his defense" had it learned of his detention prior to trial. Bustillo insisted that the consulate could have helped him locate Sirena prior to trial. His habeas petition also argued, as part of a claim of ineffective assistance of counsel, that his attorney should have advised him of his right to notify the Honduran Consulate of his arrest and detention.

The state habeas court dismissed Bustillo's Vienna Convention claim as "procedurally barred" because he had failed to raise the issue at trial or on appeal. The court also denied Bustillo's claim of ineffective assistance of counsel, ruling that his belated claim that counsel should have informed him of his Vienna Convention rights was barred by the applicable statute of limitations and also meritless under *Strickland v. Washington*, 466 U.S. 668 (1984). In an order refusing Bustillo's petition for appeal, the Supreme Court of Virginia found "no reversible error" in the habeas court's dismissal of the Vienna Convention claim. We granted certiorari to consider the Vienna Convention issue.

II

We granted certiorari as to three questions presented in these cases: (1) whether Article 36 of the Vienna Convention grants rights that may be invoked by individuals in a judicial proceeding; (2) whether suppression of evidence is a proper remedy for a violation of Article 36; and (3) whether an Article 36 claim may be deemed forfeited under state procedural rules because a defendant failed to raise the claim at trial.

As a predicate to their claims for relief, Sanchez-Llamas and Bustillo each argue that Article 36 grants them an individually enforceable right to request that their consular officers be notified of their detention, and an accompanying right to be informed by authorities of the availability of consular notification. Respondents and the United States, as *amicus curiae,* strongly dispute this contention. They argue that "there is a presumption that a treaty will be enforced through political and diplomatic channels, rather than through the courts." Because we conclude that Sanchez-Llamas and Bustillo are not in any event entitled to relief on their claims, we find it unnecessary to resolve the question whether the Vienna Convention grants individuals enforceable rights. Therefore, for purposes of addressing petitioners' claims, we assume, without deciding, that Article 36 does grant Bustillo and Sanchez-Llamas such rights.

A

Sanchez-Llamas argues that the trial court was required to suppress his statements to police because authorities never told him of his rights under Article 36. He refrains, however, from arguing that the Vienna Convention itself mandates suppression. We think this a wise concession. The Convention does not prescribe specific remedies for violations of Article 36. Rather, it expressly leaves the implementation of Article 36 to domestic law: Rights under Article 36 are to "be exercised in conformity with the laws and regulations of the receiving State." Art. 36(2). As far as the text of the Convention is concerned, the question of the availability of the exclusionary rule for Article 36 violations is a matter of domestic law. . . .

For good reason then, Sanchez-Llamas argues only that suppression is required because it is the appropriate remedy for an Article 36 violation under United States law, and urges us to require suppression for Article 36 violations as a matter of our "authority to develop remedies for the enforcement of federal law in state-court criminal proceedings."

For their part, the State of Oregon and the United States, as *amicus curiae,* contend that we lack any such authority over state-court proceedings. They argue that our cases suppressing evidence obtained in violation of federal statutes are grounded in our supervisory authority over the federal courts – an authority that does not extend to state-court proceedings. Unless required to do so by the Convention itself, they argue, we cannot direct Oregon courts to exclude Sanchez-Llamas' statements from his criminal trial.

To the extent Sanchez-Llamas argues that we should invoke our supervisory authority, the law is clear: "It is beyond dispute that we do not hold a supervisory power over the courts of the several States." The cases on which Sanchez-Llamas principally relies are inapplicable in light of the limited reach of our supervisory powers. *Mallory* and *McNabb* plainly rest on our supervisory authority. And while *Miller* is not clear about its authority for requiring suppression, we have understood it to have a similar basis.

We also agree with the State of Oregon and the United States that our authority to create a judicial remedy applicable in state court must lie, if anywhere, in the treaty itself. Under the Constitution, the President has the power, "by and with the Advice and Consent of the Senate, to make Treaties." The United States ratified the Convention with the expectation that it would be interpreted according to its terms. If we were to require suppression for Article 36 violations without some authority in the Convention, we would in effect be supplementing those terms by enlarging the obligations of the United States under the Convention. This is entirely inconsistent with the judicial function.

Of course, it is well established that a self-executing treaty binds the States pursuant to the Supremacy Clause, and that the States therefore must recognize the force of the treaty in the course of adjudicating the rights of litigants. And where a treaty provides for a particular judicial remedy, there is no issue of intruding on the constitutional prerogatives of the States or the other federal branches. Courts must apply the remedy as a requirement of federal law. But where a treaty does not provide a particular remedy, either expressly or implicitly, it is not for the federal courts to impose one on the States through lawmaking of their own.

Sanchez-Llamas argues that the language of the Convention implicitly requires a judicial remedy because it states that the laws and regulations governing the exercise of Article 36 rights "must enable *full effect* to be given to the purposes for which the rights . . . are intended," Art. 36(2). In his view, although "full effect" may not automatically require an exclusionary rule, it does require an appropriate judicial remedy of *some* kind. There is reason to doubt this interpretation. In particular, there is little indication that other parties to the Convention have interpreted Article 36 to require a judicial remedy in the context of criminal prosecutions.

Nevertheless, even if Sanchez-Llamas is correct that Article 36 implicitly requires a judicial remedy, the Convention equally states that Article 36 rights "shall be exercised in conformity with the laws and regulations of the receiving State." Art. 36(2). Under our domestic law, the exclusionary rule is not a remedy we apply lightly. "[O]ur cases have repeatedly emphasized that the rule's 'costly toll' upon truth-seeking and law enforcement objectives presents a high obstacle for those urging application of the rule." Because the rule's social costs are considerable, suppression is warranted only where the rule's "remedial objectives are thought most efficaciously served."

We have applied the exclusionary rule primarily to deter constitutional violations. In particular, we have ruled that the Constitution requires the exclusion of evidence obtained by certain violations of the Fourth Amendment, and confessions exacted by police in violation of the right against compelled self-incrimination or due process.

The few cases in which we have suppressed evidence for statutory violations do not help Sanchez-Llamas. In those cases, the excluded evidence arose directly out of statutory violations that implicated important Fourth and Fifth Amendment interests. *McNabb*, for example, involved the suppression of incriminating statements obtained during a prolonged detention of the defendants, in violation of a statute requiring persons arrested without a warrant to be promptly presented to a judicial officer. We noted that the statutory right was intended to "avoid all the evil implications of secret interrogation of persons accused of crime," and later stated that *McNabb* was "responsive to the same considerations of Fifth Amendment policy that . . . face[d] us . . . as to the states" in *Miranda*. Similarly, in *Miller,* we required suppression of evidence that was the product of a search incident to an unlawful arrest.

The violation of the right to consular notification, in contrast, is at best remotely connected to the gathering of evidence. Article 36 has nothing whatsoever to do with searches or interrogations. Indeed, Article 36 does not guarantee defendants *any* assistance at all. The provision secures only a right of foreign nationals to have their consulate *informed* of their arrest or detention – not to have their consulate intervene, or to have law enforcement authorities cease their investigation pending any such notice or intervention. In most circumstances, there is likely to be little connection between an Article 36 violation and evidence or statements obtained by police.

Moreover, the reasons we often require suppression for Fourth and Fifth Amendment violations are entirely absent from the consular notification context. We require exclusion of coerced confessions both because we disapprove of such coercion and because such confessions tend to be unreliable. We exclude the fruits of unreasonable searches on the theory that without a strong deterrent, the constraints of the Fourth Amendment might be too easily disregarded by law enforcement. The situation here is quite different. The failure to inform a defendant of his Article 36 rights is unlikely, with any frequency, to produce unreliable confessions. And unlike the search-and-seizure context – where the need to obtain valuable evidence may tempt authorities to transgress Fourth Amendment limitations – police win little, if any, practical advantage from violating Article 36. Suppression would be a vastly disproportionate remedy for an Article 36 violation.

Sanchez-Llamas counters that the failure to inform defendants of their right to consular notification gives them "a misleadingly incomplete picture of [their] legal options," and that suppression will give authorities an incentive to abide by Article 36.

Leaving aside the suggestion that it is the role of police generally to advise defendants of their legal options, we think other constitutional and statutory requirements effectively protect the interests served, in Sanchez-Llamas' view, by Article 36. A foreign national detained on suspicion of crime, like anyone else in our country, enjoys under our system the protections of the Due Process Clause. Among other things, he is entitled to an attorney, and is protected against compelled self-incrimination. Article 36 adds little to these "legal options," and we think it unnecessary to apply the exclusionary rule where other constitutional and statutory protections – many of them already enforced by the exclusionary rule – safeguard the same interests Sanchez-Llamas claims are advanced by Article 36.

Finally, suppression is not the only means of vindicating Vienna Convention rights. A defendant can raise an Article 36 claim as part of a broader challenge to the voluntariness of his statements to police. If he raises an Article 36 violation at trial, a court can make appropriate accommodations to ensure that the defendant secures, to the extent possible, the benefits of consular assistance. Of course, diplomatic avenues – the primary means of enforcing the Convention – also remain open.

In sum, neither the Vienna Convention itself nor our precedents applying the exclusionary rule support suppression of Sanchez-Llamas' statements to police.

B

The Virginia courts denied petitioner Bustillo's Article 36 claim on the ground that he failed to raise it at trial or on direct appeal. The general rule in federal habeas cases is that a defendant who fails to raise a claim on direct appeal is barred from raising the claim on collateral review. There is an exception if a defendant can demonstrate both "cause" for not raising the claim at trial, and "prejudice" from not having done so. Like many States, Virginia applies a similar rule in state postconviction proceedings, and did so here to bar Bustillo's Vienna Convention claim. Normally, in our review of state-court judgments, such rules constitute an adequate and independent state-law ground preventing us from reviewing the federal claim. Bustillo contends, however, that state procedural default rules cannot apply to Article 36 claims. He argues that the Convention requires that Article 36 rights be given " full effect " and that Virginia's procedural default rules "prevented any effect (much less 'full effect') from being given to" those rights.

This is not the first time we have been asked to set aside procedural default rules for a Vienna Convention claim. Respondent Johnson and the United States persuasively argue that this question is controlled by our decision in *Breard v. Greene,* 523 U.S. 371 (1998) (*per curiam*). In *Breard*, the petitioner failed to raise an Article 36 claim in state court – at trial or on collateral review – and then sought to have the claim heard in a subsequent federal habeas proceeding. He argued that "the Convention is the 'supreme law of the land' and thus trumps the procedural default doctrine." We rejected this argument as "plainly incorrect," for two reasons. First, we observed, "it has been recognized in international law that, absent a clear and express statement to the contrary, the procedural rules of the forum State govern the implementation of the treaty in that State." Furthermore, we reasoned that while treaty protections such as Article 36 may constitute supreme federal law, this is "no less true of provisions of the Constitution itself, to which rules of procedural default apply." In light of *Breard*'s holding, Bustillo faces an uphill task in arguing that the Convention requires States to set aside their procedural default rules for Article 36 claims.

Bustillo offers two reasons why *Breard* does not control his case. He first argues that *Breard*'s holding concerning procedural default was "unnecessary to the result," because the petitioner there could not demonstrate prejudice from the default and because, in any event, a subsequent federal statute – the Antiterrorism and Effective Death Penalty Act of 1996, – superseded any right the petitioner had under the Vienna Convention to have his claim heard on collateral review. We find Bustillo's contention unpersuasive. Our resolution of the procedural default question in *Breard* was the principal reason for the denial of the petitioner's claim, and the discussion of the issue occupied the bulk of our reasoning. It is no answer to argue, as Bustillo does, that the holding in *Breard* was "unnecessary" simply because the petitioner in that case had several ways to lose.

Bustillo's second reason is less easily dismissed. He argues that since *Breard*, the ICJ has interpreted the Vienna Convention to preclude the application of procedural default rules to Article 36 claims. The *LaGrand Case (F.R. G.v.U. S.),* 2001 I.C.J. 466 (Judgment of June 27) (*LaGrand*), and the *Case Concerning Avena and other Mexican Nationals (Mex.v.U.S.),* 2004 I.C.J. No. 128 (Judgment of Mar. 31) (*Avena*), were brought before the ICJ by the governments of Germany and Mexico, respectively, on behalf of several of their nationals facing death sentences in the United States. The foreign governments claimed that their nationals had not been informed of their right to consular notification. They further argued that application of the procedural default rule to their nationals' Vienna Convention claims failed to give "full effect" to the purposes of the Convention, as required by Article 36. The ICJ agreed, explaining that the defendants had procedurally defaulted their claims "because of the failure of the American authorities to comply with their obligation under Article 36." Application of the procedural default rule in such circumstances, the ICJ reasoned, "prevented [courts] from attaching any legal significance" to the fact that the violation of Article 36 kept the foreign governments from assisting in their nationals' defense.

Bustillo argues that *LaGrand* and *Avena* warrant revisiting the procedural default holding of *Breard*. In a similar vein, several *amici* contend that "the United States is *obligated* to comply with the Convention, *as interpreted by the ICJ*." We disagree. Although the ICJ's interpretation deserves "respectful consideration," we conclude that it does not compel us to reconsider our understanding of the Convention in *Breard*.

Under our Constitution, "[t]he judicial Power of the United States" is "vested in one supreme Court, and in such inferior Courts as the Congress may from time to time ordain and establish." Art. III, § 1. That "judicial Power . . . extend[s] to . . . Treaties." *Id., § 2. And, as Chief Justice Marshall famously explained, that judicial power includes the duty "to say what the law is." *Marbury v. Madison,* 1 Cranch 137 (1803). If treaties are to be given effect as federal law under our legal system, determining their meaning as a matter of federal law "is emphatically the province and duty of the judicial department," headed by the "one supreme Court" established by the Constitution. It is against this background that the United States ratified, and the Senate gave its advice and consent to, the various agreements that govern referral of Vienna Convention disputes to the ICJ.

Nothing in the structure or purpose of the ICJ suggests that its interpretations were intended to be conclusive on our courts. The ICJ's decisions have " *no binding force* except between the parties and in respect of that particular case," Statute of the International Court of Justice, Art. 59, 59 Stat. 1062, T.S. No. 993 (1945) (emphasis added). Any interpretation of law the ICJ renders in the course of resolving particular disputes is thus not binding precedent *even as to the ICJ itself;* there is accordingly little reason to think that such interpretations were intended to be controlling on our courts. The ICJ's principal purpose is to arbitrate particular disputes between national governments. ("Only states [*i.e.,* countries] may be parties in cases before the Court"). While each member of the United Nations has agreed to comply with decisions of the ICJ "in any case to which it is a party," United Nations Charter, Art. the Charter's procedure for noncompliance – referral to the Security Council by the aggrieved state – contemplates quintessentially *international* remedies, Art. 94(2).

In addition, "[w]hile courts interpret treaties for themselves, the meaning given them by the departments of government particularly charged with their negotiation and enforcement is given great weight." *Kolovrat v. Oregon,* 366 U.S. 187, 194 (1961). Although the United States has agreed to "discharge its international obligations" in having state courts give effect to the decision in *Avena,* it has not taken the view that the ICJ's interpretation of Article 36 is binding on our courts. Moreover, shortly after *Avena,* the United States withdrew from the Optional Protocol concerning Vienna Convention disputes. Whatever the effect of *Avena* and *LaGrand* before this withdrawal, it is doubtful that our courts should give decisive weight to the interpretation of a tribunal whose jurisdiction in this area is no longer recognized by the United States.

LaGrand and *Avena* are therefore entitled only to the "respectful consideration" due an interpretation of an international agreement by an international court. Even according such consideration, the ICJ's interpretation cannot overcome the plain import of Article 36. As we explained in *Breard,* the procedural rules of domestic law generally govern the implementation of an international treaty. In addition, Article 36 makes clear that the rights it provides "shall be exercised in conformity with the laws and regulations of the receiving State" provided that "full effect . . . be given to the purposes for which the rights accorded under this Article are intended." Art. 36(2). In the United States, this means that the rule of procedural default – which applies even to claimed violations of our Constitution – applies also to Vienna Convention claims. Bustillo points to nothing in the drafting history of Article 36 or in the contemporary practice of other signatories that undermines this conclusion.

The ICJ concluded that where a defendant was not notified of his rights under Article 36, application of the procedural default rule failed to give "full effect" to the purposes of Article 36 because it prevented courts from attaching "legal significance" to the Article 36 violation. This reasoning overlooks the importance of procedural default rules in an adversary system, which relies chiefly on the *parties* to raise significant issues and present them to the courts in the appropriate manner at the appropriate time for adjudication. Procedural default rules are designed to encourage parties to raise their claims promptly and to vindicate "the law's important interest in the finality of judgments." The consequence of failing to raise a claim for adjudication at the proper time is generally forfeiture of that claim. As a result, rules such as procedural default routinely deny "legal significance" – in the *Avena* and *LaGrand* sense – to otherwise viable legal claims.

Procedural default rules generally take on greater importance in an adversary system such as ours than in the sort of magistrate-directed, inquisitorial legal system characteristic of many of the other countries that are signatories to the Vienna Convention. "What makes a system adversarial rather than inquisitorial is . . . the presence of a judge who does not (as an inquisitor does) conduct the factual and legal investigation himself, but instead decides on the basis of facts and arguments pro and con adduced by the parties." In an inquisitorial system, the failure to raise a legal error can in part be attributed to the magistrate, and thus to the state itself. In our system, however, the responsibility for failing to raise an issue generally rests with the parties themselves.

The ICJ's interpretation of Article 36 is inconsistent with the basic framework of an adversary system. Under the ICJ's reading of "full effect," Article 36 claims could trump not only procedural default rules, but any number of other rules requiring parties to present their legal claims at the appropriate time for adjudication. If the State's failure to inform the defendant of his Article 36 rights generally excuses the defendant's failure to comply with relevant procedural rules, then presumably rules such as statutes of limitations and prohibitions against filing successive habeas petitions must also yield in the face of Article 36 claims. This sweeps too broadly, for it reads the "full effect" proviso in a way that leaves little room for

Article 36's clear instruction that Article 36 rights "shall be exercised in conformity with the laws and regulations of the receiving State."

Much as Sanchez-Llamas cannot show that suppression is an appropriate remedy for Article 36 violations under domestic law principles, so too Bustillo cannot show that normally applicable procedural default rules should be suspended in light of the type of right he claims. In this regard, a comparison of Article 36 and a suspect's rights under *Miranda* disposes of Bustillo's claim. Bustillo contends that applying procedural default rules to Article 36 rights denies such rights "full effect" because the violation itself – *i.e.,* the failure to inform defendants of their right to consular notification – prevents them from becoming aware of their Article 36 rights and asserting them at trial. Of course, precisely the same thing is true of rights under *Miranda*. Police are required to advise suspects that they have a right to remain silent and a right to an attorney. If police do not give such warnings, and counsel fails to object, it is equally true that a suspect may not be "aware he even *had* such rights until well after his trial had concluded." Nevertheless, it is well established that where a defendant fails to raise a *Miranda* claim at trial, procedural default rules may bar him from raising the claim in a subsequent postconviction proceeding.

Bustillo responds that an Article 36 claim more closely resembles a claim, under *Brady v. Maryland,* 373 U.S. 83 (1963), that the prosecution failed to disclose exculpatory evidence – a type of claim that often can be asserted for the first time only in postconviction proceedings. The analogy is inapt. In the case of a *Brady* claim, it is impossible for the defendant to know as a *factual* matter that a violation has occurred before the exculpatory evidence is disclosed. By contrast, a defendant is well aware of the fact that he was not informed of his Article 36 rights, even if the *legal* significance of that fact eludes him.

Finally, relying on *Massaro v. United States,* 538 U.S. 500, Bustillo argues that Article 36 claims "are most appropriately raised post-trial or on collateral review." *Massaro* held that claims of ineffective assistance of counsel may be raised for the first time in a proceeding under 28 U.S.C. § 2255. That decision, however, involved the question of the proper forum for *federal* habeas claims. Bustillo, by contrast, asks us to require the *States* to hear Vienna Convention claims raised for the first time in *state* postconviction proceedings. Given that the Convention itself imposes no such requirement, we do not perceive any grounds for us to revise state procedural rules in this fashion.

We therefore conclude, as we did in *Breard,* that claims under Article 36 of the Vienna Convention may be subjected to the same procedural default rules that apply generally to other federal-law claims. . . .

Although these cases involve the delicate question of the application of an international treaty, the issues in many ways turn on established principles of domestic law. Our holding in no way disparages the importance of the Vienna Convention. The relief petitioners request is, by any measure, extraordinary. Sanchez-Llamas seeks a suppression remedy for an asserted right with little if any connection to the gathering of evidence; Bustillo requests an exception to procedural rules that is accorded to almost no other right, including many of our most fundamental constitutional protections. It is no slight to the Convention to deny petitioners' claims under the same principles we would apply to an Act of Congress, or to the Constitution itself.

The judgments of the Supreme Court of Oregon and the Supreme Court of Virginia are affirmed.

Medellin v. Texas
128 S.Ct. 1346 (2008)

Chief Justice ROBERTS delivered the opinion of the Court.

The International Court of Justice (ICJ), located in the Hague, is a tribunal established pursuant to the United Nations Charter to adjudicate disputes between member states. *In the Case Concerning Avena and Other Mexican Nationals* (Mex.v.U.S.), 2004 I.C.J. 12 (Judgment of Mar. 31) (*Avena*), that tribunal considered a claim brought by Mexico against the United States. The ICJ held that, based on violations of the Vienna Convention, 51 named Mexican nationals were entitled to review and reconsideration of their state-court convictions and sentences in the United States. This was so regardless of any forfeiture of the right to raise Vienna Convention claims because of a failure to comply with generally applicable state rules governing challenges to criminal convictions.

In *Sanchez-Llamas v. Oregon*, 548 U.S. 331 (2006) – issued after *Avena* but involving individuals who were not named in the *Avena* judgment – we held that, contrary to the ICJ's determination, the Vienna Convention did not preclude the application of state default rules. After the *Avena* decision, President George W. Bush determined, through a Memorandum to the Attorney General (Feb. 28, 2005), that the United States would "discharge its international obligations" under *Avena* "by having State courts give effect to the decision."

Petitioner José Ernesto Medellín, who had been convicted and sentenced in Texas state court for murder, is one of the 51 Mexican nationals named in the *Avena* decision. Relying on the ICJ's decision and the President's Memorandum, Medellín filed an application for a writ of habeas corpus in state court. The Texas Court of Criminal Appeals dismissed Medellín's application as an abuse of the writ under state law, given Medellín's failure to raise his Vienna Convention claim in a timely manner under state law. We granted certiorari to decide two questions. First, is the ICJ's judgment in *Avena* directly enforceable as domestic law in a state court in the United States? Second, does the President's Memorandum independently require the States to provide review and reconsideration of the claims of the 51 Mexican nationals named in Avena without regard to state procedural default rules? We conclude that neither

Avena nor the President's Memorandum constitutes directly enforceable federal law that pre-empts state limitations on the filing of successive habeas petitions. We therefore affirm the decision below.

I

A

In 1969, the United States, upon the advice and consent of the Senate, ratified the Vienna Convention on Consular Relations (Vienna Convention or Convention), and the Optional Protocol Concerning the Compulsory Settlement of Disputes to the Vienna Convention. . . . Article 36 of the Convention was drafted to "facilitat [e] the exercise of consular functions." It provides that if a person detained by a foreign country "so requests, the competent authorities of the receiving State shall, without delay, inform the consular post of the sending State" of such detention, and "inform the [detainee] of his righ[t]" to request assistance from the consul of his own state.

The Optional Protocol provides a venue for the resolution of disputes arising out of the interpretation or application of the Vienna Convention. Under the Protocol, such disputes "shall lie within the compulsory jurisdiction of the International Court of Justice" and "may accordingly be brought before the [ICJ] . . . by any party to the dispute being a Party to the present Protocol."

The ICJ is "the principal judicial organ of the United Nations." It was established in 1945 pursuant to the United Nations Charter. The ICJ Statute-annexed to the U.N. Charter-provides the organizational framework and governing procedures for cases brought before the ICJ. Statute of the International Court of Justice (ICJ Statute). . . .

B

Petitioner José Ernesto Medellín, a Mexican national, has lived in the United States since preschool. A member of the "Black and Whites" gang, Medellín was convicted of capital murder and sentenced to death in Texas for the gang rape and brutal murders of two Houston teenagers. . . .

Medellín was arrested at approximately 4 a.m. on June 29, 1993. A few hours later, between 5:54 and 7:23 a.m., Medellín was given *Miranda* warnings; he then signed a written waiver and gave a detailed written confession. Local law enforcement officers did not, however, inform Medellín of his Vienna Convention right to notify the Mexican consulate of his detention. Medellín was convicted of capital murder and sentenced to death; his conviction and sentence were affirmed on appeal.

Medellín first raised his Vienna Convention claim in his first application for state postconviction relief. The state trial court held that the claim was procedurally defaulted because Medellín had failed to raise it at trial or on direct review. The trial court also rejected the Vienna Convention claim on the merits, finding that Medellín had "fail[ed] to show that any non-notification of the Mexican authorities impacted on the validity of his conviction or punishment." The Texas Court of Criminal Appeals affirmed.

Medellín then filed a habeas petition in Federal District Court. The District Court denied relief, holding that Medellín's Vienna Convention claim was procedurally defaulted and that Medellín had failed to show prejudice arising from the Vienna Convention violation.

While Medellín's application for a certificate of appealability was pending in the Fifth Circuit, the ICJ issued its decision in *Avena*. The ICJ held that the United States had violated Article 36(1)(b) of the Vienna Convention by failing to inform the 51 named Mexican nationals, including Medellín, of their Vienna Convention rights. In the ICJ's determination, the United States was obligated "to provide, by means of its own choosing, review and reconsideration of the convictions and sentences of the [affected] Mexican nationals." The ICJ indicated that such review was required without regard to state procedural default rules. . . .

This Court granted certiorari. *Medellín v. Dretke,* 544 U.S. 660, 661 (2005) (per curiam) (*Medellín I*). Before we heard oral argument, however, President George W. Bush issued his Memorandum to the United States Attorney General, providing:

> I have determined, pursuant to the authority vested in me as President by the Constitution and the laws of the United States of America, that the United States will discharge its international obligations under the decision of the International Court of Justice in [*Avena*], by having State courts give effect to the decision in accordance with general principles of comity in cases filed by the 51 Mexican nationals addressed in that decision.

Medellín, relying on the President's Memorandum and the ICJ's decision in *Avena*, filed a second application for habeas relief in state court. Because the state-court proceedings might have provided Medellín with the review and reconsideration he requested, and because his claim for federal relief might otherwise have been barred, we dismissed his petition for certiorari as improvidently granted.

The Texas Court of Criminal Appeals subsequently dismissed Medellín's second state habeas application as an abuse of the writ. In the court's view, neither the *Avena* decision nor the President's Memorandum was "binding federal law" that could displace the State's limitations on the filing of successive habeas applications. We again granted certiorari.

II

Medellín first contends that the ICJ's judgment in *Avena* constitutes a "binding" obligation on the state and federal courts of the United States. He argues that "by virtue of the Supremacy Clause, the treaties requiring compliance with the *Avena* judgment are already the

'Law of the Land' by which all state and federal courts in this country are 'bound.'" Accordingly, Medellín argues, *Avena* is a binding federal rule of decision that pre-empts contrary state limitations on successive habeas petitions. . . .

D

[After concluding that the treaties and international agreements at issue did not create a binding federal law and after reviewing the text and history of the Optional Protocol, the United Nations Charter, Article 94 of the United Nations Charter, which deals with the effect of ICJ decisions, and the ICJ statute, the Court concluded:] In sum, while the ICJ's judgment in *Avena* creates an international law obligation on the part of the United States, it does not of its own force constitute binding federal law that pre-empts state restrictions on the filing of successive habeas petitions. As we noted in *Sanchez-Llamas*, a contrary conclusion would be extraordinary, given that basic rights guaranteed by our own Constitution do not have the effect of displacing state procedural rules. Nothing in the text, background, negotiating and drafting history, or practice among signatory nations suggests that the President or Senate intended the improbable result of giving the judgments of an international tribunal a higher status than that enjoyed by "many of our most fundamental constitutional protections."

III

Medellín next argues that the ICJ's judgment in *Avena* is binding on state courts by virtue of the President's February 28, 2005 Memorandum. The United States contends that while the *Avena* judgment does not of its own force require domestic courts to set aside ordinary rules of procedural default, that judgment became the law of the land with precisely that effect pursuant to the President's Memorandum and his power "to establish binding rules of decision that preempt contrary state law." Accordingly, we must decide whether the President's declaration alters our conclusion that the *Avena* judgment is not a rule of domestic law binding in state and federal courts.

A

The United States maintains that the President's constitutional role "uniquely qualifies" him to resolve the sensitive foreign policy decisions that bear on compliance with an ICJ decision and "to do so expeditiously." In this case, the President seeks to vindicate United States interests in ensuring the reciprocal observance of the Vienna Convention, protecting relations with foreign governments, and demonstrating commitment to the role of international law. These interests are plainly compelling.

Such considerations, however, do not allow us to set aside first principles. The President's authority to act, as with the exercise of any governmental power, "must stem either from an act of Congress or from the Constitution itself." *Youngstown, supra*, at 585; *Dames & Moore v. Regan*, 453 U.S. 654 (1981).

Justice Jackson's familiar tripartite scheme provides the accepted framework for evaluating executive action in this area. First, "[w]hen the President acts pursuant to an express or implied authorization of Congress, his authority is at its maximum, for it includes all that he possesses in his own right plus all that Congress can delegate." *Youngstown*, 343 U.S., at 635 (Jackson, J., concurring). Second, "[w]hen the President acts in absence of either a congressional grant or denial of authority, he can only rely upon his own independent powers, but there is a zone of twilight in which he and Congress may have concurrent authority, or in which its distribution is uncertain." In this circumstance, Presidential authority can derive support from "congressional inertia, indifference or quiescence." Finally, "[w]hen the President takes measures incompatible with the expressed or implied will of Congress, his power is at its lowest ebb," and the Court can sustain his actions "only by disabling the Congress from acting upon the subject."

B

The United States marshals two principal arguments in favor of the President's authority "to establish binding rules of decision that preempt contrary state law." The Solicitor General first argues that the relevant treaties give the President the authority to implement the *Avena* judgment and that Congress has acquiesced in the exercise of such authority. The United States also relies upon an "independent" international dispute-resolution power wholly apart from the asserted authority based on the pertinent treaties. Medellín adds the additional argument that the President's Memorandum is a valid exercise of his power to take care that the laws be faithfully executed.

1

The United States maintains that the President's Memorandum is authorized by the Optional Protocol and the U.N. Charter. That is, because the relevant treaties "create an obligation to comply with Avena," they "implicitly give the President authority to implement that treaty-based obligation." As a result, the President's Memorandum is well grounded in the first category of the *Youngstown* framework.

We disagree. The President has an array of political and diplomatic means available to enforce international obligations, but unilaterally converting a non-self-executing treaty into a self-executing one is not among them. The responsibility for transforming an international obligation arising from a non-self-executing treaty into domestic law falls to Congress. . . .

. . . At bottom, none of the sources of authority identified by the United States supports the President's claim that Congress has acquiesced in his asserted power to establish on his own federal law or to override state law.

None of this is to say, however, that the combination of a non-self-executing treaty and the lack of implementing legislation precludes the President from acting to comply with an international treaty obligation. It is only to say that the Executive cannot unilaterally execute a non-self-executing treaty by giving it domestic effect. That is, the non-self-executing character of a treaty constrains the President's ability to comply with treaty commitments by unilaterally making the treaty binding on domestic courts. The President may comply with the treaty's obligations by some other means, so long as they are consistent with the Constitution. But he may not rely upon a non-self-executing treaty to "establish binding rules of decision that preempt contrary state law."

Note

Despite pleas from the White House and the State Department, and notwithstanding an International Court of Justice order to review their cases, Texas announced plans to go forward with the executions of the five Mexican nationals on Texas' death row. Jose Ernesto Medellin, convicted of the 1993 rape and murder of two teenage girls, was scheduled to die by lethal injection on August 5, 2008. State Department officials expressed concern that the execution of the five convicted murderers could hamper the ability of the United States to assist Americans accused of crimes abroad. McKinley, "Texas Turns Aside Pressure on Execution of 5 Mexicans," New York Times (July 18, 2008).

SELECTED STATUTES

PART I. FEDERAL HABEAS CORPUS

Statutes and Rules

A. Federal Habeas Corpus Statutes As Amended By The Anti-Terrorism and Effective Death Penalty Act of 1996

28 U.S.C. § 2241. *Power to grant writ*

(a) Writs of habeas corpus may be granted by the Supreme Court, any justice thereof, the district courts and any circuit judge within their respective jurisdictions. The order of a circuit judge shall be entered in the records of the district court of the district wherein the restraint complained of is had.

(b) The Supreme Court, any justice thereof, and any circuit judge may decline to entertain an application for a writ of habeas corpus and may transfer the application for hearing and determination to the district court having jurisdiction to entertain it.

(c) The writ of habeas corpus shall not extend to a prisoner unless–

(1) He is in custody under or by color of the authority of the United States or is committed for trial before some court thereof; or

(2) He is in custody for an act done or omitted in pursuance of an Act of Congress, or an order, process, judgment or decree of a court or judge of the United States; or

(3) He is in custody in violation of the Constitution or laws or treaties of the United States; or

(4) He, being a citizen of a foreign state and domiciled therein is in custody for an act done or omitted under any alleged right, title, authority, privilege, protection, or exemption claimed under the commission, order or sanction of any foreign state, or under color thereof, the validity and effect of which depend upon the law of nations; or

(5) It is necessary to bring him into court to testify or for trial.

(d) Where an application for a writ of habeas corpus is made by a person in custody under the judgment and sentence of a State court of a State which contains two or more Federal judicial districts, the application may be filed in the district court for the district wherein such person is in custody or in the district court for the district within which the State court was held which convicted and sentenced him and each of such district courts shall have concurrent jurisdiction to entertain the application. The district court for the district wherein such an application is filed in the exercise of its discretion and in furtherance of justice may transfer the application to the other district court for hearing and determination.

(e)(1) No court, justice, or judge shall have jurisdiction to hear or consider an application for a writ of habeas corpus filed by or on behalf of an alien detained by the United States who has been determined by the United States to have been properly detained as an enemy combatant or is awaiting such determination.

(2) Except as provided in paragraphs (2) and (3) of section 1005(e) of the Detainee Treatment Act of 2005 (10 U.S.C. 801 note), no court, justice, or judge shall have jurisdiction to hear or consider any other action against the United States or its agents relating to any aspect of the detention, transfer, treatment, trial, or conditions of confinement of an alien who is or was detained by the United States and has been determined by the United States to have been properly detained as an enemy combatant or is awaiting such determination.

28 U.S.C. § 2242. *Application*
Application for a writ of habeas corpus shall be in writing signed and verified by the person for whose relief it is intended or by someone acting in his behalf.

It shall allege the facts concerning the applicant's commitment or detention, the name of the person who has custody over him and by virtue of what claim or authority, if known.

It may be amended or supplemented as provided in the rules of procedure applicable to civil actions.

If addressed to the Supreme Court, a justice thereof or a circuit judge it shall state the reasons for not making application to the district court of the district in which the applicant is held.

28 U.S.C. § 2243. *Issuance of writ; return; hearing; decision*
A court, justice or judge entertaining an application for a writ of habeas corpus shall forthwith award the writ or issue an order directing the respondent to show cause why the writ should not be granted, unless it appears from the application that the applicant or person detained is not entitled thereto.

The writ, or order to show cause shall be directed to the person having custody of the person detained. It shall be returned within three days unless for good cause additional time, not exceeding twenty days, is allowed.

The person to whom the writ or order is directed shall make a return certifying the true cause of the detention.

When the writ or order is returned a day shall be set for hearing, not more than five days after the return unless for good cause additional time is allowed.

Unless the application for the writ and the return present only issues of law the person to whom the writ is directed shall be required to produce at the hearing the body of the person detained.

The applicant or the person detained may, under oath, deny any of the facts set forth in the return or allege any other material facts.

The return and all suggestions made against it may be amended, by leave of court, before or after being filed.

The court shall summarily hear and determine the facts, and dispose of the matter as law and justice require.

28 U.S.C. § 2244. *Finality of determination*

(a) No circuit or district judge shall be required to entertain an application for a writ of habeas corpus to inquire into the detention of a person pursuant to a judgment of a court of the United States if it appears that the legality of such detention has been determined by a judge or court of the United States on a prior application for a writ of habeas corpus, except as provided in section 2255.

(b)(1) A claim presented in a second or successive habeas corpus application under section 2254 that was presented in a prior application shall be dismissed.

(2) A claim presented in a second or successive habeas corpus application under section 2254 that was not presented in a prior application shall be dismissed unless–

(A) the applicant shows that the claim relies on a new rule of constitutional law, made retroactive to cases on collateral review by the Supreme Court, that was previously unavailable; or

(B)(i) the factual predicate for the claim could not have been discovered previously through the exercise of due diligence; and

(ii) the facts underlying the claim, if proven and viewed in light of the evidence as a whole, would be sufficient to establish by clear and convincing evidence that, but for constitutional error, no reasonable factfinder would have found the applicant guilty of the underlying offense.

(3)(A) Before a second or successive application permitted by this section is filed in the district court, the applicant shall move in the appropriate court of appeals for an order authorizing the district court to consider the application.

(B) A motion in the court of appeals for an order authorizing the district court to consider a second or successive application shall be determined by a three-judge panel of the court of appeals.

(C) The court of appeals may authorize the filing of a second or successive application only if it determines that the application makes a prima facie showing that the application satisfies the requirements of this subsection.

(D) The court of appeals shall grant or deny the authorization to file a second or successive application not later than 30 days after the filing of the motion.

(E) The grant or denial of an authorization by a court of appeals to file a second or successive application shall not be appealable and shall not be the subject of a petition for rehearing or for a writ of certiorari.

(4) A district court shall dismiss any claim presented in a second or successive application that the court of appeals has authorized to be filed unless the applicant shows that the claim satisfies the requirements of this section.

(c) In a habeas corpus proceeding brought in behalf of a person in custody pursuant to the judgment of a State court, a prior judgment of the Supreme Court of the United States on an appeal or review by a writ of certiorari at the instance of the prisoner of the decision of such State court, shall be conclusive as to all issues of fact or law with respect to an asserted denial of a Federal right which constitutes ground for discharge in a habeas corpus proceeding, actually adjudicated by the Supreme Court therein, unless the applicant for the writ of habeas corpus shall plead and the court shall find the existence of a material and controlling fact which did not appear in the record of the proceeding in the Supreme Court and the court shall further find that the applicant for the writ of habeas corpus could not have caused such fact to appear in such record by the exercise of reasonable diligence.

(d)(1) A 1-year period of limitation shall apply to an application for a writ of habeas corpus by a person in custody pursuant to the judgment of a State court. The limitation period shall run from the latest of–

(A) the date on which the judgment became final by the conclusion of direct review or the expiration of the time for seeking such review;

(B) the date on which the impediment to filing an application created by State action in violation of the Constitution or laws of the United States is removed, if the applicant was prevented from filing by such State action;

(C) the date on which the constitutional right asserted was initially recognized by the Supreme Court, if the right has been newly recognized by the Supreme Court and made retroactively applicable to cases on collateral review; or

(D) the date on which the factual predicate of the claim or claims presented could have been discovered through the exercise of due diligence.

(2) The time during which a properly filed application for State post- conviction or other collateral review with respect to the pertinent judgment or claim is pending shall not be counted toward any period of limitation under this subsection.

28 U.S.C. § 2245. *Certificate of trial judge admissible in evidence*

On the hearing of an application for a writ of habeas corpus to inquire into the legality of the detention of a person pursuant to a judgment the certificate of the judge who presided at the trial resulting in the judgment, setting forth the facts occurring at the trial, shall be admissible in evidence. Copies of the certificate shall be filed with the court in which the application is pending and in the court in which the trial took place.

28 U.S.C. § 2246. *Evidence; depositions; affidavits*

On application for a writ of habeas corpus, evidence may be taken orally or by deposition, or, in the discretion of the judge, by affidavit. If affidavits are admitted any party shall have the right to propound written interrogatories to the affiants, or to file answering affidavits.

28 U.S.C. § 2247. *Documentary evidence*

On application for a writ of habeas corpus documentary evidence, transcripts of proceedings upon arraignment, plea and sentence and a transcript of the oral testimony introduced on any previous similar application by or in behalf of the same petitioner, shall be admissible in evidence.

28 U.S.C. § 2248. *Return or answer; conclusiveness*

The allegations of a return to the writ of habeas corpus or of an answer to an order to show cause in a habeas corpus proceeding, if not traversed, shall be accepted as true except to the extent that the judge finds from the evidence that they are not true.

28 U.S.C. § 2249. *Certified copies of indictment, plea and judgment; duty of respondent*

On application for a writ of habeas corpus to inquire into the detention of any person pursuant to a judgment of a court of the United States, the respondent shall promptly file with the court certified copies of the indictment, plea of petitioner and the judgment, or such of them as may be material to the questions raised, if the petitioner fails to attach them to his petition, and same shall be attached to the return to the writ, or to the answer to the order to show cause.

28 U.S.C. § 2250. *Indigent petitioner entitled to documents without cost*

If on any application for a writ of habeas corpus an order has been made permitting the petitioner to prosecute the application in forma pauperis, the clerk of any court of the United States shall furnish to the petitioner without cost certified copies of such documents or parts of the record on file in his office as may be required by order of the judge before whom the application is pending.

28 U.S.C. § 2251. *Stay of State court proceedings*

(a) In general.–

(1) Pending matters.– A justice or judge of the United States before whom a habeas corpus proceeding is pending, may, before final judgment or after final judgment of discharge, or pending appeal, stay any proceeding against the person detained in any State court or by or under the authority of any State for any matter involved in the habeas corpus proceeding.

(2) Matter not pending.– For purposes of this section, a habeas corpus proceeding is not pending until the application is filed.

(3) Application for appointment of counsel.– If a State prisoner sentenced to death applies for appointment of counsel pursuant to section 3599(a)(2) of title 18 in a court that would have jurisdiction to entertain a habeas corpus application regarding that sentence, that court may stay execution of the sentence of death, but such stay shall terminate not later than 90 days after counsel is appointed or the application for appointment of counsel is withdrawn or denied.

(b) No further proceedings.– After the granting of such a stay, any such proceeding in any State court or by or under the authority of any State shall be void. If no stay is granted, any such proceeding shall be as valid as if no habeas corpus proceedings or appeal were pending.

28 U.S.C. § 2252. *Notice*

Prior to the hearing of a habeas corpus proceeding in behalf of a person in custody of State officers or by virtue of State laws notice shall be served on the attorney general or other appropriate officer of such State as the justice or judge at the time of issuing the writ shall direct.

28 U.S.C. § 2253. *Appeal*

(a) In a habeas corpus proceeding or a proceeding under section 2255 before a district judge, the final order shall be subject to review, on appeal, by the court of appeals for the circuit in which the proceeding is held.

(b) There shall be no right of appeal from a final order in a proceeding to test the validity of a warrant to remove to another district or place for commitment or trial a person charged with a criminal offense against the United States, or to test the validity of such person's detention pending removal proceedings.

(c)(1) Unless a circuit justice or judge issues a certificate of appealability, an appeal may not be taken to the court of appeals from–

(A) the final order in a habeas corpus proceeding in which the detention complained of arises out of process issued by a State court; or

(B) the final order in a proceeding under section 2255.

(2) A certificate of appealability may issue under paragraph (1) only if the applicant has made a substantial showing of the denial of a constitutional right.

(3) The certificate of appealability under paragraph (1) shall indicate which specific issue or issues satisfy the showing required by paragraph (2).

28 U.S.C. § 2254. *State custody; remedies in Federal courts*

(a) The Supreme Court, a Justice thereof, a circuit judge, or a district court shall entertain an application for a writ of habeas corpus in behalf of a person in custody pursuant to the judgment of a State court only on the ground that he is in custody in violation of the Constitution or laws or treaties of the United States.

(b)(1) An application for a writ of habeas corpus on behalf of a person in custody pursuant to the judgment of a State court shall not be granted unless it appears that–

(A) the applicant has exhausted the remedies available in the courts of the State; or

(B)(i) there is an absence of available State corrective process; or

(ii) circumstances exist that render such process ineffective to protect the rights of the applicant.

161

(2) An application for a writ of habeas corpus may be denied on the merits, notwithstanding the failure of the applicant to exhaust the remedies available in the courts of the State.

(3) A State shall not be deemed to have waived the exhaustion requirement or be estopped from reliance upon the requirement unless the State, through counsel, expressly waives the requirement.

(c) An applicant shall not be deemed to have exhausted the remedies available in the courts of the State, within the meaning of this section, if he has the right under the law of the State to raise, by any available procedure, the question presented.

(d) An application for a writ of habeas corpus on behalf of a person in custody pursuant to the judgment of a State court shall not be granted with respect to any claim that was adjudicated on the merits in State court proceedings unless the adjudication of the claim–

(1) resulted in a decision that was contrary to, or involved an unreasonable application of, clearly established Federal law, as determined by the Supreme Court of the United States; or

(2) resulted in a decision that was based on an unreasonable determination of the facts in light of the evidence presented in the State court proceeding.

(e)(1) In a proceeding instituted by an application for a writ of habeas corpus by a person in custody pursuant to the judgment of a State court, a determination of a factual issue made by a State court shall be presumed to be correct. The applicant shall have the burden of rebutting the presumption of correctness by clear and convincing evidence.

(2) If the applicant has failed to develop the factual basis of a claim in State court proceedings, the court shall not hold an evidentiary hearing on the claim unless the applicant shows that–

(A) the claim relies on–

(i) a new rule of constitutional law, made retroactive to cases on collateral review by the Supreme Court, that was previously unavailable; or

(ii) a factual predicate that could not have been previously discovered through the exercise of due diligence; and

(B) the facts underlying the claim would be sufficient to establish by clear and convincing evidence that but for constitutional error, no reasonable factfinder would have found the applicant guilty of the underlying offense.

(f) If the applicant challenges the sufficiency of the evidence adduced in such State court proceeding to support the State court's determination of a factual issue made therein, the applicant, if able, shall produce that part of the record pertinent to a determination of the sufficiency of the evidence to support such determination. If the applicant, because of indigency or other reason is unable to produce such part of the record, then the State shall produce such part of the record and the Federal court shall direct the State to do so by order directed to an appropriate State official. If the State cannot provide such pertinent part of the record, then the court shall determine under the existing facts and circumstances what weight shall be given to the State court's factual determination.

(g) A copy of the official records of the State court, duly certified by the clerk of such court to be a true and correct copy of a finding, judicial opinion, or other reliable written indicia showing such a factual determination by the State court shall be admissible in the Federal court proceeding.

(h) Except as provided in section 408 of the Controlled Substances Act, in all proceedings brought under this section, and any subsequent proceedings on review, the court may appoint counsel for an applicant who is or becomes financially unable to afford counsel, except as provided by a rule promulgated by the Supreme Court pursuant to statutory authority. Appointment of counsel under this section shall be governed by section 3006A of title 18.

(i) The ineffectiveness or incompetence of counsel during Federal or State collateral post-conviction proceedings shall not be a ground for relief in a proceeding arising under section 2254.

28 U.S.C. § 2255. *Federal custody; remedies on motion attacking sentence*
A prisoner in custody under sentence of a court established by Act of Congress claiming the right to be released upon the ground that the sentence was imposed in violation of the Constitution or laws of the United States, or that the court was without jurisdiction to impose such sentence, or that the sentence was in excess of the maximum authorized by law, or is otherwise subject to collateral attack, may move the court which imposed the sentence to vacate, set aside or correct the sentence.

Unless the motion and the files and records of the case conclusively show that the prisoner is entitled to no relief, the court shall cause notice thereof to be served upon the United States attorney, grant a prompt hearing thereon, determine the issues and make findings of fact and conclusions of law with respect thereto. If the court finds that the judgment was rendered without jurisdiction, or that the sentence imposed was not authorized by law or otherwise open to collateral attack, or that there has been such a denial or infringement of the constitutional rights of the prisoner as to render the judgment vulnerable to collateral attack, the court shall vacate and set the judgment aside and shall discharge the prisoner or resentence him or grant a new trial or correct the sentence as may appear appropriate.

A court may entertain and determine such motion without requiring the production of the prisoner at the hearing.

An appeal may be taken to the court of appeals from the order entered on the motion as from a final judgment on application for a writ of habeas corpus.

An application for a writ of habeas corpus in behalf of a prisoner who is authorized to apply for relief by motion pursuant to this section, shall not be entertained if it appears that the applicant has failed to apply for relief, by motion, to the court which sentenced him, or that such court has denied him relief, unless it also appears that the remedy by motion is inadequate or ineffective to test the legality of his detention.

A 1-year period of limitation shall apply to a motion under this section. The limitation period shall run from the latest of–

(1) the date on which the judgment of conviction becomes final;

(2) the date on which the impediment to making a motion created by governmental action in violation of the Constitution or laws of the United States is removed, if the movant was prevented from making a motion by such governmental action;

(3) the date on which the right asserted was initially recognized by the Supreme Court, if that right has been newly recognized by the Supreme Court and made retroactively applicable to cases on collateral review; or

(4) the date on which the facts supporting the claim or claims presented could have been discovered through the exercise of due diligence.

Except as provided in section 408 of the Controlled Substances Act, in all proceedings brought under this section, and any subsequent proceedings on review, the court may appoint counsel, except as provided by a rule promulgated by the Supreme Court pursuant to statutory authority. Appointment of counsel under this section shall be governed by section 3006A of title 18.

A second or successive motion must be certified as provided in section 2244 by a panel of the appropriate court of appeals to contain–

(1) newly discovered evidence that, if proven and viewed in light of the evidence as a whole, would be sufficient to establish by clear and convincing evidence that no reasonable factfinder would have found the movant guilty of the offense; or

(2) a new rule of constitutional law, made retroactive to cases on collateral review by the Supreme Court, that was previously unavailable.

B. Special Habeas Corpus Procedures in Capital Cases

28 U.S.C. § 2261. *Prisoners in State custody subject to capital sentence; appointment of counsel; requirement of rule of court or statute; procedures for appointment*

(a) This chapter shall apply to cases arising under section 2254 brought by prisoners in State custody who are subject to a capital sentence. It shall apply only if the provisions of subsections (b) and (c) are satisfied.

(b) Counsel.– This chapter is applicable if-
    (1) the Attorney General of the United States certifies that a State has established a mechanism for providing counsel in postconviction proceedings as provided in section 2265; and

    (2) counsel was appointed pursuant to that mechanism, petitioner validly waived counsel, petitioner retained counsel, or petitioner was found not to be indigent.

(c) Any mechanism for the appointment, compensation, and reimbursement of counsel as provided in subsection (b) must offer counsel to all State prisoners under capital sentence and must provide for the entry of an order by a court of record–

    (1) appointing one or more counsels to represent the prisoner upon a finding that the prisoner is indigent and accepted the offer or is unable competently to decide whether to accept or reject the offer;

    (2) finding, after a hearing if necessary, that the prisoner rejected the offer of counsel and made the decision with an understanding of its legal consequences; or
    (3) denying the appointment of counsel upon a finding that the prisoner is not indigent.

(d) No counsel appointed pursuant to subsections (b) and (c) to represent a State prisoner under capital sentence shall have previously represented the prisoner at trial in the case for which the appointment is made unless the prisoner and counsel expressly request continued representation.

(e) The ineffectiveness or incompetence of counsel during State or Federal post-conviction proceedings in a capital case shall not be a ground for relief in a proceeding arising under section 2254. This limitation shall not preclude the appointment of different counsel, on the court's own motion or at the request of the prisoner, at any phase of State or Federal post-conviction proceedings on the basis of the ineffectiveness or incompetence of counsel in such proceedings.

28 U.S.C. § 2262. *Mandatory stay of execution; duration; limits on stays of execution; successive petitions*

(a) Upon the entry in the appropriate State court of record of an order under section 2261(c), a warrant or order setting an execution date for a State prisoner shall be stayed upon application to any court that would have jurisdiction over any proceedings filed under section 2254. The application shall recite that the State has invoked the post-conviction review procedures of this chapter and that the scheduled execution is subject to stay.

(b) A stay of execution granted pursuant to subsection (a) shall expire if–

(1) a State prisoner fails to file a habeas corpus application under section 2254 within the time required in section 2263;

(2) before a court of competent jurisdiction, in the presence of counsel, unless the prisoner has competently and knowingly waived such counsel, and after having been advised of the consequences, a State prisoner under capital sentence waives the right to pursue habeas corpus review under section 2254; or

(3) a State prisoner files a habeas corpus petition under section 2254 within the time required by section 2263 and fails to make a substantial showing of the denial of a Federal right or is denied relief in the district court or at any subsequent stage of review.

(c) If one of the conditions in subsection (b) has occurred, no Federal court thereafter shall have the authority to enter a stay of execution in the case, unless the court of appeals approves the filing of a second or successive application under section 2244(b).

28 U.S.C. § 2263. *Filing of habeas corpus application; time requirements; tolling rules*

(a) Any application under this chapter for habeas corpus relief under section 2254 must be filed in the appropriate district court not later than 180 days after final State court affirmance of the conviction and sentence on direct review or the expiration of the time for seeking such review.

(b) The time requirements established by subsection (a) shall be tolled–

(1) from the date that a petition for certiorari is filed in the Supreme Court until the date of final disposition of the petition if a State prisoner files the petition to secure review

by the Supreme Court of the affirmance of a capital sentence on direct review by the court of last resort of the State or other final State court decision on direct review;

(2) from the date on which the first petition for post-conviction review or other collateral relief is filed until the final State court disposition of such petition; and

(3) during an additional period not to exceed 30 days, if–

> (A) a motion for an extension of time is filed in the Federal district court that would have jurisdiction over the case upon the filing of a habeas corpus application under section 2254; and

> (B) a showing of good cause is made for the failure to file the habeas corpus application within the time period established by this section.

28 U.S.C. § 2264. *Scope of Federal review; district court adjudications*

(a) Whenever a State prisoner under capital sentence files a petition for habeas corpus relief to which this chapter applies, the district court shall only consider a claim or claims that have been raised and decided on the merits in the State courts, unless the failure to raise the claim properly is–

(1) the result of State action in violation of the Constitution or laws of the United States;

(2) the result of the Supreme Court's recognition of a new Federal right that is made retroactively applicable; or

(3) based on a factual predicate that could not have been discovered through the exercise of due diligence in time to present the claim for State or Federal post-conviction review.

(b) Following review subject to subsections (a), (d), and (e) of section 2254, the court shall rule on the claims properly before it.

28 U.S.C. § 2265. *Certification and judicial review*

(a) Certification.–

(1) In general.– If requested by an appropriate State official, the Attorney General of the United States shall determine –
> (A) whether the State has established a mechanism for the appointment, compensation, and payment of reasonable litigation expenses of competent

counsel in State postconviction proceedings brought by indigent prisoners who have been sentenced to death;

(B) the date on which the mechanism described in subparagraph (A) was established; and

(C) whether the State provides standards of competency for the appointment of counsel in proceedings described in subparagraph (A).

(2) Effective date.– The date the mechanism described in paragraph (1)(A) was established shall be the effective date of the certification under this subsection.

(3) Only express requirements.– There are no requirements for certification or for application of this chapter other than those expressly stated in this chapter.

(b) Regulations.– The Attorney General shall promulgate regulations to implement the certification procedure under subsection (a).

(c) Review of certification.–

(1) In general.– The determination by the Attorney General regarding whether to certify a State under this section is subject to review exclusively as provided under chapter 158 of this title.

(2) Venue.– The Court of Appeals for the District of Columbia Circuit shall have exclusive jurisdiction over matters under paragraph (1), subject to review by the Supreme Court under section 2350 of this title.

(3) Standard of review.– The determination by the Attorney General regarding whether to certify a State under this section shall be subject to de novo review.

28 U.S.C. § 2266. *Limitation periods for determining applications and motion*

(a) The adjudication of any application under section 2254 that is subject to this chapter, and the adjudication of any motion under section 2255 by a person under sentence of death, shall be given priority by the district court and by the court of appeals over all noncapital matters.

(b)(1)(A) A district court shall render a final determination and enter a final judgment on any application for a writ of habeas corpus brought under this chapter in a capital case not later than 450 days after the date on which the application is filed, or 60 days after the date on which the case is submitted for decision, whichever is earlier.

(B) A district court shall afford the parties at least 120 days in which to complete all actions, including the preparation of all pleadings and briefs, and if necessary, a hearing, prior to the submission of the case for decision.

(C)(i) A district court may delay for not more than one additional 30-day period beyond the period specified in subparagraph (A), the rendering of a determination of an application for a writ of habeas corpus if the court issues a written order making a finding, and stating the reasons for the finding, that the ends of justice that would be served by allowing the delay outweigh the best interests of the public and the applicant in a speedy disposition of the application.

(ii) The factors, among others, that a court shall consider in determining whether a delay in the disposition of an application is warranted are as follows:

(I) Whether the failure to allow the delay would be likely to result in a miscarriage of justice.

(II) Whether the case is so unusual or so complex, due to the number of defendants, the nature of the prosecution, or the existence of novel questions of fact or law, that it is unreasonable to expect adequate briefing within the time limitations established by subparagraph (A).

(III) Whether the failure to allow a delay in a case that, taken as a whole, is not so unusual or so complex as described in subclause (II), but would otherwise deny the applicant reasonable time to obtain counsel, would unreasonably deny the applicant or the government continuity of counsel, or would deny counsel for the applicant or the government the reasonable time necessary for effective preparation, taking into account the exercise of due diligence.

(iii) No delay in disposition shall be permissible because of general congestion of the court's calendar.

C. Federal Habeas Corpus Statutes Prior to 1996 Amendments

28 U.S.C. § 2241. *Power to grant writ*
    (a) Writs of habeas corpus may be granted by the Supreme Court, any justice thereof, the district courts and any circuit judge within their respective jurisdictions. The order of a circuit judge shall be entered in the records of the district court of the district wherein the restraint complained of is had.

    (b) The Supreme Court, any justice thereof, and any circuit judge may decline to entertain an application for a writ of habeas corpus and may transfer the application for hearing and determination to the district court having jurisdiction to entertain it.

    (c) The writ of habeas corpus shall not extend to a prisoner unless–

(1) He is in custody under or by color of the authority of the United States or is committed for trial before some court thereof; or

(2) He is in custody for an act done or omitted in pursuance of an Act of Congress, or an order, process, judgment or decree of a court or judge of the United States; or

(3) He is in custody in violation of the Constitution or laws or treaties of the United States; or

(4) He, being a citizen of a foreign state and domiciled therein is in custody for an act done or omitted under any alleged right, title, authority, privilege, protection, or exemption claimed under the commission, order or sanction of any foreign state, or under color thereof, the validity and effect of which depend upon the law of nations; or

(5) It is necessary to bring him into court to testify or for trial.

(d) Where an application for a writ of habeas corpus is made by a person in custody under the judgment and sentence of a State court of a State which contains two or more Federal judicial districts, the application may be filed in the district court for the district wherein such person is in custody or in the district court for the district within which the State court was held which convicted and sentenced him and each of such district courts shall have concurrent jurisdiction to entertain the application. The district court for the district wherein such an application is filed in the exercise of its discretion and in furtherance of justice may transfer the application to the other district court for hearing and determination.

28 U.S.C. § 2242. *Application*

Application for a writ of habeas corpus shall be in writing, signed and verified by the person for whose relief it is intended or by someone acting in his behalf.

It shall allege the facts concerning the applicant's commitment or detention, the name of the person who has custody over him and by virtue of what claim or authority, if known.

It may be amended or supplemented as provided in the rules of procedure applicable to civil actions.

If addressed to the Supreme Court, a Justice thereof or a circuit judge it shall state the reasons for not making application to the district court of the district in which the applicant is held.

28 U.S.C. § 2243. *Issuance of writ; return; hearing; decision*

A court, justice or judge entertaining an application for a writ of habeas corpus shall forthwith award the writ or issue an order directing the respondent to show cause why the writ should not be granted, unless it appears from the application that the applicant or person detained is not entitled thereto.

The writ, or order to show cause shall be directed to the person having custody of the person detained. It shall be returned within three days unless for good cause additional time, not exceeding twenty days, is allowed.

The person to whom the writ or order is directed shall make a return certifying the true cause of the detention.

When the writ or order is returned a day shall be set for hearing, not more than five days after the return unless for good cause additional time is allowed.

Unless the application for the writ and the return present only issues of law the person to whom the writ is directed shall be required to produce at the hearing the body of the person detained.

The applicant or the person detained may, under oath, deny any of the facts set forth in the return or allege any other material facts. The return and all suggestions made against it may be amended, by leave of court, before or after being filed.

The court shall summarily hear and determine the facts, and dispose of the matter as law and justice require.

28 U.S.C. § 2244. *Finality of determination*

(a) No circuit or district judge shall be required to entertain an application for a writ of habeas corpus to inquire into the detention of a person pursuant to a judgment of a court of the United States if it appears that the legality of such detention has been determined by a judge or court of the United States on a prior application for a writ of habeas corpus and the petition presents no new ground not heretofore presented and determined, and the judge or court is satisfied that the ends of justice will not be served by such inquiry.

(b) When after an evidentiary hearing on the merits of a material factual issue, or after a hearing on the merits of an issue of law, a person in custody pursuant to the judgment of a State court has been denied by a court of the United States or a justice or judge of the United States release from custody or other remedy on an application for a writ of habeas corpus, a subsequent application for a writ of habeas corpus in behalf of such person need not be entertained by a court of the United States or a justice or judge of the United States unless the application alleges and is predicated on a factual or other ground not adjudicated on the hearing of the earlier application for the writ, and unless the court, justice, or judge is satisfied that the applicant has not on the earlier application deliberately withheld the newly asserted ground or otherwise abused the writ.

(c) In a habeas corpus proceeding brought in behalf of a person in custody pursuant to the judgment of a State court, a prior judgment of the Supreme Court of the United States on an appeal or review by a writ of certiorari at the instance of the prisoner of the decision of such State court, shall be conclusive as to all issues of fact or law with respect to an asserted denial of a Federal right which constitutes ground for discharge in a habeas corpus proceeding, actually adjudicated by the Supreme Court therein, unless the applicant for the writ of habeas corpus shall plead and the court shall find the existence of a material and controlling fact which did not appear in the record of the proceeding in the Supreme Court and the court shall further find that the applicant for the writ of habeas corpus could not have caused such fact to appear in such record by the exercise of reasonable diligence.

28 U.S.C. § 2245. *Certificate of trial judge admissible in evidence*

On the hearing of an application for a writ of habeas corpus to inquire into the legality of the detention of a person pursuant to a judgment the certificate of the judge who presided at the trial resulting in the judgment, setting forth the facts occurring at the trial, shall be admissible in evidence. Copies of the certificate shall be filed with the court in which the application is pending and in the court in which the trial took place.

28 U.S.C. § 2246. *Evidence; depositions; affidavits*

On application for a writ of habeas corpus, evidence may be taken orally or by deposition, or, in the discretion of the judge, by affidavit. If affidavits are admitted any party shall have the right to propound written interrogatories to the affiants, or to file answering affidavits.

28 U.S.C. § 2247. *Documentary evidence*

On application for a writ of habeas corpus documentary evidence, transcripts of proceedings upon arraignment, plea and sentence and a transcript of the oral testimony introduced on any previous similar application by or in behalf of the same petitioner, shall be admissible in evidence.

28 U.S.C. § 2248. *Return or answer; conclusiveness*

The allegations of a return to the writ of habeas corpus or of an answer to an order to show cause in a habeas corpus proceeding, if not traversed, shall be accepted as true except to the extent that the judge finds from the evidence that they are not true.

28 U.S.C. § 2249. *Certified copies of indictment, plea and judgment; duty of respondent*

On application for a writ of habeas corpus to inquire into the detention of any person pursuant to a judgment of a court of the United States, the respondent shall promptly file with the court certified copies of the indictment, plea of petitioner and the judgment, or such of them as may be material to the questions raised, if the petitioner fails to attach them to his petition, and same shall be attached to the return to the writ, or to the answer to the order to show cause.

28 U.S.C. § 2250. *Indigent petitioner entitled to documents without cost*

If on any application for a writ of habeas corpus an order has been made permitting the petitioner to prosecute the application in forma pauperis, the clerk of any court of the United States shall furnish to the petitioner without cost certified copies of such documents or parts of the record on file in his office as may be required by order of the judge before whom the application is pending.

28 U.S.C. § 2251. *Stay of State court proceedings*

A justice or judge of the United States before whom a habeas corpus proceeding is pending may, before final judgment or after final judgment of discharge, or pending appeal, stay any proceeding against the person detained in any State court or by or under the authority of any State for any matter involved in the habeas corpus proceeding.

After the granting of such a stay, any such proceeding in any State court or by or under the authority of any State shall be void. If no stay is granted, any such proceeding shall be as valid as if no habeas corpus proceedings or appeal were pending.

28 U.S.C. § 2252. *Notice*

Prior to the hearing of a habeas corpus proceeding in behalf of a person in custody of State officers or by virtue of State laws notice shall be served on the attorney general or other appropriate officer of such State as the justice or judge at the time of issuing the writ shall direct.

28 U.S.C. § 2253. *Appeal*

In a habeas corpus proceeding before a circuit or district judge, the final order shall be subject to review, on appeal, by the court of appeals for the circuit where the proceeding is had.

There shall be no right of appeal from such an order in a proceeding to test the validity of a warrant to remove, to another district or place for commitment or trial, a person charged with a criminal offense against the United States, or to test the validity of his detention pending removal proceedings.

An appeal may not be taken to the court of appeals from the final order in a habeas corpus proceeding where the detention complained of arises out of process issued by a State court, unless the justice or judge who rendered the order or a circuit justice or judge issues a certificate of probable cause.

28 U.S.C. § 2254. *State custody; remedies in Federal courts*

(a) The Supreme Court, a Justice thereof, a circuit judge, or a district court shall entertain an application for a writ of habeas corpus in behalf of a person in custody pursuant to the judgment of a State court only on the ground that he is in custody in violation of the Constitution or laws or treaties of the United States.

(b) An application for a writ of habeas corpus in behalf of a person in custody pursuant to the judgment of a State court shall not be granted unless it appears that the applicant has exhausted the remedies available in the courts of the State, or that there is either an absence of available State corrective process or the existence of circumstances rendering such process ineffective to protect the rights of the prisoner.

(c) An applicant shall not be deemed to have exhausted the remedies available in the courts of the State, within the meaning of this section, if he has the right under the law of the State to raise, by any available procedure, the question presented.

(d) In any proceeding instituted in a Federal court by an application for a writ of habeas corpus by a person in custody pursuant to the judgment of a State court, a determination after a hearing on the merits of a factual issue, made by a State court of competent jurisdiction in a proceeding to which the applicant for the writ and the State or an officer or agent thereof were parties, evidenced by a written finding, written opinion, or other reliable and adequate written indicia, shall be presumed to be correct, unless the applicant shall establish or it shall otherwise appear, or the respondent shall admit–

(1) that the merits of the factual dispute were not resolved in the State court hearing;

(2) that the factfinding procedure employed by the State court was not adequate to afford a full and fair hearing:

(3) that the material facts were not adequately developed at the State court hearing;

(4) that the State court lacked jurisdiction of the subject matter or over the person of the applicant in the State court proceeding;

(5) that the applicant was an indigent and the State court, in deprivation of his constitutional right, failed to appoint counsel to represent him in the State court proceeding;

(6) that the applicant did not receive a full, fair, and adequate hearing in the State court proceeding; or

(7) that the applicant was otherwise denied due process of law in the State court proceeding;

(8) or unless the part of the record of the State court proceeding in which the determination of such factual issue was made, pertinent to a determination of the sufficiency of the evidence to support such factual determination, is produced as provided for hereinafter, and the Federal court on a consideration of such part of the record as a whole concludes that such factual determination is not fairly supported by the record:

And in an evidentiary hearing in the proceeding in the Federal court, when due proof of such factual determination has been made, unless the evidence of one or more of the circumstances respectively set forth in paragraphs numbered (1) to (7), inclusive, is shown by the applicant, otherwise appears, or is admitted by the respondent, or unless the court concludes pursuant to the provisions of paragraph numbered (8) that the record in the State court proceeding, considered as a whole, does not fairly support such factual determination, the burden shall rest upon the applicant to establish by convincing evidence that the factual determination by the State court was erroneous.

(e) If the applicant challenges the sufficiency of the evidence adduced in such State court proceeding to support the State court's determination of a factual issue made therein, the applicant, if able, shall produce that part of the record pertinent to a determination of the sufficiency of the evidence to support such determination. If the applicant, because of indigency or other reason is unable to produce such part of the record, then the State shall produce such part of the record and the Federal court shall direct the State to do so by order directed to an appropriate State official. If the State cannot provide such pertinent part of the record, then the court shall determine under the existing facts and circumstances what weight shall be given to the State court's factual determination.

(f) A copy of the official records of the State court, duly certified by the clerk of such court to be a true and correct copy of a finding, judicial opinion, or other reliable written indicia showing such a factual determination by the State court shall be admissible in the Federal court proceeding.

28 U.S.C. § 2255. *Federal custody; remedies on motion attacking sentence*

A prisoner in custody under sentence of a court established by Act of Congress claiming the right to be released upon the ground that the sentence was imposed in violation of the Constitution or laws of the United States, or that the court was without jurisdiction to impose such sentence, or that the sentence was in excess of the maximum authorized by law, or is otherwise subject to collateral attack, may move the court which imposed the sentence to vacate, set aside or correct the sentence.

A motion for such relief may be made at any time.

Unless the motion and the files and records of the case conclusively show that the prisoner is entitled to no relief, the court shall cause notice thereof to be served upon the United States attorney, grant a prompt hearing thereon, determine the issues and make findings of fact and conclusions of law with respect thereto. If the court finds that the judgment was rendered without jurisdiction, or that the sentence imposed was not authorized by law or otherwise open to collateral attack, or that there has been such a denial or infringement of the constitutional rights of the prisoner as to render the judgment vulnerable to collateral attack, the court shall vacate and set the judgment aside and shall discharge the prisoner or resentence him or grant a new trial or correct the sentence as may appear appropriate.

A court may entertain and determine such motion without requiring the production of the prisoner at the hearing.

The sentencing court shall not be required to entertain a second or successive motion for similar relief on behalf of the same prisoner.

An appeal may be taken to the court of appeals from the order entered on the motion as from a final judgment on application for a writ of habeas corpus.

An application for a writ of habeas corpus in behalf of a prisoner who is authorized to apply for relief by motion pursuant to this section, shall not be entertained if it appears that the applicant has failed to apply for relief, by motion, to the court which sentenced him, or that such court has denied him relief, unless it also appears that the remedy by motion is inadequate or ineffective to test the legality of his detention.

PART II. ANTI-DRUG ABUSE ACT OF 1988

21 U.S.C. § 848. *Continuing criminal enterprise (Selected portions)*

    (c) Continuing criminal enterprise defined. For purposes of subsection (a) of this section, a person is engaged in a continuing criminal enterprise if–

    (1) he violates any provision of this subchapter or subchapter II of this chapter the punishment for which is a felony, and

    (2) such violation is a part of a continuing series of violations of this subchapter or subchapter II of this chapter–

        (A) which are undertaken by such person in concert with five or more other persons with respect to whom such person occupies a position of organizer, a supervisory position, or any other position of management, and

        (B) from which such person obtains substantial income or resources. . . .

    (e) Death penalty

    (1) In addition to the other penalties set forth in this section–

        (A) any person engaging in or working in furtherance of a continuing criminal enterprise, or any person engaging in an offense punishable under section 841(b)(1)(A) or section 960(b)(1) who intentionally kills or counsels, commands, induces, procures, or causes the intentional killing of an individual and such killing results, shall be sentenced to any term of imprisonment, which shall not be less than 20 years, and which may be up to life imprisonment, or may be sentenced to death; and

        (B) any person, during the commission of, in furtherance of, or while attempting to avoid apprehension, prosecution or service of a prison sentence for, a felony violation of this subchapter or subchapter II of this chapter who intentionally kills or counsels, commands, induces, procures, or causes the intentional killing of any Federal, State, or local law enforcement officer engaged in, or on account of, the performance of such officer's official duties and such killing results, shall be sentenced to any term of imprisonment, which shall not be less than 20 years, and which may be up to life imprisonment, or may be sentenced to death. . . .

PART III. FEDERAL DEATH PENALTY ACT OF 1994

18 U.S.C. § 3591. *Sentence of death*

(a) A defendant who has been found guilty of–

(1) an offense described in section 794 or section 2381; or

(2) any other offense for which a sentence of death is provided, if the defendant, as determined beyond a reasonable doubt at the hearing under section 3593–

(A) intentionally killed the victim;

(B) intentionally inflicted serious bodily injury that resulted in the death of the victim;

(C) intentionally participated in an act, contemplating that the life of a person would be taken or intending that lethal force would be used in connection with a person, other than one of the participants in the offense, and the victim died as a direct result of the act; or

(D) intentionally and specifically engaged in an act of violence, knowing that the act created a grave risk of death to a person, other than one of the participants in the offense, such that participation in the act constituted a reckless disregard for human life and the victim died as a direct result of the act, shall be sentenced to death if, after consideration of the factors set forth in section 3592 in the course of a hearing held pursuant to section 3593, it is determined that imposition of a sentence of death is justified, except that no person may be sentenced to death who was less than 18 years of age at the time of the offense.

(b) A defendant who has been found guilty of–

(1) an offense referred to in section 408(c)(1) of the Controlled Substances Act (21 U.S.C. 848(c)(1)), committed as part of a continuing criminal enterprise offense under the conditions described in subsection (b) of that section which involved not less than twice the quantity of controlled substance described in subsection (b)(2)(A) or twice the gross receipts described in subsection (b)(2)(B); or

(2) an offense referred to in section 408(c)(1) of the Controlled Substances Act (21 U.S.C. 848(c)(1)), committed as part of a continuing criminal enterprise offense under that section, where the defendant is a principal administrator, organizer, or leader of such an enterprise, and the defendant, in order to obstruct the investigation or prosecution of the enterprise or an offense involved in the enterprise, attempts to kill or knowingly directs, advises, authorizes, or assists another to attempt to kill any public officer, juror, witness, or members of the family or household of such a person, shall

be sentenced to death if, after consideration of the factors set forth in section 3592 in the course of a hearing held pursuant to section 3593, it is determined that imposition of a sentence of death is justified, except that no person may be sentenced to death who was less than 18 years of age at the time of the offense.

18 U.S.C. § 3592. *Mitigating and aggravating factors to be considered in determining whether a sentence of death is justified*

(a) Mitigating factors.– n determining whether a sentence of death is to be imposed on a defendant, the finder of fact shall consider any mitigating factor, including the following:

    (1) Impaired capacity.–The defendant's capacity to appreciate the wrongfulness of the defendant's conduct or to conform conduct to the requirements of law was significantly impaired, regardless of whether the capacity was so impaired as to constitute a defense to the charge.
    (2) Duress.–The defendant was under unusual and substantial duress, regardless of whether the duress was of such a degree as to constitute a defense to the charge.
    (3) Minor participation.–The defendant is punishable as a principal in the offense, which was committed by another, but the defendant's participation was relatively minor, regardless of whether the participation was so minor as to constitute a defense to the charge.
    (4) Equally culpable defendants.–Another defendant or defendants, equally culpable in the crime, will not be punished by death.
    (5) No prior criminal record.–The defendant did not have a significant prior history of other criminal conduct.
    (6) Disturbance.–The defendant committed the offense under severe mental or emotional disturbance.
    (7) Victim's consent.–The victim consented to the criminal conduct that resulted in the victim's death.
    (8) Other factors.–Other factors in the defendant's background, record, or character or any other circumstance of the offense that mitigate against imposition of the death sentence.

(b) Aggravating factors for espionage and treason.–In determining whether a sentence of death is justified for an offense described in section 3591(a)(1), the jury, or if there is no jury, the court, shall consider each of the following aggravating factors for which notice has been given and determine which, if any, exist:
    (1) Prior espionage or treason offense.–The defendant has previously been convicted of another offense involving espionage or treason for which a sentence of either life imprisonment or death was authorized by law.
    (2) Grave risk to national security.–In the commission of the offense the defendant knowingly created a grave risk of substantial danger to the national security.
    (3) Grave risk of death.–In the commission of the offense the defendant knowingly created a grave risk of death to another person.

The jury, or if there is no jury, the court, may consider whether any other aggravating factor for which notice has been given exists.

(c) Aggravating factors for homicide.–In determining whether a sentence of death is justified for an offense described in section 3591(a)(2), the jury, or if there is no jury, the court, shall consider each of the following aggravating factors for which notice has been given and determine which, if any, exist:

(1) Death during commission of another crime.–The death, or injury resulting in death, occurred during the commission or attempted commission of, or during the immediate flight from the commission of, an offense under section 32 (destruction of aircraft or aircraft facilities), section 33 (destruction of motor vehicles or motor vehicle facilities), section 37 (violence at international airports), section 351 (violence against Members of Congress, Cabinet officers, or Supreme Court Justices), an offense under section 751 (prisoners in custody of institution or officer), section 794 (gathering or delivering defense information to aid foreign government), section 844(d) (transportation of explosives in interstate commerce for certain purposes), section 844(f) (destruction of Government property by explosives), section 1118 (prisoners serving life term), section 1201 (kidnapping), section 844(i) (destruction of property affecting interstate commerce by explosives), section 1116 (killing or attempted killing of diplomats), section 1203 (hostage taking), section 1992 (wrecking trains), section 2245 (offenses resulting in death), section 2280 (maritime violence), section 2281 (maritime platform violence), section 2332 (terrorist acts abroad against United States nationals), section 2332a (use of weapons of mass destruction), or section 2381 (treason) of this title, or section 46502 of title 49, United States Code (aircraft piracy).

(2) Previous conviction of violent felony involving firearm.–For any offense, other than an offense for which a sentence of death is sought on the basis of section 924(c), the defendant has previously been convicted of a Federal or State offense punishable by a term of imprisonment of more than 1 year, involving the use or attempted or threatened use of a firearm (as defined in section 921) against another person.

(3) Previous conviction of offense for which a sentence of death or life imprisonment was authorized.–The defendant has previously been convicted of another Federal or State offense resulting in the death of a person, for which a sentence of life imprisonment or a sentence of death was authorized by statute.

(4) Previous conviction of other serious offenses.–The defendant has previously been convicted of 2 or more Federal or State offenses, punishable by a term of imprisonment of more than 1 year, committed on different occasions, involving the infliction of, or attempted infliction of, serious bodily injury or death upon another person.

(5) Grave risk of death to additional persons.–The defendant, in the commission of the offense, or in escaping apprehension for the violation of the offense, knowingly created a grave risk of death to 1 or more persons in addition to the victim of the offense.

(6) Heinous, cruel, or depraved manner of committing offense.–The defendant committed the offense in an especially heinous, cruel, or depraved manner in that it involved torture or serious physical abuse to the victim.

(7) Procurement of offense by payment.–The defendant procured the commission of the offense by payment, or promise of payment, of anything of pecuniary value.

(8) Pecuniary gain.–The defendant committed the offense as consideration for the receipt, or in the expectation of the receipt, of anything of pecuniary value.

(9) Substantial planning and premeditation.–The defendant committed the offense after substantial planning and premeditation to cause the death of a person or commit an act of terrorism.

(10) Conviction for two felony drug offenses.–The defendant has previously been convicted of 2 or more State or Federal offenses punishable by a term of imprisonment of more than one year, committed on different occasions, involving the distribution of a controlled substance.

(11) Vulnerability of victim.–The victim was particularly vulnerable due to old age, youth, or infirmity.

(12) Conviction for serious Federal drug offenses.–The defendant had previously been convicted of violating title II or III of the Comprehensive Drug Abuse Prevention and Control Act of 1970 for which a sentence of 5 or more years may be imposed or had previously been convicted of engaging in a continuing criminal enterprise.

(13) Continuing criminal enterprise involving drug sales to minors.–The defendant committed the offense in the course of engaging in a continuing criminal enterprise in violation of section 408(c) of the Controlled Substances Act (21 U.S.C. 848(c)), and that violation involved the distribution of drugs to persons under the age of 21 in violation of section 418 of that Act (21 U.S.C. 859).

(14) High public officials.–The defendant committed the offense against–

    (A) the President of the United States, the President-elect, the Vice President, the Vice President-elect, the Vice President-designate, or, if there is no Vice President, the officer next in order of succession to the office of the President of the United States, or any person who is acting as President under the Constitution and laws of the United States;

    (B) a chief of state, head of government, or the political equivalent, of a foreign nation;

    (C) a foreign official listed in section 1116(b)(3)(A), if the official is in the United States on official business; or

    (D) a Federal public servant who is a judge, a law enforcement officer, or an employee of a United States penal or correctional institution–

        (i) while he or she is engaged in the performance of his or her official duties;

        (ii) because of the performance of his or her official duties; or

        (iii) because of his or her status as a public servant.

For purposes of this subparagraph, a "law enforcement officer" is a public servant authorized by law or by a Government agency or Congress to conduct or engage in the prevention, investigation, or prosecution or adjudication of an offense, and includes those engaged in corrections, parole, or probation functions.

(15) Prior conviction of sexual assault or child molestation.–In the case of an offense under chapter 109A (sexual abuse) or chapter 110 (sexual abuse of children), the defendant has previously been convicted of a crime of sexual assault or crime of child molestation.

(16) Multiple killings or attempted killings.–The defendant intentionally killed or attempted to kill more than one person in a single criminal episode.

The jury, or if there is no jury, the court, may consider whether any other aggravating factor for which notice has been given exists.

(d) Aggravating factors for drug offense death penalty.–In determining whether a sentence of death is justified for an offense described in section 3591(b), the jury, or if there is no jury, the court, shall consider each of the following aggravating factors for which notice has been given and determine which, if any, exist:

(1) Previous conviction of offense for which a sentence of death or life imprisonment was authorized.–The defendant has previously been convicted of another Federal or State offense resulting in the death of a person, for which a sentence of life imprisonment or death was authorized by statute.

(2) Previous conviction of other serious offenses.–The defendant has previously been convicted of two or more Federal or State offenses, each punishable by a term of imprisonment of more than one year, committed on different occasions, involving the importation, manufacture, or distribution of a controlled substance (as defined in section 102 of the Controlled Substances Act (21 U.S.C. 802)) or the infliction of, or attempted infliction of, serious bodily injury or death upon another person.

(3) Previous serious drug felony conviction.–The defendant has previously been convicted of another Federal or State offense involving the manufacture, distribution, importation, or possession of a controlled substance (as defined in section 102 of the Controlled Substances Act (21 U.S.C. 802)) for which a sentence of five or more years of imprisonment was authorized by statute.

(4) Use of firearm.–In committing the offense, or in furtherance of a continuing criminal enterprise of which the offense was a part, the defendant used a firearm or knowingly directed, advised, authorized, or assisted another to use a firearm to threaten, intimidate, assault, or injure a person.

(5) Distribution to persons under 21.–The offense, or a continuing criminal enterprise of which the offense was a part, involved conduct proscribed by section 418 of the Controlled Substances Act (21 U.S.C. 859) which was committed directly by the defendant.

(6) Distribution near schools.–The offense, or a continuing criminal enterprise of which the offense was a part, involved conduct proscribed by section 419 of the Controlled Substances Act (21 U.S.C. 860) which was committed directly by the defendant.

(7) Using minors in trafficking.–The offense, or a continuing criminal enterprise of which the offense was a part, involved conduct proscribed by section 420 of the Controlled Substances Act (21 U.S.C. 861) which was committed directly by the defendant.

(8) Lethal adulterant.–The offense involved the importation, manufacture, or distribution of a controlled substance (as defined in section 102 of the Controlled Substances

Act (21 U.S.C. 802)), mixed with a potentially lethal adulterant, and the defendant was aware of the presence of the adulterant.

The jury, or if there is no jury, the court, may consider whether any other aggravating factor for which notice has been given exists.

18 U.S.C. § 3592. *Mitigating and aggravating factors to be considered in determining whether a sentence of death is justified*

(a) Mitigating factors.–In determining whether a sentence of death is to be imposed on a defendant, the finder of fact shall consider any mitigating factor, including the following:

> (1) Impaired capacity.–The defendant's capacity to appreciate the wrongfulness of the defendant's conduct or to conform conduct to the requirements of law was significantly impaired, regardless of whether the capacity was so impaired as to constitute a defense to the charge.
> (2) Duress.–The defendant was under unusual and substantial duress, regardless of whether the duress was of such a degree as to constitute a defense to the charge.
> (3) Minor participation.–The defendant is punishable as a principal in the offense, which was committed by another, but the defendant's participation was relatively minor, regardless of whether the participation was so minor as to constitute a defense to the charge.
> (4) Equally culpable defendants.–Another defendant or defendants, equally culpable in the crime, will not be punished by death.
> (5) No prior criminal record.–The defendant did not have a significant prior history of other criminal conduct.
> (6) Disturbance.–The defendant committed the offense under severe mental or emotional disturbance.
> (7) Victim's consent.–The victim consented to the criminal conduct that resulted in the victim's death.
> (8) Other factors.–Other factors in the defendant's background, record, or character or any other circumstance of the offense that mitigate against imposition of the death sentence.

(b) Aggravating factors for espionage and treason.–In determining whether a sentence of death is justified for an offense described in section 3591(a)(1), the jury, or if there is no jury, the court, shall consider each of the following aggravating factors for which notice has been given and determine which, if any, exist:

> (1) Prior espionage or treason offense.–The defendant has previously been convicted of another offense involving espionage or treason for which a sentence of either life imprisonment or death was authorized by law.

184

(2) Grave risk to national security.–In the commission of the offense the defendant knowingly created a grave risk of substantial danger to the national security.

(3) Grave risk of death.–In the commission of the offense the defendant knowingly created a grave risk of death to another person.

The jury, or if there is no jury, the court, may consider whether any other aggravating factor for which notice has been given exists.

(c) Aggravating factors for homicide.–In determining whether a sentence of death is justified for an offense described in section 3591(a)(2), the jury, or if there is no jury, the court, shall consider each of the following aggravating factors for which notice has been given and determine which, if any, exist:

(1) Death during commission of another crime.–The death, or injury resulting in death, occurred during the commission or attempted commission of, or during the immediate flight from the commission of, an offense under section 32 (destruction of aircraft or aircraft facilities), section 33 (destruction of motor vehicles or motor vehicle facilities), section 37 (violence at international airports), section 351 (violence against Members of Congress, Cabinet officers, or Supreme Court Justices), an offense under section 751 (prisoners in custody of institution or officer), section 794 (gathering or delivering defense information to aid foreign government), section 844(d) (transportation of explosives in interstate commerce for certain purposes), section 844(f) (destruction of Government property by explosives), section 1118 (prisoners serving life term), section 1201 (kidnapping), section 844(i) (destruction of property affecting interstate commerce by explosives), section 1116 (killing or attempted killing of diplomats), section 1203 (hostage taking), section 1992 (wrecking trains), section 2245 (offenses resulting in death), section 2280 (maritime violence), section 2281 (maritime platform violence), section 2332 (terrorist acts abroad against United States nationals), section 2332a (use of weapons of mass destruction), or section 2381 (treason) of this title, or section 46502 of title 49, United States Code (aircraft piracy).

(2) Previous conviction of violent felony involving firearm.–For any offense, other than an offense for which a sentence of death is sought on the basis of section 924(c), the defendant has previously been convicted of a Federal or State offense punishable by a term of imprisonment of more than 1 year, involving the use or attempted or threatened use of a firearm (as defined in section 921) against another person.

(3) Previous conviction of offense for which a sentence of death or life imprisonment was authorized.–The defendant has previously been convicted of another Federal or State offense resulting in the death of a person, for which a sentence of life imprisonment or a sentence of death was authorized by statute.

(4) Previous conviction of other serious offenses.–The defendant has previously been convicted of 2 or more Federal or State offenses, punishable by a term of imprisonment of more than 1 year, committed on different occasions, involving the infliction of, or attempted infliction of, serious bodily injury or death upon another person.

185

(5) Grave risk of death to additional persons.–The defendant, in the commission of the offense, or in escaping apprehension for the violation of the offense, knowingly created a grave risk of death to 1 or more persons in addition to the victim of the offense.

(6) Heinous, cruel, or depraved manner of committing offense.–The defendant committed the offense in an especially heinous, cruel, or depraved manner in that it involved torture orserious physical abuse to the victim.

(7) Procurement of offense by payment.–The defendant procured the commission of the offense by payment, or promise of payment, of anything of pecuniary value.

(8) Pecuniary gain.–The defendant committed the offense as consideration for the receipt, or in the expectation of the receipt, of anything of pecuniary value.

(9) Substantial planning and premeditation.–The defendant committed the offense after substantial planning and premeditation to cause the death of a person or commit an act of terrorism.

(10) Conviction for two felony drug offenses.–The defendant has previously been convicted of 2 or more State or Federal offenses punishable by a term of imprisonment of more than one year, committed on different occasions, involving the distribution of a controlled substance.

(11) Vulnerability of victim.–The victim was particularly vulnerable due to old age, youth, or infirmity.

(12) Conviction for serious Federal drug offenses.–The defendant had previously been convicted of violating title II or III of the Comprehensive Drug Abuse Prevention and Control Act of 1970 for which a sentence of 5 or more years may be imposed or had previously been convicted of engaging in a continuing criminal enterprise.

(13) Continuing criminal enterprise involving drug sales to minors.–The defendant committed the offense in the course of engaging in a continuing criminal enterprise in violation of section 408(c) of the Controlled Substances Act (21 U.S.C. 848(c)), and that violation involved the distribution of drugs to persons under the age of 21 in violation of section 418 of that Act (21 U.S.C. 859).

(14) High public officials.–The defendant committed the offense against–

> (A) the President of the United States, the President-elect, the Vice President, the Vice President-elect, the Vice President-designate, or, if there is no Vice President, the officer next in order of succession to the office of the President of the United States, or any person who is acting as President under the Constitution and laws of the United States;
>
> (B) a chief of state, head of government, or the political equivalent, of a foreign nation;
>
> (C) a foreign official listed in section 1116(b)(3)(A), if the official is in the United States on official business; or
>
> (D) a Federal public servant who is a judge, a law enforcement officer, or an employee of a United States penal or correctional institution–
>
>> (i) while he or she is engaged in the performance of his or her official duties;

(ii) because of the performance of his or her official duties; or

(iii) because of his or her status as a public servant.

For purposes of this subparagraph, a "law enforcement officer" is a public servant authorized by law or by a Government agency or Congress to conduct or engage in the prevention, investigation, or prosecution or adjudication of an offense, and includes those engaged in corrections, parole, or probation functions.

(15) Prior conviction of sexual assault or child molestation.–In the case of an offense under chapter 109A (sexual abuse) or chapter 110 (sexual abuse of children), the defendant has previously been convicted of a crime of sexual assault or crime of child molestation.

(16) Multiple killings or attempted killings.–The defendant intentionally killed or attempted to kill more than one person in a single criminal episode.

The jury, or if there is no jury, the court, may consider whether any other aggravating factor for which notice has been given exists.

(d) Aggravating factors for drug offense death penalty.–In determining whether a sentence of death is justified for an offense described in section 3591(b), the jury, or if there is no jury, the court, shall consider each of the following aggravating factors for which notice has been given and determine which, if any, exist:

(1) Previous conviction of offense for which a sentence of death or life imprisonment was authorized.–The defendant has previously been convicted of another Federal or State offense resulting in the death of a person, for which a sentence of life imprisonment or death was authorized by statute.

(2) Previous conviction of other serious offenses.–The defendant has previously been convicted of two or more Federal or State offenses, each punishable by a term of imprisonment of more than one year, committed on different occasions, involving the importation, manufacture, or distribution of a controlled substance (as defined in section 102 of the Controlled Substances Act (21 U.S.C. 802)) or the infliction of, or attempted infliction of, serious bodily injury or death upon another person.

(3) Previous serious drug felony conviction.–The defendant has previously been convicted of another Federal or State offense involving the manufacture, distribution, importation, or possession of a controlled substance (as defined in section 102 of the Controlled Substances Act (21 U.S.C. 802)) for which a sentence of five or more years of imprisonment was authorized by statute.

(4) Use of firearm.–In committing the offense, or in furtherance of a continuing criminal enterprise of which the offense was a part, the defendant used a firearm or

knowingly directed, advised, authorized, or assisted another to use a firearm to threaten, intimidate, assault, or injure a person.

(5) Distribution to persons under 21.–The offense, or a continuing criminal enterprise of which the offense was a part, involved conduct proscribed by section 418 of the Controlled Substances Act (21 U.S.C. 859) which was committed directly by the defendant.

(6) Distribution near schools.–The offense, or a continuing criminal enterprise of which the offense was a part, involved conduct proscribed by section 419 of the Controlled Substances Act (21 U.S.C. 860) which was committed directly by the defendant.

(7) Using minors in trafficking.–The offense, or a continuing criminal enterprise of which the offense was a part, involved conduct proscribed by section 420 of the Controlled Substances Act (21 U.S.C. 861) which was committed directly by the defendant.

(8) Lethal adulterant.–The offense involved the importation, manufacture, or distribution of a controlled substance (as defined in section 102 of the Controlled Substances Act (21 U.S.C. 802)), mixed with a potentially lethal adulterant, and the defendant was aware of the presence of the adulterant.

The jury, or if there is no jury, the court, may consider whether any other aggravating factor for which notice has been given exists.

18 U.S.C. § 3593. *Special Hearing to Determine Whether a Sentence of Death is Justified*

(a) Notice by the government.--If, in a case involving an offense described in section 3591, the attorney for the government believes that the circumstances of the offense are such that a sentence of death is justified under this chapter, the attorney shall, a reasonable time before the trial or before acceptance by the court of a plea of guilty, sign and file with the court, and serve on the defendant, a notice–

(1) stating that the government believes that the circumstances of the offense are such that, if the defendant is convicted, a sentence of death is justified under this chapter and that the government will seek the sentence of death; and

(2) setting forth the aggravating factor or factors that the government, if the defendant is convicted, proposes to prove as justifying a sentence of death.

The factors for which notice is provided under this subsection may include factors concerning the effect of the offense on the victim and the victim's family, and may include oral testimony, a victim impact statement that identifies the victim of the offense and the extent and scope of the injury and loss suffered by the victim and the victim's family, and any other relevant information. The court may permit the attorney for the government to amend the notice upon a showing of good cause.

(b) Hearing before a court or jury.--If the attorney for the government has filed a notice as required under subsection (a) and the defendant is found guilty of or pleads guilty to an offense described in section 3591, the judge who presided at the trial or before whom the guilty plea was entered, or another judge if that judge is unavailable, shall conduct a separate sentencing hearing to determine the punishment to be imposed. The hearing shall be conducted–

(1) before the jury that determined the defendant's guilt;

(2) before a jury impaneled for the purpose of the hearing if–

(A) the defendant was convicted upon a plea of guilty;

(B) the defendant was convicted after a trial before the court sitting without a jury;

(C) the jury that determined the defendant's guilt was discharged for good cause; or

(D) after initial imposition of a sentence under this section, reconsideration of the sentence under this section is necessary; or

(3) before the court alone, upon the motion of the defendant and with the approval of the attorney for the government.

A jury impaneled pursuant to paragraph (2) shall consist of 12 members, unless, at any time before the conclusion of the hearing, the parties stipulate, with the approval of the court, that it shall consist of a lesser number.

(c) Proof of mitigating and aggravating factors.--Notwithstanding rule 32 of the Federal Rules of Criminal Procedure, when a defendant is found guilty or pleads guilty to an offense under section 3591, no presentence report shall be prepared. At the sentencing hearing, information may be presented as to any matter relevant to the sentence, including any mitigating or aggravating factor permitted or required to be considered under section 3592. Information presented may include the trial transcript and exhibits if the hearing is held before a jury or judge not present during the trial, or at the trial judge's discretion. The defendant may present any information relevant to a mitigating factor. The government may present any information relevant to an aggravating factor for which notice has been provided under subsection (a). Information is admissible regardless of its admissibility under the rules governing admission of evidence at criminal trials except that information may be excluded if its probative value is outweighed by the danger of creating unfair prejudice, confusing the issues, or misleading the jury. For the purposes of the preceding sentence, the fact that a victim, as defined in section 3510, attended or observed the trial shall not be construed to pose a danger of creating unfair prejudice, confusing the issues, or misleading the jury. The government and the defendant shall be permitted to rebut any information received at the hearing, and shall be given fair opportunity to present argument as to the adequacy of the information to establish the existence of any aggravating or mitigating factor, and as to the appropriateness in the case of imposing a sentence of death. The government shall open the argument. The defendant shall be permitted to reply. The government shall then be permitted to reply in rebuttal. The burden of establishing the existence of any aggravating factor is on the government, and is not satisfied unless the existence of such a factor is established beyond a reasonable doubt. The burden of establishing the existence of any mitigating factor is on the defendant, and is not satisfied unless the existence of such a factor is established by a preponderance of the information.

(d) Return of special findings.--The jury, or if there is no jury, the court, shall consider all the information received during the hearing. It shall return special findings identifying any aggravating factor or factors set forth in section 3592 found to exist and any other aggravating factor for which notice has been provided under subsection (a) found to exist. A finding with respect to a mitigating factor may be made by 1 or more members of the jury, and any member of the jury who finds the existence of a mitigating factor may consider such factor established for purposes of this section regardless of the number of jurors who concur that the factor has been established. A finding with respect to any aggravating factor must be unanimous. If no aggravating factor set forth in section 3592 is found to exist, the court shall impose a sentence other than death authorized by law.

(e) Return of a finding concerning a sentence of death.--If, in the case of–

(1) an offense described in section 3591(a)(1), an aggravating factor required to be considered under section 3592(b) is found to exist;

(2) an offense described in section 3591(a)(2), an aggravating factor required to be considered under section 3592(c) is found to exist; or

(3) an offense described in section 3591(b), an aggravating factor required to be considered under section 3592(d) is found to exist, the jury, or if there is no jury, the court, shall consider whether all the aggravating factor or factors found to exist sufficiently outweigh all the mitigating factor or factors found to exist to justify a sentence of death, or, in the absence of a mitigating factor, whether the aggravating factor or factors alone are sufficient to justify a sentence of death. Based upon this consideration, the jury by unanimous vote, or if there is no jury, the court, shall

recommend whether the defendant should be sentenced to death, to life imprisonment without possibility of release or some other lesser sentence.

(f) Special precaution to ensure against discrimination.--In a hearing held before a jury, the court, prior to the return of a finding under subsection (e), shall instruct the jury that, in considering whether a sentence of death is justified, it shall not consider the race, color, religious beliefs, national origin, or sex of the defendant or of any victim and that the jury is not to recommend a sentence of death unless it has concluded that it would recommend a sentence of death for the crime in question no matter what the race, color, religious beliefs, national origin, or sex of the defendant or of any victim may be. The jury, upon return of a finding under subsection (e), shall also return to the court a certificate, signed by each juror, that consideration of the race, color, religious beliefs, national origin, or sex of the defendant or any victim was not involved in reaching his or her individual decision and that the individual juror would have made the same recommendation regarding a sentence for the crime in question no matter what the race, color, religious beliefs, national origin, or sex of the defendant or any victim may be.

18 U.S.C. § 3594. *Imposition of a Sentence of Death*
Upon a recommendation under section 3593(e) that the defendant should be sentenced to death or life imprisonment without possibility of release, the court shall sentence the defendant accordingly. Otherwise, the court shall impose any lesser sentence that is authorized by law. Notwithstanding any other law, if the maximum term of imprisonment for the offense is life imprisonment, the court may impose a sentence of life imprisonment without possibility of release.

18 U.S.C. § 3595. *Review of a Sentence of Death*
(a) Appeal.--In a case in which a sentence of death is imposed, the sentence shall be subject to review by the court of appeals upon appeal by the defendant. Notice of appeal must be filed within the time specified for the filing of a notice of appeal. An appeal under this section may be consolidated with an appeal of the judgment of conviction and shall have priority over all other cases.

(b) Review.--The court of appeals shall review the entire record in the case, including–

(1) the evidence submitted during the trial;

(2) the information submitted during the sentencing hearing;

(3) the procedures employed in the sentencing hearing; and

(4) the special findings returned under section 3593(d).

(c) Decision and disposition.--

(1) The court of appeals shall address all substantive and procedural issues raised on the appeal of a sentence of death, and shall consider whether the sentence of death was imposed under the influence of passion, prejudice, or any other arbitrary factor and whether the evidence supports the special finding of the existence of an aggravating factor required to be considered under section 3592.

(2) Whenever the court of appeals finds that–

(A) the sentence of death was imposed under the influence of passion, prejudice, or any other arbitrary factor;

(B) the admissible evidence and information adduced does not support the special finding of the existence of the required aggravating factor; or

(C) the proceedings involved any other legal error requiring reversal of the sentence that was properly preserved for appeal under the rules of criminal procedure, the court shall remand the case for reconsideration under section 3593 or imposition of a sentence other than death. The court of appeals shall not reverse or vacate a sentence of death on account of any error which can be harmless, including any erroneous special finding of an aggravating factor, where the Government establishes beyond a reasonable doubt that the error was harmless.

(3) The court of appeals shall state in writing the reasons for its disposition of an appeal of a sentence of death under this section.

18 U.S.C. § 3596. *Implementation of a Sentence of Death*

(a) In general.--A person who has been sentenced to death pursuant to this chapter shall be committed to the custody of the Attorney General until exhaustion of the procedures for appeal of the judgment of conviction and for review of the sentence. When the sentence is to be implemented, the Attorney General shall release the person sentenced to death to the custody of a United States marshal, who shall supervise implementation of the sentence in the manner prescribed by the law of the State in which the sentence is imposed. If the law of the State does not provide for implementation of a sentence of death, the court shall designate another State, the law of which does provide for the implementation of a sentence of death, and the sentence shall be implemented in the latter State in the manner prescribed by such law.

(b) Pregnant woman.--A sentence of death shall not be carried out upon a woman while she is pregnant.

(c) Mental capacity.--A sentence of death shall not be carried out upon a person who is mentally retarded. A sentence of death shall not be carried out upon a person who, as a result of mental disability, lacks the mental capacity to understand the death penalty and why it was imposed on that person.

18 U.S.C. § 3597. *Use of State Facilities*

(a) In general.--A United States marshal charged with supervising the implementation of a sentence of death may use appropriate State or local facilities for the purpose, may use the services of an appropriate State or local official or of a person such an official employs for the purpose, and shall pay the costs thereof in an amount approved by the Attorney General.

(b) Excuse of an employee on moral or religious grounds.--No employee of any State department of corrections, the United States Department of Justice, the Federal Bureau of Prisons, or the United States Marshals Service, and no employee providing services to that department, bureau, or service under contract shall be required, as a condition of that employment or contractual obligation, to be in attendance at or to participate in any prosecution or execution under this section if such participation is contrary to the moral or religious convictions of the employee. In this subsection, "participation in executions" includes personal preparation of the condemned individual and the apparatus used for execution and supervision of the activities of other personnel in carrying out such activities.

18 U.S.C. § 3598. *Special Provisions for Indian Country*

Notwithstanding sections 1152 and 1153, no person subject to the criminal jurisdiction of an Indian tribal government shall be subject to a capital sentence under this chapter for any offense the Federal jurisdiction for which is predicated solely on Indian country (as defined in section 1151 of this title) and which has occurred within the boundaries of Indian country, unless the governing body of the tribe has elected that this chapter have effect over land and persons subject to its criminal jurisdiction.